Life for Dreams

by

Vera Stanek

ISBN: 1-4140-2987-X (e-book)
ISBN: 1-4140-2988-8 (Paperback)
ISBN: 1-4140-2989-6 (Dust Jacket)

Library of Congress Number: 2003098001

This book is printed on acid free paper.

Printed in the United States of America
Bloomington, IN

1st Books - rev. 02/27/04

To Eva and David

Acknowledgments

I would like to thank the following persons for their help with my book.

My first thanks goes to Chris Cowan who encouraged me to write this book. I am very thankful to her because without her I would probably not have believed in myself enough to write it.

Very special thanks to my daughter Eva who started the editing of my book. I thank her from my whole heart because she knew about many of the events and could put herself in my position very well.

My thanks for the final editing of my book goes to Mindy Reed, The Author's Assistant. Without her hard work it would have been impossible for me to bring this book to the readers. I am still ashamed of all the grammar errors I made and I am terribly grateful to her.

I would like to say "Thank you" to La Toya Baker of 1st Books Library who helped me in taking the most important step and encouraging me until I signed the contract.

I am grateful to Amy Barnes and to the production team of 1st Books Library who contributed to the publishing of this book.

Last, but not least, I thank my husband Frank for being there for me every day of our life together. And that is more than 40 years.

Table of Contents

Chapter 1

July 5th, 1967.

The bus made the last stop.
The last stop before we would cross the border.
In the distance the barricade was already visible .

How much farther to freedom? One mile or less?
Better not to think about it.
We have to go through the last step, the most difficult one; now we will be interrogated by the border guards.

The door of the bus opened silently.
The bus was modern and designed only for trips to West Germany.
It was important to show the West that Czechoslovakia is not the *poor relative.*

Two guards came to the bus.
"Prepare your travel documents, please," one of them told us.
I opened my bag. My hands shook so much that I couldn't pick up my passport. So I held one hand with the other and tried to calm myself.
'Just for the next ten minutes, maybe just five,' I told myself.
I did not look at Frank.
I didn't want him to see the panic in my eyes. I wanted to be cool and fearless so I clenched my teeth.

The guards slowly moved through the bus.

My brain stopped working.
I could not think about anything, just the barricade and getting past it.
'Maybe if I concentrate on it, it will happen,' I thought.

Vera Stanek

The guards were already by our seats.
They took Frank's passport first, then mine.
The world stopped moving.
And then I heard the words, "Please, take your bags and come with us."
"Oh, no....please no, " I cried in my soul.
It was a silent cry.
Nobody listened to it.
Nobody responded.

Shuffling like elderly persons, the three of us: Frank, our daughter Eva, and I left the bus.
Our suitcases were already unloaded.
This was no coincidence, they were already prepared for us.

Why?
Who betrayed us?
It was not the moment to torment myself with questions for which I had no answers.

Out of the corner of my eye I saw the bus drive off.
But without us.
How near we were!
What happens now?

We were brought to the border control house where Frank and I were separated. Frank to the left and I to the right.
Three-year-old Eva had to stay waiting in the entrance room.
She did not protest.
She did not cry.
She remained alone.

What if I would not see her again?

I was taken into a gray room.
There was only one table with a chair, more chairs by the wall, and two ladies in border guard uniforms. Nothing more.

The interrogation began.
First, the usual questions about my life and person.
Second, the questions about my relatives we had wanted to visit in West Germany.
Third, they told me I would have to go through a strip search.
"Why?" I asked, "I am not a criminal!"

They only laughed with a knowing leer, because they knew my type.

After the interrogation they began to inspect my travel bag.
They took one piece after another from the bag, opening every cosmetic container; lipstick, eye-shadow, powder box.
And then... they found it!
The 10 Deutsche Mark I had in a box. Frank got them from one of his business friends and we did not write it on our customs declaration.
Why?
It was forbidden.
You could only bring with you 60 Deutsche Marks per person for your personal expenses, and not one Deutsche Mark more.

I could tell they were pleased with themselves and happy with the discovery.
I was a criminal after all.

"We go on with the examination of your clothing," they told me.
I did not protest; I was paralyzed with horror.

Slowly, I took off my jacket.
Both of them threw themselves onto it. With experienced hands they looked in every pocket, inspected every stitch of the lining. In the same way they inspected my skirt and my blouse.
I stood there only in panties and a bra.
"Take the rest off too, " they ordered.
"Please, please no," I begged in vain.
"Ha, ha...," they laughed.

So I took the rest off too.

And with it I lost control.
I began to cry.

With the first tears went away the years of hope, the hours of
planning the escape.

I cried for Frank, for Eva, for myself.
I felt humiliated.
I did not know what would happen now.
Would they put me in jail?
What would happen to Eva?
Who would take care of her?
I did not know the answers to these questions.

What I knew positively was quite simple.

It was all over!

Chapter 2

The communist society is historically inevitable.
(Karl Marx)

Maybe you are curious as to why we wanted to escape.

The answer is anything but simple.

Yes, we did want to escape the socialistic Czechoslovakia.
Although it meant leaving our parents and our homeland.
To abandon our apartment that we furnished with love for every detail.
To leave the city Prague.
The city where we studied at the university, worked and lived.
The place where we met, married, and our daughter, Eva, was born and where we had few friends, that we had to abandon without saying goodbye to them.

Yes, we did yearn to leave socialism.
To go away from the system where the Party decides your fate.
To go away from the Party that tells you what you should say.
Do not think!
The Party tells you what is white and what is black.

To guide you along the proper path the Party begins in kindergarten.
To educate children is easier than to educate adults, because adults might have their own thoughts.

But children are a good material to work with.

The Party starts to teach them to address people as *comrade*.

Vera Stanek

No Mister, no Mrs., no Miss.
We are all comrades; we all belong to the working class.
And children are like parrots.
It is no longer father, but Comrade Father.
It is no longer Santa Claus, but Comrade Santa Claus.
Some people laugh about it.
Some cry.

It does not stop in kindergarten.
It continues with you through your whole life.
In school, of course, the pressure is very strong.

Would you like to go to high school ?
Then you have to be a Pioneer, the youngest communist.
You are required to wear a red scarf, a mark of your membership.
You greet with the right arm bent at the elbow and pulled up before
your face and you say, "Always Ready !"

Would you like to study at the university ?
Then you have to be a member of the Youth Organization.
An organization of the Young Communists.
You have to wear a blue shirt, because the blue is the color of the
working class. You have to wear it for special occasions like Labor
Day, or Liberation Day, or any public holiday.

Would you like to have a good job?
Then you have to be a Party member.
Are you?
No?

Then it is your own fault that you do not have a good job.
It does not matter that you are good or even excellent!
The important thing is that you are not a Party member.

So your boss in a research institute may be a former hairdresser or
blacksmith.
But he knew what to do; he joined the Party.

The Party needs people with a class-consciousness. People without their own thoughts, people willing to obey.
They then have the *right* to have a new flat or a car.
But not you.
Because you are not a Party member.

And why we, Frank and I, were not Party members?

Because we wanted to think for ourself.
We did not like the practices of socialism, we did not like the ideology, and we did not like it when other people made decisions for us.
Or simply, because we did not like to do anything that was against our convictions.

And what were our convictions?

That all people should be free to say what they think, have the right to choose a school or job after their abilities and skills.
That all people should be free to choose a country they want to live, travel abroad, study or live there without restriction and punishment.
But first and foremost.
It does not matter if we are Party members or not, because the Party does not make us human beings.
All of us should have the same right to live our lives as we choose.

Maybe we will not make the smartest decisions.
We would make mistakes.
So what? It is our life!
We will learn from our mistakes and if we are smart enough, we will try to not repeat them.

It would be the life we chose.
And we, only we, would be responsible for our actions.

This is what we learned from our fathers.

Vera Stanek

We could not betray them.
We could not forget them.

It was written in our hearts.

The love to be free.

Chapter 3

When a human is born, a new star appears on the night sky.
When a human dies, the star disappears.

My star was born with me.
It is still there.
For how long yet?

It has nothing to do with astronomy.

It is just what my father told me.

I could not have been born in the night.
It had to be a nice spring day with a blue sky and lots of sunshine.
Why?
Because I love the sun.
It gives me energy to work.
A sunny day brings a smile to my face when I wake up.
In these moments I love the world, I love life.

It was probably the time of the full moon.
Because I love the moon.
There is no person in the world that could change my mind about the moon. It has round face, full of mystery, and it looks directly at me!
Do not tell me it is just my fantasy.
I will not believe you.

I was the first child born to my father, Oldrich, and mother, Marie.

They were very different from each other.

My mother was a petite lady, always nicely dressed.
She was very happy in the city of Brno where I was born.

She loved the people in the streets, the shop windows, the atmosphere of evenings with the lights, theaters, and restaurants. It was the life she wanted.

My father was not too much taller than she.
He was a village boy.
He loved the forest with its silence, birds, and animals... the country life. The peacefullness of the nature he loved so much lent a balance to his life.
Brno was for him only a place to work.

How could my parents come together?

It was easy.
My father had deep green eyes.
My mother's eyes were dark brown.
And they just fell in love.

It was not important that my father was Czech and mother German.
In these times it was normal.
These two nations had lived together for centuries and nobody cared who was married to whom.
You want to marry a German? It is OK.
You want to marry a Czech? It is OK, too.

So they married.

Then I was born and they were happy to have me.
It did not matter to them that it was not good timing.
Why?
For many reasons...

Times were hard economically.
My father, trained as a druggist, was unemployed.
Because the family needed money, my mother, a skilled dressmaker, continued to work almost to the last day of her pregnancy.

Soon after I was born, she left me in the arms of my father and went back to work again.

My father took care of me for about two years.

Sometimes he would find a temporary job.
Then I would stay with my grandmother on my mother's side; quiet, petite, and inconspicuous lady.
We all lived together in an old house in the middle of the city, in a courtyard gallery with a water tap in the corridor outside the apartment.
The rooms were dark and small, and the apartment had no bathroom. There was only one toilet for the whole floor.
But all of us had a roof over our head, a place we called home.

The time I spent with my father was a very happy time.

He took me to the parks, showed me the birds, flowers, and fountains with their fine spray of water sparkling in the sun.
He talked to me about all the beauty of nature.
He told me stories of fairy creatures and taught me my first steps and my first words.
He loved me very much.

In addition to the economics, times were difficult for another reason as well.
Politics.

Five months after I was born, Hitler stretched out his arms to Czechoslovakia to *take care* of the Germans in the border regions between Czechoslovakia and Germany.
According to Hitler the Germans there had right of self-determination.
They required return to the German Reich.

Why now?
The answer was simple: the time was ripe for annexation.

Hitler became stronger day after day.

Where were our allies, France and England?

They negotiated with Hitler.
They arranged conditions to surrender the border regions of
Czechoslovakia to Germany. Satisfied with the results, they
announced proudly, "We did everything to prevent a war. We saved
the peace in Europe."

How foolish could they be?
How could they believe that giving us away could stop Hitler?
It was like trying to satisfy the hunger of an ox with a single cherry.

It would be quite clear to them very soon.

Six months later Hitler annexed the rest of Czechoslovakia to the
German Reich. Other countries followed, one after another.
The war began.
Europe exploded.
People died.
Seven years of horror had just begun...

There were big changes in our family, too.

After three years of looking for a real job, my father got an offer to
leave Brno for a smaller city about fifty miles away, Prerov.
He would represent a company that sold paints and be his own
boss.
He was extremely happy.
Naturally.

My mother was extremely unhappy.
Naturally.
She had to quit the job she loved and go to a smaller city and to her
absolute horror, to live in the suburbs, in reality just a village!

But my parents moved, together with grandmother and myself.

Our new apartment on the first floor of the two-apartment house was wonderful. We had two big bright rooms, huge kitchen with running water and our own bathroom.

Outside we had a half of a small yard.

My father began to grow vegetables such as lettuce, onion, carrots, dill and radishes, all of them in neat rows.
I got a small watering can and in the summer evenings, I would water the radishes. I promised myself that they would be the biggest and sweetest ones.
When the right time came, I pulled one of them out.
I washed the earth away and then? Ooooh... the first bite!
It was the best I ever ate, for sure.

For the first time in my young life I came into contact with animals.

There was Punta, our dog.
Punta was a mutt, the sum of all dog breeds in the neighborhood.
We got him a small kennel, and he had to stay outside and keep watch.
Sometimes my father let him run free in our yard and then I could stroke his coat.
However, I was a little afraid of him.
Maybe I was more the daughter of my mother, a city lady, than I was prepared to admit.

And of course there were the rabbits.
We had them in small hutches.
White or black or multicolored, it had no influence on how sweet they were.
Together with my father I took care of them, changed the water in their bowls and fed them.

Vera Stanek

Through the wire on the hutch I pushed dandelion leaves and waited. The rabbits began to nibble; their faces moved quickly until a leaf completely disappeared in their mouths. And then another one and...
They seemed so comical to me.
I really enjoyed watching them.

In no time our food supplies dwindled.
War was around the corner.

So my father began to slaughter our rabbits to put meat on the Sunday table.
In the beginning I cried about this loss. But, as time passed, I found that the smell and taste of a roasted rabbit was stronger than my grief.
The instinct of self-preservation prevailed.

I did not know yet in those days how many times I would come to rely upon this instinct.

Shortly after we moved to this new place, on a foggy winter day, my grandmother died.

Everything was so strange.
Our flat full of people in black, my aunt and uncle so solemn.
The whole family with unsmiling faces.
"Sit down, play quietly with your dolls. Be a good girl," I was told.
I obeyed.
I was used to obeying.

During the ceremony my father held me in his arms.
Grandmother's casket was pushed into a big hole in the earth at the cemetery.
I was told that people who die sleep there from now on, but I did not understand. I wondered how someone could sleep in such cold weather in a hole.

But I did not ask why.

From that day every All Souls Day, my mother, father, and I went to the cemetery where we put flowers and lit candles on my grandmother's grave.
With several seconds of silence we remembered her.

My mother slowly tried to accept her fate and her new village life. She was able to hire a woman from the neighborhood, named Pavla, to help her with the weekly clean-up.

Pavla cleaned the flat and did the laundry.

Especially the laundry in our laundry room in the cellar was for me a big event.
Pavla put lots of water in a huge boiler and threw in the white laundry. Then she made a fire to bring the water to a boil.
After a while she pulled the boiled laundry from the boiler and rubbed the separate pieces on the washboard in the washtub.
The whole room was full of steam.

Usually I stood on one end of the washtub.
I watched how her skilled hands moved from one piece to another.
Afterwards, we hung together the laundry on the clothes-line either outside in the yard, if the weather was good, or inside, in the laundry room.
It was a special day for me every time.
I loved the smell of fresh clothes, towels, linens...
I buried my face in them, overwhelmed with pleasure.

Whenever Pavla cleaned our flat it was another exciting time for me.
After she washed the floor in the kitchen, she waxed the linoleum.
Then it was my turn. I jumped on her back and she polished and waxed with me.
I laughed with joy.

Vera Stanek

We had a great time together.

My joy and pleasure with her did not last long.

With the war going on my parents were short on money, and
mother had to do the housework alone.
She hated the work, but it had to be done.

Mother loved to sew new dresses for me, and I found a new source
of joy watching her.
I watched her hands measure the fabric and draw the form with
chalk, cut it and stitch the pieces together.
I wondered, 'How does she know which one? She has to be very
smart.'
She really was.

In only a short time, a new dress was ready for fitting.
I hated this part of her work .
I had to put on the dress and obey orders.
"Keep your shoulders straight! Do not move! Turn slowly left, but
s l o w l y!"
In the end the dress fitted perfectly.
Then mother sewed on the sewing machine.
She stepped on the pedal; the wheel began to turn and the needle
began to sew. Soon I had a new dress.

It did not cross my mind that the time would come when I would be
so thankful that she had let me watch her work.

I didn't know that I too would sew one day.
That I would visualize her hands before my eyes and I would ask
myself, "How would my mother do it?"
And I would find the answer every time.
I would see her by the machine.
I would remember.

There was more that my mother gave to me.

The love for books.

Mother was a passionate reader.
I estimated that she had read almost every book in our village
library; four to five books each week. She was eager to bury herself
in a world of imagination.
Who knows?
Maybe she was not as happy with her life in our village, as I thought
she was.

Later when I learned to read, I began to experience the same
passion for books.

I can see my mother like it was yesterday.
Sitting on a small chair by the oven warming her hands, a book on
her lap...not moving...not paying attention to the growing darkness
in the room.
Then I heard my father say, "You will ruin your eyes. Believe me."

Father could not know in these times, how right his words ones
would be.
Due to years of reading in the dark and sewing by poor light, my
mother's eyesight slowly diminished.
Eye surgery was necessary.
However, the surgery was unsuccessful, and my mother became
almost blind. She remained this way for about ten years until the
day she died.

Mother did not fully recover from this tragedy.

It was not only my mother that I learned much from.

My father taught me different things.
He began to educate me in skills, considered in those days as "boy"
skills. It did not matter to him that I was a girl.

Vera Stanek

Father built a workshop in the cellar.
He was an excellent handyman.
On Saturdays and Sundays he worked on his projects, with me next to him.
I was excited to see how new shelves grew under his hands, how the windows got new paint, how the old bicycle became new again.

I loved the smell of all his paints.
I learned how to take care of brushes.
I knew what turpentine was, how to hold a screwdriver, plane, rasp.
I liked how raw wood smelled.

I loved the hours spent with my father.

I did not know that the time would come when it would be necessary to remember.
To remember his hands, to remember his words.
About forty years later, when I found a job making display samples, I would draw on these skills.

The war began to escalate in 1943.
Food was short in supply, winter was terribly cold.

We could heat only one room, the kitchen.
There, life took place in daily routines; mother was sewing or reading, I was playing with dolls, father was listening to the radio.

Our coal supply slowly diminished.
We had only enough coal for one week; there was no more to buy.
Everything went to the front.

Our house was near the railroad tracks. One train after another passed, full with black coal from the coal mine nearby.
For the German.
Not for us.

Some of the trains, escorted by soldiers that watched over their essential cargo, stopped in front of our home because of traffic jams on the rails.
And these stops brought my father and our neighbors into action.

One night with no moon in the sky a group of men met in our yard.
There was severe frost and snow.
The men had sleds and shovels.
They waited patiently.

In the distance the train hooted.
Now! The men sprang forward, quickly ran the short distance to the track and hid under the embankment.
The train stopped.
Because of the cold night, the soldiers did not come out as usual.
On a night like this everyone stayed inside.
Or maybe not?

Not these men.
They worked in silence, quickly and efficiently.
Some climbed onto freight cars and threw down the coal. The rest picked it up and loaded it on sleds. In a short time the sleds were full of nice black coal.
The coal that belonged to the Germans.
The coal that would heat the flats of the Czechs.

My father made this trip many times that winter, and soon our cellar was full to the ceiling with black coal.

But my mother suffered.
Every time my father went on one of his trips, she was scared to death. She feared my father would be shot by the soldiers and she would not see him again.

And my father?
He knew it was a risk, a terrible risk.
But it was necessary, because the people he loved so much had

suffered.

He was the man in the family. He felt responsible for every one and every thing. And there was nothing else to do.

No choice.

In 1944, two events happened that could have changed our whole life.

It was time for me to go to school.
My parents sent the application to a Czech school.
Why Czech school when my mother was of German origin?
But why not?

Before the war nobody cared what school your child attended.
It was the decision of the parents.
But not now.
We were in a war and the Germans had the power to decide our fate, and they wanted me in a German school.

School officers tried to persuade my parents.
No way. My father was stubborn.

The pressure began.
Letters and visits from school officers became more frequent, but nothing changed my father's mind.

Then came the letter.
A short announcement to my father to get ready to work in Germany. It was common to take people from the annexed countries and send them to Germany to work in the war industry. They replaced the German men that were fighting on the front.

The letter was like receiving a ticket to your own funeral.

In Germany there were the bombs...
The bombs that the Allies dropped on the German war industry.

There was hunger and diseases, terrible housing conditions for the foreign workers.
Few men survived.

Why my father?

The Gestapo had decided.
Period.

The family was broken with this catastrophe; there was no way out!
Surprisingly another letter came with the invitation to go to the Gestapo for one last talk.
What could they possibly want from us?
My parents were in shock, but it was necessary to obey, to go and not ask why.

The Gestapo's headquarters were in one of the nicest villas in Prerov.
The Jews to whom it belonged were sent to the concentration camp and the Germans moved in.
Private rooms and offices of the commanders were established on the first floor, interrogation rooms were in the cellar.

We were brought to a small room in the cellar that had a tiny window up high near the ceiling. The walls were yellow on the upper part; the lower part was painted in green oil paint about five feet from the floor.
In one corner of the room was a coal stove that emitted enormous heat.

I was wearing a rabbit fur coat, made of course from the fur of our nice rabbits.
My mother unbuttoned my coat and told me, "Please sit. Be patient and courageous. You are our big girl already."
I obeyed.

My parents left, escorted by a soldier in a black uniform.

I stayed alone, scared and confused.
I longed to be at home with my parents next to me.
I was only six years old in a strange house with noises I didn't recognize or understand. A feeling came over me that something horrible was going to happen to my parents.
I tried so hard not to cry.

After a long time my parents came back.
My mother was crying.
I saw tears in her eyes and a red nose from all the crying she had done. However, they were not tears of despair, but of relief.
She gave me a big hug and buttoned up my coat.
We went home.

After a long time I put together the many fragments said here and there.

My parents had been taken to the officer who was in charge of the city.
My father told him the story about the school.
The officer listened.
Then he took the letter of my father's deportation, folded it, and tore it into tiny, little pieces. He told them, "If every such problem were solved in this way, who would work here for us?"
Then he sent us all home.

So I went to the Czech school and my father stayed with us.

How did this happen that my father was not deported?
Because among the beasts was one person who had retained a shred of humanity.

We are all born to be human beings, but sometimes something goes wrong.
Parents with no love for you, bad friends or just a society with its ideology.

It changes you.

The human being becomes a beast.

History is full of beasts.
We remember them better than we do the human beings.
Do you recall who was the Nobel Prize winner for literature last year?
But you know who Hitler was.
Do you recall the man who discovered penicillin?
But you know who Stalin was.

It is not necessary to go on, is it?

The second event happened in the fall of the same year.
My mother and I went to Brno again to visit Aunt Trudy and Uncle Franzi.
Both of them had married German partners. Both of them still lived in Brno.
Brno... my mother's vain dream.

Maybe my mother just needed a change.
Just a few days in the city, and then she could return to our village with renewed energy to face her everyday life.
Or maybe she wanted to tell them that she was pregnant again.

I looked forward to going to Brno.
I loved these visits.

We lodged in the big flat of Aunt Trudy. There she lived with Uncle Erich, my two cousins, Gerhard and Werni, and a maid that took care of us.
This was a luxury I didn't have at home.
Uncle Franzi and his wife, Greta, and my cousin, Liza, however had a life more like ours.

Vera Stanek

My Aunt Trudy owned a shop located on the main street of Brno.
A small exclusive shop in the front and a factory in the back. There
about 20 girls sewed women's underwear including shirts, panties,
night gowns...
I loved this place.

I loved to watch the skilled hands of the girls working with silk and
lace and embroidered fabric.
My soul laughed.
Do you know how many remnants I found to use for my dolls?
Every time I visited my aunt I left with a big package.
My dolls had exquisite dresses after I sewed them.

Aunt Trudy, my mother, and I had just arrived in the factory.
Suddenly we heard the alarm of sirens. It was something we knew
very well.
It meant, stop the work, and go to the cellar... the bombers are near.

The girls escaped very quickly, but not us.
Aunt Trudy told us, "It will be a false alarm like every day. They will
just fly over."
So we didn't go to the cellar.
The sisters continued their small talk.

Aunt Trudy was wrong this time.

First the awful blow.
Then more blows with no time in between.
Not knowing what was happening, I began to cry very loud
My mother reacted impulsively. She pushed me under a sewing
machine and knelt next to me to protect me with her body.
It was horrible and it felt like an eternity until it stopped.

When we crawled out from our hiding places we did not believe our
eyes.
The windows were blown away. There was no light, just
semidarkness with dust.

Pieces of bricks and glass were scattered over all.

Aunt Trudy was in shock.
Her shop, her pride, did not exist anymore.
In the middle of it all were just the three of us.
"Quickly, we have to leave. We do not know how long the building will stay together," Aunt Trudy told us.

She was right this time.

After about a week we heard that a bomb had fallen into the room.
It had jammed into the wall but did not explode.
Sometimes a miracle happens and you stay alive.

So we left.
But where to go?

Aunt Trudy wanted to go home to check on her family.
My mother, almost hysterical, refused to go along.
No, she said, she would not go there now; she would go when it was over, but not now. Now she wanted to find a bomb shelter.

The streets were full of terrified people and ruins.
They were full of water that escaped from the cracks in the pipelines, full with fire from burning buildings, but with no firemen to save them.

It was chaos.
Unadulterated, unmitigated chaos.
People stumbled through craters and everyone tried to find a hiding place.
What if the bombers came back?

The streets were chaotic, but the overfilled cellars were even worse.

A stranger had helped my mother and myself to get through the

ruins and brought us into a cellar.
Fear, panic, and powerlessness hung in the air.
Written in the eyes of people kneeling on the floor and praying loudly.
Visible on the faces of people huddled together.
The entire space was full of smoke from candles.
Full of dust.
Full of horror.

I can still see one man.
The bearded one with a crucifix in his hands.
Sitting on the floor, with an emptiness in his eyes.
What was he seeing in his mind?
What had happened to him?
He did not speak.
He was in his own world where nobody could catch him.
Where there were no bombs anymore.

We stayed in this cellar until the sirens announced that the air was clear.
Then we started for Aunt Trudy's apartment.

What a great surprise to find the whole family together, in an undamaged flat, in an undamaged building.
For today, the Allies had chosen another part of the city.
Everything was fine.

The next day, Uncle Erich made a decision about our safety.
He was a member of Hitler's Party and it was the main reason why my father disliked him.

But on that day, he decided to take all of us to the secret shelter of the *pure race*.
Its existence and location was known only to the best of the best.

There was only one problem, me.

I did not speak German.
So the order was clear, "Do not say a word under any circumstances. Do you understand?"
I nodded.

The shock from the day before was still in me.

In Brno there was a medieval castle, built high up on a hill of solid rock. Beneath the castle was a labyrinth of passageways.
They had been used for centuries as secret places for hiding and for escape.
Now the castle was the main headquarters for the highest of Hitler's command.
The Gestapo.

We went there.

Before we reached the inner courtyard, there was a small door leading directly into the rock.
Inside were steps that took us down.
First into the rock, and finally, into an underground tunnel.
Suddenly we were in a big cave where some people were present.
The ladies boasted their furs and jewelry on hands and necks.
The men wore uniforms.

Uncle Erich quickly found a place for us in a distant corner.
He and Aunt Trudy mixed with the people while my cousins played together with other children .

Only my mother and I remained in the corner.
The poor relatives nobody cared about, but today thankful to be there.
The experience from the previous day was too fresh and strong.
But my mother was resolute.
We would survive.

After a few hours we left the cave and went back to Aunt Trudy's

apartment.
The Allies had bombed only the industrial part of the city today.
We had survived another day.

The next morning, my mother refused to stay any longer in the city.
She wanted go back to Oldrich, but it was impossible.
The tracks had been bombed and there were no trains running.

My mother discovered that she could at least send a card to my
father to tell him that we were alive.
Such postcards were sold in the market.
On them were printed in a bold red only three words: "We are
alive."
Nothing more.
Just sign it and write the address.

My parents kept this card for the rest of their lives.
Sometimes when I visited them later on, I secretly opened the
drawer that the card was in.
I pulled out the card and read the words "We are alive."
With all my heart I longed for a life where such cards did not exist.
Because no one would need them.

My mother had made a plan to get us back from Brno.
The two of us would go to a small village between the forests near
Brno, where another part of our family lived, my father's side.
We would escape to Lelekovice.

It was not easy for her to go there.
They did not like her. She was this city lady and what was more, a
German.
How could Oldrich marry her?

However, my mother had only one thought in mind.
To escape to safety with me and her unborn child.

We started out early in the morning .
Mother carried only one bag with food and water in one hand and
held my hand with the other one.
She chose a longer but safer route.
We would go around the city, instead of through it.

We walked, one hour, two hours... We did not care.
From time to time we stopped, took a little food, drank some water
and continued.
My legs began to hurt.
I was not very brave and whined.
But we had to keep going.

When we passed one house on the outskirts of Brno, a woman
graciously offered us to take rest for a while in her home.
Mother agreed to accept this kind invitation.
She saw, that we both were tired.
We needed a break.

But very soon my mother became anxious.
Time had fled too quickly and our destination was still a long way
away. We continued.

Soon we got lucky.
A man with a horse-and-cart caught up with us and took us in his
cart. I was so excited.
The man drove us almost to the village of Lelekovice.
There we got on our feet again.
Now we could see our destination. Maybe only one hour more and
we would be there.

Our journey ended at Aunt Ema's, Aunt Mina's, and my
grandfather's home.
My grandmother had died already.
I remember very little of her.
In my mind she remains as a plump little lady who cooked very well.

Thanks be to heaven she passed her cooking skills on to my Aunt Ema.

At least two times a year I visited these relatives.
I liked to be there.
It was so different from our home.

I went with my grandfather, a small man with a mustache, to the forest. We picked edible mushrooms and berries, and gathered wood and pine cones for the fire.
Then there were the animals; a dog, chickens, two cats and even a pig.
But I could never forget the food.
The smell of kolaches filled the house.
The skin of the roasted duck on the Sunday table was nice and crisp. The dumplings were big and airy.
What a life!
Nobody cared if I washed my hands.
Nobody told me not to go outside.

I was happy there.

But this time I was not there for a visit.
I was with my mother, not my father and everything was different.
Our relatives took us in, put food in front of us and gave us shelter.
We were not just people in need.
We were family.

After a few days, the trains began to run again.
We said thanks and goodbye and left Lelekovice for home.

The end of war was near.
The resistance of the Germans was strong.

Shortly after our experience with war in Brno, the German Army placed anti-aircraft guns about 500 feet from our house.

The possibility grew that our house might be bombed by the Allies.

So my father decided that we would go *underground*.
He built a room in our cellar where we would hide and survive.
Maybe.
He put sandbags in front of the windows. He built a plank bed for
me and another one for mother and himself.
The china and crystal were packed and stored in the cellar, together
with the carpets, blankets, some clothing, and water.
We were prepared.

During this difficult time, my father and I got sick.
Ulcers began to grow on my knees and buttocks and on my father's
back.
The doctor told us it was because of food, lack of vitamins, and
poor nourishment.

The only help was ichtyol, a stinking ointment, like tar.

The treatment was quite simple.
Put the ointment on the ulcer.
Let it ripen.
Then squeeze the pus out.

It was very painful.
My mother tried to help me with a chamomile infusion, one of the
old house remedies.
But it did not help very much.

My father tried to ignore it, but something was very wrong with him.
About twenty ulcers began to grow together into one big one on his
back.
He became crazy with pain.
During the night he would cry.
"Give me a gun. I can't hold on anymore," he would scream to my
mother.
"Please, hold on. Just one more night... just one more day," she

begged, tears rolling down her face.
What could she do?

It was just a few days after the birth of my sister Eva and we were all in the cellar.

Eva was born on a quite and clear night.
With no planes in the sky, and no sirens calling out.
Luckily, my mother could give birth in her own bed upstairs in the house with the help of a midwife.
Only twenty four hours later, my little sister shared the cellar with us, wrapped in pieces of cotton gauze.

My father was no help to the mother.
He himself needed help.
He needed every ounce of energy he had left just to endure the pain from his ulcers.

The beginning of May brought an end to the war.
Was it a reality?
Yes. Yes.

The men were called to help rebuild the bridges the Germans had blown up as they fled before the Russian Army.
My father decided to go also.
Against the protests of my mother, "You can't go on in this condition. You are sick."
But he said, "I am going," and left.

We were very worried about him.
In the evening my mother would go to the window every five minutes to watch for my father coming back.
Later she began to cry.
She was certain in her mind, that something terrible had happened to him.

Finally he returned.

The man who opened the door was not the man who left with his
face twisted from pain.
Now here he was.
His eyes deathly tired, but clear.
His whole shirt soaked with pus.
The hard work had caused that his ulcers erupted and that saved
his life.

The recovery took a long time.
But father had won his life back.

Our life changed dramatically now.
We could creep from the cellar like moles and enjoy the fresh air,
the sunshine, and peace again

What a wonderful time it was, to sleep in my own bed.
No bombers in the sky.
No sirens anymore.

How sweet freedom tasted.

In only a few days the Russian Army reached our village.

The part of the army that came to our village was from the Ukraine.
They were tired but very happy that the war was over.
They would go home very soon.

But now they were here, the army that won the war.
They were the heroes.
We admired them and would do anything for them.

My parents cleared one room in our apartment.
They moved furniture into the hallway and the now empty cellar.
They made the room available to the army, complete with water and
a toilet.

Vera Stanek

Twenty soldiers moved in with armfuls of hay to sleep on.

They were good people.
They even shared what little food they had with us.
We had almost nothing.

In the evenings, they lit fires in the street.
All children were invited to join them.
Mostly we sat on their laps and listened to the melancholy songs
they sang, accompanied by an accordion.
The war was over.
This was peace.

We were sad when they left after spending fourteen days with us.

Not everyone was so lucky as we were.

The biggest trouble was in Brno and the surrounding vicinity.
The part of the Russian Army that went there had been formed of
criminals.
"Fight against the Germans. You will be pardoned," they were told.
They had fought like lions.
Now they behaved like predators.

Nothing was safe from them.
They raped the women and girls.
They stole the last food people had.
They burned people's houses when they tried to stop them.
The horror continued with every step they took.

The people fled to the forests.
The men built second walls in their houses, creating hiding spaces
for their wives and daughters.

How could this happen?

We have survived the war.

We have peace.
Why should this happen to us now ?

You can find the answer for yourself.

They were all human beings but in some of them there was not enough of the human.

Simply, too much of the beasts.

Chapter 4

A child was born.
A boy.

In the first night he got a visit.
The three Fates.

The First spoke :
"I give you faith in people.
You will be a human person.
But people will betray you sometimes and it will hurt you."

The Second spoke :
"I give you wisdom.
You will be a thinker.
But you will fight the human ignorance your whole life."

The Third spoke :
"I give you the love for freedom.
But your way to it will be hard and long."

It is just an old legend.

Or not?

Frank was born six years and thirty seven days before me.
To mother Bozena and father Frantisek in Prague.
But the family lived in the small town near Prague, Podebrady.

His mother was a short young lady with green eyes and light-colored hair.
She was very proud to give birth to a son.
Because a son is the heir.

Frank's father was an imposing figure and had the same blue eyes as his newborn son.
He was sixteen years older then the mother.
A special man in every respect.

Born into a farmer's family, he learned artistic smith work.
He could turn a piece of glowing iron into a fence, forge the leaves of a rose, or create a gate to the castle.
After he got his diploma, he left home to discover the world.
Not exactly the whole one, just the Austrian-Hungary Empire, which was almost a quarter of Europe then. There he gathered many experiences.

He lived in the belief, "If you want to succeed, you have to work hard."

Frantisek knew what it meant to work hard.

When he returned home from his travels, he bought a big hole in the ground on the periphery of Podebrady.
The pit was what remained after a sand mine.
Soon he was a laughing stock.
"What a fool he is!"
"To buy a hole!"
"He is crazy!"
All the people around laughed at him.

Frantisek ignored them.

He made an agreement with the city and soon the trucks began to fill the hole with rubbish.
Suddenly the people stopped laughing.
The smile froze on their faces.

In only a short time Frantisek had a piece of land where he could materialize his plans.

First, he built a wooden workshop and began to repair bicycles.
Later, he visited the company where the bicycles were made.
He presented them an offer, "Give me 1000 bikes and I will sell
them."
They hesitated at first, but then agreed.

Frantisek tried hard but the result was devastating.
After five months he sold only two bicycles.
Only two out of the thousand!
Did he want too much ?

No, no, he just had to work harder!

So he worked harder.
All of sudden events took an unexpected turn.
In the following two months he sold the rest.
He had made enough profit to think about what he would do next.

"If bicycles worked so well, what about motorcycles?" he asked
himself.
From thought to action was a short way for Frantisek.
He decided to follow the same plan with the motorcycles.
The result was better.
More money.
More profit.

After these two successful sales experiences, Frantisek came to
the conclusion, that the time was ripe for something bigger.
'What about cars?' he thought, 'It is time for people own one.'
In 1925, an automobile was a sign of wealth.

Frantisek assumed that for his new venture a new building would
be necessary.
He began to realize his vision.

First he made a deal with the car company.
Then he borrowed money and built a building.

The huge modern building had a showroom and offices on the ground level and two apartments on the second level.
One apartment was for himself, the second one was for his brother who became a salesman.

Finally, Frantisek employed a young lady named Bozena.
She became the love of his life.

Frank was born to the happy couple.

But both of Frank's parents had to work, take care of the company, pay debts.
What to do with Frank?

The problem was solved to the satisfaction of everyone.

Bozena's mother, Anna, offered to help.
Her last child, a son Lada, was only nine years older than Frank.
She agreed to take Frank under her care.
So Bozena returned to work and Grandmother Anna cared for both, Lada and Frank .

Anna was a small but resolute lady; the mother of five children.

During her life she acquired the wisdom of people who live in the country.
She knew exactly which herb to put on an injured thumb or burned finger.
She could tend the chickens or grow tomatoes.
She was a whirlwind; in the kitchen, in the yard, around the house.
And she loved Frank.
She tried hard, even if sometimes in vain, to prevent him from the naughty influence of the older Lada.
But when this happened, she knew exactly what to do.

"Have you been smoking?" she asked Frank one day after seeing him with a cob of reed in his mouth.

She did not wait for an answer and reacted on the spot.
Without warning Frank got two slaps. His *cigar* fell to the ground
and Grandmother Anna trampled it down until nothing was left.
She was a woman of action.

Frank's life was the life of a village boy.

He took part in all street games.
He threw stones, played soccer with the boys in the neighborhood,
swam in the river in summer and skated on frozen ponds in winter.
But everything he did, was with one goal in mind; to be like his
hero, Lada.
It did not matter to him that he was a child and Lada was a
teenager.

How excited Frank was when he found that Lada and his friends
had declared a *war* on a neighbor they all disliked.

This neighbor did not like Frank.
He did not like Lada either.
He did not like the children in neighboring houses.

He put broken glass where the children played.
Without mercy he slashed the ball some unlucky child tossed into
his yard.
And he complained to all the parents on the street.
He was a mean old geezer.

"Revenge was necessary," decided the boys.

One cold winter day, Lada and his friends took action.
Silently, the boys climbed up the roof of the neighbor's house and
put a glass plate on the top of the chimney.
Afterwards they quickly hid behind a corner and waited impatiently
to see what would happen.
They didn't have to wait too long.

In a short time thick smoke escaped through hurriedly opened windows.
The man appeared in the door, coughing and gasping for breath, with eyes full of tears.
He did not know what happened.
After a short search around the house he noticed the boys.
Cursing them and the whole world he finally climbed up a ladder and removed the plate.
The boys beamed with happiness.

But this was not their last prank.

One day the neighbor left to go shopping.
While he was gone, the boys prepared a surprise for him.
They tied up the tips of all his trees, which grew near the fence, to the fence.
Then they waited for the man's return.
Afterwards the boys laughed with a pleasure as they watched the man, shouting with rage, as he cut the ropes.
He knew whose work it was.

"He got what he deserved," was the unanimous opinion of the events.

Soon the boys lost interest in the neighbor.
There were so many other things to do.

And then one day a miracle happened.

The same neighbor asked Frank to come out of the house.
In his hands he held a pair of stilts, nice new stilts that he had carved out of a piece of wood.
"Take them," he told Frank and for the first time, he smiled.

It had long been Frank's secret dream to have stilts.
Now he held them in his hands.
But he did not know what to say, how to react on this generous gift.

"Thank you," he smiled back at the neighbor, turned on his heels and left.

Only an idea was turning over in his mind, 'What does he want?'

Maybe it was a gesture of peace, maybe not.
Who knows.
Sometimes you cannot explain the behavior of people.
You have to take it or leave it.
Nothing more.

Even more than playing in the street, Frank loved cars.

The finest hours were those he spent in his father's garage,
watching the hands of mechanics who repaired the vehicles.
He wanted to be there when a car got a new life, when an engine
roared once again.
He loved the smell of gas and oil.
He liked the view of red iron hammered into a shape of a new tie
rod.

It was Frank's world.

He quickly learned how to pump a tire.
When to shift into another gear.
Where to put the gas.
He was only a boy and he knew all this

All this before I was born.

When I was born, Frank was in the first grade of elementary school.
It was still in the good old First Republic.
But these days did not last long.

The day arrived when Hitler occupied the border regions of

Czechoslovakia.
With this event the family faced their first problem.
It was Frank's Uncle Joseph and his family, who came
unexpectedly to Podebrady, excited, tired and unhappy.

Uncle Joseph was a customs officer on the border with Germany.
He loved his job, and he loved his neighbors.
All of them, Czech and German, equally with no exception.
He drank beer on the German side because the beer was better
there, but he visited the pub on the Czech side because the pub
was better.
Who cared!

The people had lived there together for centuries.
Like the people in Brno.

But then Hitler's army marched into the village and everything
changed.

The neighbor next door a friend yesterday, was now an enemy.
Stones were thrown into the yard of Uncle Joseph.
Then at the house.
In the windows.
Finally at the children.
Why?
It was quite simple, he was Czech.

There was only one way to solve this problem.
To escape, and quickly.

The family came to Podebrady and found refuge with Frank's
family.
Frank was happy, not just because he had new pals, but also
because of Uncle Joseph.
Uncle Joseph loved children; he played with them, invented new
games, told great stories and especially he laughed with them.
He was a merry man who everyone loved.

Uncle Joseph's family found a small house near Prague and a new job for the uncle. He became a policeman.

Soon afterwards, Hitler marched into Prague.

One morning Frank's grandmother and mother were listening to the radio and crying.
Confused Frank stood there not knowing what happened. But it was clear to him it had to be something bad if his grandmother was crying.

The changes started soon.

First, in the schools, of course.
Although taught by Czech teachers, the elective German language was now mandatory already from the third grade.
For some of the teachers it was an acid test.
Would they change or not?

It was only a question of bravery, character and personality.
Two of them were Frank's teachers.

The first one remained loyal to the ideas he believed in.
Although he taught the German language, at every opportunity he switched to Czech history.
He taught the children about the Czech kings, their cultural heredity, the glory of the Czech Empire through the centuries...
He loved being a Czech.

He knew he risked more than his job.

After the communists took over in 1948, they threw him out of the school.
They justified this act with his unreliability to teach.

The second teacher was very eager to show his adaptability.
He had a swastika on his lapel and he greeted the children with

Vera Stanek

"Heil Hitler!"
"A fine example of teacher," the German appraised his behavior.

After the war, this second teacher disappeared from Podebrady.

Ten years later, Frank saw a big picture of him in the newspaper
with a headline "National artist, comrade..." and his name.
It was obvious that he had adapted again.
This time to the new Communist regime.

They exist.
People like that.
Today a Nazi, tomorrow a Communist.
They just change the coat and everything is fine again.

You can find them in every nation, every regime.
Life goes smooth by for them.
They just do not have the backbone.
But it does not matter to them.

To others, though, it does matter.
Life is not easy for them, then.
Especially if they are Russian professors, like the few in Podebrady.

There was a group of intellectuals who had escaped earlier from
the Communist regime in Russia.
What should they do now, escape again?
How could they escape from Hitler?
Where to go in Europe, with the war spread overall?

So they stayed and suffered the consequences.
They were the first that the Germans fired from their jobs and soon
they were penniless with no idea how to survive.

A group of Podebrady citizens tried to help in a simple way.
They sent their children to them for Russian lessons.
Nobody thought about if it was good for the children because it was

---

not a question of learning Russian.
It was only to help.

This was the reason that Frank could already speak Russian, the language of the winners, by the time the war was over.

Until it was a reality, there was still a long way to go.

The changes were on every step.

Since the beginning of the war, there had been changes in the Frank's hometown.
Similar changes like in every another place in Czechoslovakia.

Podebrady was a spa resort with natural springs of water.
The water was good for one's heart, although it smelled like rotten eggs.
It was a well-known town.
With little industry and with green parks and promenades.
The focus on health could be felt everywhere.

The town was now very favorable for the Germans.

They closed the hotels, inns, schools for the Czechs.
They accomodated there their own young people, the Hitler Youth Organization.
Young people in brown shirts with knives in their belts, singing militant songs while marching through the town.

The people of the town hated them.
Mostly Lada and his friends, young, proud Czech men.
They were prepared to fight the Germans at every opportunity and with no concern about the knives and the superiority.
They only had to be smarter than they were.

Often, Lada came home at night with cut wounds.

He needed all the healing skills of his mother, Anna, who always helped him, without asking.
It was not easy for either of them.
She knew and understood.
But she was scared.

When the Germans closed the schools, the classes were moved to the small villages around Podebrady.

The time in class was cut to the minimum, the homework had the priority.
The situation got worse in the winter.
There was not enough coal to heat the rooms. So teaching was reduced to just two hours per week.
Sometimes it was held in the pub, sometimes in the rectory.

Despite this situation, Frank's parents decided that it would be better for Frank to change schools and go to the school at higher level than his village school.

But Frank failed the admission exams.

On the tests, he drew the swastika, the Nazi symbol, with the bends turned in the opposite direction.
It did not matter that he was the best in all other disciplines.
"The boy is not qualified for this school," wrote the officials.

Frank walked on air.
He did not want to be away from his friends, from the bike rides to school and from his handball team.
Also, it gave him more time for playing the violin.

Frank had played the violin for many years already.
He visited his teacher, an unusual man, once a week.
His teacher was the son of the famous composer, Kmoch, a man the whole world surely knew.

Even today, Kmoch's marches, polkas and waltzes make faces
smile, legs dance, and hearts happy.

The son of Kmoch taught Frank not just play the violin.
He taught him to love his instrument.
To make it sing.
To understand the music he played.
To forget his own problems and listen, and be happy.

But life in these times was full of surprises.

During one of his lessons, the teacher told Frank,
"This is the last lesson. I have to leave for the front. Do not forget
my advice, Frank, when your life is difficult just pick up your violin.
The music will bring peace to your mind again."

But why did he have to go to the front when he was Czech?

Because this son of a famous father had adapted to the new
situation at the beginning of war. He took the German citizenship so
that he would not have any problems.
His citizeship was the reason that he was sent to the front.
He never came back.
He laid his life down for a nation he nor his ancestors belonged to.

However his words remained in the soul of a boy who never forgot
them.

Another teacher took over Frank's violin lessons.

Life went on.

The war changed the company of Frank's father, Frantisek, too.
The company he represented, stopped the production of private
cars and produced trucks and tanks.
Frantisek got orders to work for the military, to repair the trucks.

Vera Stanek

It was a crazy time for a driver.
Just three gallons of gas for a car per month, not more.
The rest went to the army.

Frantisek solved this problem in his own way.
He converted his 1932 Chrysler car to one that drove on wood gas.

On the rear end of his car, Frantisek attached a boiler.
He filled it with small oak blocks, stacked up on a base of wood shavings for better ignition.
Then all he had to do was release a ventilator and strike a match.
The gas that was released by burning of the wood, carbon monoxide, was routed to the engine.
The car moved!

For a 30 mile trip to Prague it was necessary to take at least three bags of wood.
Toward the end of the war oak wood was in short supply.
Frantisek had to use any kind of wood he could find.
And with it came other problems.
At red lights in Prague, the burning would suddenly stop and when the lights changed to green, the car would not move.
It was necessary to get out of the car and with the poker stir the fire.
It was an adventure.

The food supply in Prague was also inadequate.

Most of people there lived in poverty, with rations for meat, sugar, flour....
But no one could buy needed food when the stores were empty.
And on the black market were the prices astronomically high.
To have relatives in a village, with the possibility to grow vegetables, or even to raise small animals was better than winning the lottery.

So Frantisek, a man from the village, tried to help.

He decided to bring food to his hungry friends.

There was, however, a small problem to solve.
How to get the food to Prague?
On every entry road to Prague were German police patrols that
confiscated all food they found in the cars.

How to find a way through the patrols?

Frantisek knew, he had to do something.
But what?

Finally he had found the answer.
In a net above the windshield he put small packages with butter.
Among wooden blocks in bags he hid the meat.
Mostly chickens and rabbits, but sometimes even a half of a pig.

The same procedure repeated without change.
A patrolman would stop his car and ask, "Do you have any food?"
"Yes, of course officer," Frantisek would answer, "Just look in the
net. It is my snack for the trip."
This small lie worked every time.
Frantisek was so convincing when he looked the patrolman in the
eye and carelessly pointed at the snack.

With nerves of steel, he was willing to take the risk for his friends.

The war approached its last stages.

Podebrady had no air raids.
There was almost no industry, just the springs with the water good
for the heart and that was not worth bombing.

Only ten miles away the situation was different; the local oil
refineries were ruthlessly bombed.
However not one bomb in Podebrady.

Vera Stanek

The people were lucky.

The end of the war was just around the corner.

In Prague an uprising against the Germans broke out.
People built barricades.
The Russian Army rushed to help from the East.
In the West, the American Army came as far as Pilsen, but had to stop there because of the demarcation line.

The Germans tried to escape.
They hurried toward the West, to Germany.
Just to be away from annexed countries, to be at home, and quickly.

In those last days the German Army brought 35 cars to Frantisek's workshop.
The order was brief: "You have three days to get them ready."
Normally it would be not a problem, but now it was a big one.

To repair the cars of the losers of war?

'How can I convince my fellow workers to do it?' Frantisek asked himself.
He talked to them.
He tried to persuade them to do this job.
And he pointed out that this would be probably the last one for the Germans.
To his surprise the workers of his garage did this job on time.
But in return they stole the clocks from all cars.

When the Germans found out, they issued another order.
"You have 24 hours to bring the clocks back. Or we take you to our barracks, and who knows..."

Some clocks were put back.
Some were not.

Nobody cared now.
How many days or hours to the end of the war?

The Germans fled from Podebrady by cars, in trucks, on freight trains, just to get away from the Russians.
It was still better to be prisoner of war of USA, than of Russians.

In the yard of Frantisek's workshop were left behind many cars.
Both, civilian and military, filled with food, clothes, bed linens, duvets,etc.

When the Russian Army finally marched into Podebrady, the first thing they looked for was alcohol.
The soldiers plundered the cars. They threw everything onto the grass in the hopes of finding a hidden bottle. Only one bottle of alcohol and they would be happy.

The war was over.
It was the Russian Army that had brought the freedom.
They were the winners, they behaved like it.

They took what they wanted.
Just one word, "Davai!" (Give), was enough.
This word and a pistol aimed at the head of Frantisek and a brand new Mercedes with blue leather seats changed owners.
Who wants to die now, when the war is over?

Above all the soldiers loved wrist watches the most.

Shortly after the war, Frank took a train to a nearby city of Kolin.

The train was full of Russian soldiers.
And one of the soldiers absolutely fascinated Frank.
The soldier sat on a bumper between two train cars.
He was young with a round Slavic face and bald shaved head. His cap was neatly folded and stuck into his left epaulette.
On his left arm, he wore watches. But not one or two.

Vera Stanek

His arm was full of them, from his wrist to his shoulder.
In his right hand he held a bayonet and with its tip he adjusted one
of his watches.

If you win the war, it does not matter what you do.
You are the hero.
You are welcome.
What can we do for you?

If you are the loser?
A German, maybe?
You die.

Die in the same way as the commanding officer of Podebrady died.
A German with a good heart who had saved the lives of many
Czech people.
Because he was not a beast.

Do you ask me what happened to him?
Do you think that the Czechs were thankful to him?
Not so!

He was killed with a pickax by a Czech policeman.

Why?

He was a German!
A loser!
It was so simple.

"An eye for an eye, a tooth for a tooth!"
Passions shook the nations.

Nobody thought about humanity, fairness or honesty.

The world was divided just into losers and winners.

But the war was over.

Chapter 5

How high is the price of freedom?

55 million people died in this war.

Seven million Germans.
21 millions Russians.
Six million Jews died in the concentration camps.

Other nations not counted.

Stop it!
Those are only numbers.

You cannot express numerically the tragedy of the war.
Because the numbers do not have a face.
They do not have a heart to feel.

They do not tell you anything about the children.

Children in the concentrations camps, behind the wire.
With tattooed number on their wrists.
Children that stopped being children and were transformed into a number.
No more Judy and David, just a number now.
Maybe13,275 and 6,452.

Look in their eyes.

They have no eyes anymore.
Just two hollow holes, with no spark of live.

Vera Stanek

They were snatched with no mercy from their mother's grip.
Crying and struggling, screaming and shouting, "Mother, please,
help!!!"

If you are quiet just for a few seconds, maybe you will hear it.
In the places where it happened.
Because the earth is soaked with tears to the core.
Forever.

The numbers do not tell you anything about the women.
Because you cannot quantify in numbers the pain of the mothers,
nor a broken heart of women in the concentration camps.
Women without men and without children.
Most of them still young but with bald scalps.

Where was their hair?
You do not know?
Their hair was put into the mattresses because it was softer than
the finest horsehair. The very best quality for the very best and
purest race in the world.

Those women were lucky to be young.
To lose only the hair.
The older women were sent without hesitation directly to the gas
chambers.
They were useless for the Nazi.

Only the gold on them was of interest.

Rings on their hands.
Given them by the men that were probably no longer alive.
Given them in times of love and dignity.

And golden teeth in their mouths.
It was so easy to break them off.
To have enough gold to make necklaces for the German women
strutting solemnly on the side of men in uniforms.

Long live Hitler!

But these women in the concentrations camps, young and old, were human beings!
And so what?
The rules were different.
Enforced from a position of strength, from the *right* to decide over the life of another creature.

This was the war.
Better say, just a small part of it.

Because there were many others.

The women and children in the places of the battles, in the ruins of their homes.
Sometimes they stayed alive.
But for what?
Was this life better than death in the artillery fire?

Could you, just for a moment, imagine how it was?

To be alive and to have nothing to eat or drink.
With the whole body twisted with hunger and crazy with thirst.
With children dying before your eyes and you cannot save them.
And how much longer can you, yourself, stay alive?

Until the next bombing, maybe.
Maybe until tomorrow if you can survive one more night in the ruins.
One endless night.

Please, God, let me die.
Quickly.

The numbers tell you nothing about the men.

Vera Stanek

The soldiers and the civilians.

The soldiers on both sides of the front.
Fighting for ideas they believed in, or maybe not.
Fighting for the world of the *pure race* where there is no place for
Jews or Gypsies.
Or fighting to protect the families and the country.

Both sides with death as a part of their lives.

Today, a friend was killed.
Is it my turn tomorrow?
Who knows?

Hope to survive today and do not think about tomorrow.
Fight and be happy that you can!
Because there were lots of them who could not.

All the Jews and all the men who died in the concentration camps.
They had been dragged to the camps with bold letters above the
entrance :
"Arbeit Macht Frei!"
"Work Sets You Free! "
How many of them survived?
Not too much.

And those who did, how could they ever be happy again?

With their eyes that saw the horror.
With their hands that carried out the bodies from the gas chambers.
With their hearts empty.

Where are their feelings?
Dead.

Where are their families?
Dead.

Where are their friends?
Dead.

What can bring them back to life again?
To love.
To smile.
To be happy.

So many of them could not handle it because the hell was too deep
in their minds.
They died then in the time of peace.
Intentionally.
Because they wanted it.
Not to think.
Not to feel.
Nothing.

They are not in these numbers.

The rest of the human race survived.
Like me.
And you.

"Arbeit Macht Frei"

Do not forget.

Remember!
Please!

Chapter 6

It is morning.
You wake up.

Through the open windows you can hear a twitter of the birds.
The first sunbeam has reached your nose.
You can almost feel it tickle.

You think, "Life is wonderful! "

It is not a dream.

It is just another day of peace.

The war was over and a new life began.
There was peace in Europe again and everyone could breathe freely.
Life was great, only we were hungry.

The help program, UNRA from the USA, was already on the way to our country. Some weeks later we got some cans of meat and peanut butter.

I was very excited about it.
American food, here in our small village in Europe, wow!
I knew even before it came, it would taste heavenly.

Then the big moment arrived.
My father opened the can, my mother put the peanut butter on slice of bread.
I had the first bite.
But what a disappointment; it was terrible.
I hated the smell, I hated the taste, and immediately I spat the bite on the table.

My parents could not understand it. They tried to persuade me to try again but without success. I clenched my teeth and remained stubborn.
No one will force me to eat it!

Even until today I have never tried peanut butter again.

At that time, it was foolish to refuse food.
Food was rare even to buy and we still had food stamps.
They gave every person the guaranteed minimum of food.
Three ounces of meat, five ounces of flour, two ounces of butter... for a week.
The stamps were the same ones as in the war and with the same problems. We could not spend them because the stores were almost empty.
The supply was slow and inadequate.
You had to be prepared to wait in long lines.
Lines for everything.

Every Friday, there was a ritual in our family.

My mother went to the butcher at 6:00 a.m. to be among the first twenty people, when the butcher opened his store at 8:00 a.m.
If she managed to be among the first few, there was at least a small selection of the meat. If she did not manage it, then there were just two possibilities.
Either, no selection and take what was left.
Or second, no meat at all.

When she came back, she began to cook.
We didn't have a refrigerator, nor did our neighbors.
The only solution was to cook the meat immediately.

In the winter, it was no problem at all.
The cooked meat was stored in the pantry and we enjoyed it in the next days.
However, what to do in summer?

The freshly cooked or baked meat was wrapped in a fabric soaked in vinegar.
Then it was put on the wooden cover of our water pump, the coolest place in the house.
One could only hope that it would remain in the same condition for about three or four days. That the bluebottles would not find it.
Just a little carelessness in the wrapping, and the meat was full of bluebottle eggs.
It meant we had to put this precious meat in the trash.

My mother cried every time it happened.
But so it is in life.
Only sometimes you think, you did not deserve it.

It was a time of struggles for everything.

But I should not complain.
We were together.
The future looked rose-colored and we had freedom.

Not everybody in our family was so lucky.

The families of my Aunt Trudy and Uncle Franzi were now paying the price of a lost war.

Uncle Erich, the Nazi, was sent to Russia to build roadways there.
To everybody's surprise, he came back after three years.

Aunt Trudy was sent to a mass camp in northern Bohemia. She was allowed to take with her her two children and one suitcase.
There were all Germans gathered, then split to groups, and later sent to different parts of Germany.

The conditions in the camp were awful.
My three-year-old cousin Werni poured a pot with boiling porridge on himself and died. There was nobody to help.

Aunt Trudy with Cousin Gerhard were then evacuated to West Germany.
So was Uncle Franzi, except that his family stayed together.

"Why did they leave Brno?" you may ask.

It was simple.

Germans belong to Germany.
Czechs belong to Czechoslovakia.
Those were the after-war rules.

My relatives were Germans so they had to go to Germany.
There they had to build a new society; strong and peaceful, without Nazis.

Only my mother was married to a Czech.
So she remained in Czechoslovakia.
It took her ten years before she could visit her siblings and it was not her fault.
She could not go because of the new Communist regime we had then.

Life was not easy in those days, but somehow we managed.

During the summer school breaks, I, and later my sister Eva, visited Lelekovice and our grandfather and aunts.
The tense relationship between them and my mother slowly melted away.
But it was mostly I who visited them.
I still liked the forest.
I loved the delicious food.
I enjoyed the easy lifestyle of my grandfather.
But I found something else...

On one rainy day, I was bored.

I slowly took a "trip" through the house, when it happened!
I found an old dresser in the attic. Curiously, I opened it.....
What a surprise!
What a wealth I discovered!

The dresser was crammed with old magazines, yet from the time
before the war.

With an unbelievable passion, I buried myself in reading.
What a new world opened for me.

The world of ranchers, cowboys, and Indians.
Texas, with its prairies and deserts, with horses and cows.
The sky was blue.
The sun was hot.
The sand swirled under the hoofs of the herds.

The story was almost the same every time.

A handsome leader of the cowboys, a ranger with a beautiful
daughter, and a villain who stole the cows.
But do not worry, the bold hero always found out who did it.
Sometimes it was work of bad Indians. But sometimes the Indians
were good and fought together with the hero to bring the right
person to justice.
However always, always Good won.
And the end?
The hero married the daughter because they were in love.

It was great.

It was my world of illusion I lived in this small house, in this little
village of a small country in the heart of Europe.

I really could not know that fifty years later I would be in Texas.

Vera Stanek

The situation of our family changed dramatically, when my father found a new job. He became the manager of big paint store in the nearby city of Olomouc.
The second biggest city in Moravia.

It took my father a couple of hours to get to work every day.

Olomouc was 18 miles from Prerov, where we lived.
Just the trip to the railway station took my father one hour on a bicycle. Then half an hour by train and another half an hour by tram in Olomouc to get to the store.

But father was happy.
He was the boss of six employees, and the owner gave him a free hand in the business.
For the first and last time of his life, father was paid very well.

Three happy years, no more!

We began to feel the advantage of having enough money.

Every Saturday afternoon father came home from Olomouc with a box from the best bakery in town in his hand.
Inside the box were three pieces of cakes for every family member.
There were cakes with real buttery cream.
Cakes with whipping cream and chocolate.
The smell of vanilla filled our kitchen.

We children were crazy about these goodies.

For me, the cakes were a statement about how good our lives were.
How *rich* we were.

Thanks to the money, my parents also changed our apartment.
They bought new furniture with a surface smooth as silk. I stroked the surface with my hand and was sure that this was the nicest

furniture I had ever seen.
Later we had new carpet and I got a piano to learn to play.

We were wealthy now.
I was convinced about it and nothing could change my mind.

We had one nice living room.
Following the good manners of these times, the room was reserved
for special occasions.
For visitors or friends.

Only I do not remember anyone coming to visit.
So this nice room remained closed.
Ready for visitors that never came.

Just once a year, at Christmas, the door opened.
The room was heated, and a Christmas tree stood there.
Underneath it were gifts, wrapped in colorful paper with names
written in big letters.
On the table was a white tablecloth and a huge plate with cookies.

There we spent Christmas days.
My sister and I played with new toys, my parents read or listened to
the radio.
Even our meals were served there.
It was very different from the daily routine.

Only I spent more time in this lovely room during the year.
My piano was there and I practiced very diligently every day.
In the winter I had a small radiator next to me so that my fingers
would not completely freeze.

To tell the truth I liked to play piano.

Especially, when my father brought me new sheet music from
Olomouc with the music he liked.
There were arias from the best operas together with film music from

the times before the war. And operetta songs, Glen Miller's songs, and of course classic Czech music.
So many different styles, but all of them full of wonderful music.
I liked playing them more than the compulsory homework.

Sometimes, I needed sheet music that was not available on the market.
Then my father made it, just for me.
Every evening, after the work, he took ink and a pen in his hand.
He wrote the notes on a paper, copying the original I borrowed from my piano teacher.
My father was very skilled and nothing was difficult for him to do for me because he loved my piano playing.

What a shame I do not have the sheet music anymore.

The time after the war was very exciting.

With the freedom came a zest for living.
My parents joined a gymnastics club that they had loved before the war. Both of them were great gymnasts, on the rings, horizontal bar, on the mat.
Soon they were instructors, and my father became the president.

We almost lived at the gym.
My sister Eva, only few months old, slept peacefully on the mat.
I trained diligently because I wanted to be as good as my parents.

In the course of time, I began to love it.
The gracefulness of a movement.
The necessity to be exact.
The lightness of a practice.

How wonderful a time it was and not only because of the gymnastics.
Our social life also changed drastically.

Summer evenings in the club were the most exciting.
Adults played ball games, children had free time for games and
were always up to some mischief.
All of us enjoyed this time together.

In the winter was a special event on the program.
A fancy-dress ball for the whole village.
Each year had another theme.
"Around the world," or "In our orchards," to name just two of them.

What did it mean?

My mother had to find the perfect dress, appropriate for this
occasion. Something not just nice, but a dress my father would not
recognize her in and with a mask on her face.
Because that was the joke.
Not to be recognizable.
Then they could enjoy the anonymity and have a great time.

It was fun, not just for our parents, but for us, children, too.

When the day arrived, we were so excited.

Father started the show.
He dressed in his black suit, only he fooled around.
He put his jacket and tie directly on his body and pretended to be
ready to go. With no shirt and just in his house shoes.

My sister Eva and I laughed hard.

When father left, another excitement began.
My mother got ready.
How breathtaking her dresses were; of course she sewed them
herself.

Vera Stanek

I was allowed to help her to get ready.
To bring her purse.
To hold her lipstick or powder box.
To bring her shoes.
I walked on air.

With my mother leaving, the fun was not over yet.

There was still a second day, the day after ball.
And for us, children, it was much more interesting than the day of ball itself.

In the morning sister Eva and I quietly sneaked from our beds.
We knew exactly what was waiting for us on the kitchen table. A full box of home-made cookies that just melted in one's mouth.

This day was an exception.
No bread and tea for breakfast, but cookies instead!
Yum, yum !

In the afternoon, when our parents were rested again, we all went to enjoy aftermath ball.
Because it was an occasion where children were allowed in.

I was very excited.
I could watch how the adults danced.
I could see how they entertained themselves.
And I could admire the dresses of the ladies.
There were more sweets, lemonade and goodies, but it was the opportunity to be there that was so tempting.
In these moments, I had only one big wish; to quickly be old enough to go to the ball, to have a nice dress and dance.

These were some of the happiest moments of my childhood.

Our whole family's existence was on the way up.

But only until February 1948, when the Communists took over in a coup.

First, they dismissed the president.
Then they took power in the government with the main orientation of the politics at the Soviet Union.
One of the most difficult times in the modern Czech history began.

Some people adapted to this new situation very well.

My father did not.
He told one day to all of us, "I will not bend my back before this mob."
Somehow I understood, that he was very serious about it.

He quit his sport club, his love and mark of freedom, because the Communists wanted the club under their control.
Most of members quit with him and shortly thereafter, the club broke up.

The Communists did not forget his action.
I would know it best and very soon.

The new government nationalized the industry.
Now everything belonged to the people.

Some business owners did not like it and protested loudly and that was wrong.
They were not allowed to disagree.
They were there to obey and to be thankful to give away their possessions.
To give everything to the people.

To disobey meant to take the consequences.
People were put in the jail with no lawsuit and no lawyer, for ten or

even twenty years of prison.
The "people's court" with a Party member as the judge decided
their fate.

The head will chill during the years in jail.
The possessions will be gone.
Simple, isn't it?

What was even worse, that the enemy were the people of the same
nationality.
The people that spoke the same language.
These people hanged in public their own people just because they
were members of another party.
They killed the uncomfortable ones and pronounced their death as
a suicide.

Nothing was safe before them.

"The path to Communism asks for sacrifice," was their ideology.

The propaganda was everywhere.
Big loudspeakers that constantly bawled Communist and Soviet
songs were put on every street corner.
I can still hear "We are the new youths ..."
I still remember it.

The rows of the Party grew and with it came a question to your
mind.
"Was the Czech nation so corrupt ?"
I do not know.
But what I know absolutely is, that there were still some people like
my father.

I never once told him how I was, and still am, proud of him for not
betraying his beliefs.
Why did I not tell him?
Because we were not used to talking about our feelings.

What a shame!
I only wish that I could tell him this before he died.

Meanwhile, everybody had to deal with the new reality.

Some people escaped to foreign countries.
Some tried to escape.
Some stayed and believed that it would not take long and that the
Communists would be overthrown again.

How wrong they were.

The borders to the West were closed.
The nation stayed behind the *Iron Curtain.*

My mother could not go and visit her siblings in West Germany.
They, on other hand, feared to come to visit her especially in
Czechoslovakia.
That was easy to understand.
There was nothing that could be done to bring the family together.

In addition, our family had *minus point* because it was suspicious to
have relatives in the West.
There were always some questions to ask.
Were you or were not a friend of socialism?
What if the relatives influenced you?
What if they shook your faith in socialism?

There were many reasons for having more *minus points*.

Maybe you did not put a Soviet flag on your house on the Day
of Victory of the Soviet Revolution and your neighbor saw it, and
reported it.
Or you told a friend that you did not like the politics of the new
government.

And why not to tell him what you really think?
He was your friend.

Only you did not know that he had changed sides.
That he was now an eager Party member.
That he notified his new pals about your point of view.

How could he change his attitude?

Maybe he wanted an easy life for his children.
Maybe he was already tired of holding his back straight.
Or maybe he wanted at least once in his life to belong to the winners.
Who knows?

It was probably the reason why our nice living room stayed empty.
Empty of friends who would talk and laugh.
Empty of human beings.

My parents had no friends because they did not know whom to trust.

The changes in politics interfered also in the life of our family.

My father lost his job.
The owner of the paint store did not hold up to the pressure of the Communists.
He decided to give his store as a *gift* to the new regime.

Father looked around.
Surprisingly, he found another job in Prerov, even closer to home.
It was a job in distribution of pharmaceutical drugs where he was responsible for the orders of pharmacies. He liked his new job very much.
In his spare time he learned about the drugs until he was an expert.

During inventory, he brought his papers home and I was allowed to help him check it.

I was so proud of myself!

As a reward for my help, my father gave me 100 Czech Krones; my first pocket money at the age of twelve.

Our *rich* times were over.

But we could live without any big problems.

Aside from school, I was involved in many activities.

I found great joy in poetry and amateur theater and I sang in the school choir.

I also participated in many athletic contests.

It was then that I fell in love with skiing.

Again it was my father who brought me to this discovery.

While cleaning out the attic, he found there his old skis. He adapted them for me, using my only pair of winter shoes.

It did not matter to me that we did not have any money for new ones.

Father began to teach me how to ski.

How to go down a slope without breaking my leg or neck. He did not regret the time he spent with me on the nearby hills.

What began as a curiosity grew to a love that remained with me my whole life.

I still love to go skiing down the slopes.

Despite that I am, perhaps, too old for this sport.

In addition to the downhill style I began cross-country skiing.

But I needed another pair of skis.

Because the family had no money, there was just one solution to my problem; I had to decide between downhill or cross-country skiing.

Cross-country skiing won for one simple reason, it was cheaper.

I could use the skis near the house, in the fields of our flat country.

Often, snow covered the ground in winter for months at a time.

My father cut off the sides of my downhill skis to make them narrower, and I began take part in cross-country skiing competitions.

I brought home some victories and my father was very proud of me.

Later, while I was at the university, my father gave me an annual gift. He paid for a one week long ski vacation for me in the mountains.

Often he had to struggle to pull the money together.

But father stayed stubborn.

And every time when he could save some extra money, he went with me.

We had a great time together.

The year 1953, was one of the most miserable for our family.

But not just for us.

The Communists put into effect the stabilization of the currency.

The rules were simple.

Five old Czech Krones were exchanged for one new Czech Krone.

But only up to 300 new ones per person.

The rest was exchanged at the rate of 50:1.

If you had some savings, maybe for coal or a new coat, suddenly you had nothing.

Everybody was poor in the same way.

The nation suffered.

Some people tried to sell their last possessions such as antique furniture, paintings or jewelry, just to have enough to eat.

Life was getting harder and harder.

My father was fired from his job for political reasons.
Sometimes he did not keep his mouth shut and he said what he
thought.
It was dangerous.
Now he knew it without doubt.
But it did not change him and he remained a rebel all his life.

Now he was put to work where the Party needed him.

And the Party needed him in a warehouse where were stored foods
such as flour, sugar, etc. All day he filled bags and loaded them
onto trucks.
It was horrible work without mechanization.
His only tools were his hands.
His reward was an unqualified laborer's pay.

The family had problems again and not just from lack of money, but
with me.

After nine years, I finished elementary school.
I wanted to go study to high school for another three years and
then, maybe, to the university.

However there were many obstacles.

For nine years I had been the best in the class.
My only problem was my father.
Because of his rebellious manner and not being loyal to the Party,
it was obvious to the people in power that I, his daughter, could not
be much different from him.

The Party members in my school found the solution.
They made me an offer; if I wanted to go study further, I needed to
change my attitude and show them my love for the regime.

How?
For two years I was to go and build the "big socialistic constructions."
To learn what it mean to be working class.

What did it mean for me?
To go away from home.
To build a dam or work in a mine or maybe in heavy industry where every hand was needed.
Why?
Because it was necessary to catch up with the imperialists, America in particular. It was not just important to catch-up with them, but to be better than they were.
This was the official propaganda.

Some young people volunteered convinced of communistic ideas.
Some were put there for punishment.

Both groups had to be prepared to work in inhuman conditions.
The young people slept in barracks with no sanitation.
For 24 hours a day they were under the influence of Communist propaganda, and had no free time at all.

More importantly, they were kept away from their families.
It was part of the reeducation. After a while the family lost their influence on a young person and then a change happened.

Many young people turned away from their families.
They were even ashamed of them and did everything to forget them.
They grew up to be enthusiastic Party members.
They walked with a Party pin on their collars.

All this was waiting for me.

My mother was devastated; I was her pride and hope for a better

future.
Now she cried and cried.

My father was furious.
He decided to go to the school offices and tell them what he really thought about it. Neither the pleading nor the tears of my mother could stop him.
She was sure that the situation would only get worse.

But my father remained stubborn.
He drove to the school district in Olomouc and found the school department.
He knocked on a nearby door and opened it.

When he looked into the room, he did not believe his eyes.

He recognized the face behind the desk immediately.
It was somebody very well known to him. A friend from the times of his train trips to Olomouc, when they used to play cards to kill the time.

"Hi Oldrich, how are you doing? I have not seen you for a long time. What can I do for you?" he greeted my father.
He was now a Communist with an influential position. Only now, out of sentimentality, he offered my father help.
Sometimes even such Communists existed.

I received the permission to go study.

The school system had just been reorganized after the school system in Soviet Union, although it was sub-standard.
Many said the Soviets were "100 years behind the apes in their education system."
But it was not open to discussion.
They were our model now.

Did I want to go study? Yes, I did.
So I had to accept it and keep my mouth shut.

I was offered to skip one class which meant I could study in high
school for only two years.
I agreed without hesitation.
Of course, I was told, to say goodbye to my good results,
because during the first year I would have to study two classes
simultaneously.

It was quite a difficult task.
But it did not change my decision.

The first year was really very hard.
I had missed a lot of instructions in mathematics, history, physics, to
name a few.
However, I worked diligently on my studies and was able to do
other activities that I really enjoyed.

I joined the school theatrical group and got to act again with a group
of friends. It was refreshing and made me happy.

I did not forget my love for skiing.
I took part in cross-country skiing competitions, this time armed with
new skis, borrowed from the school.
I managed to win some of the contests and had fun.

Finally there were dancing lessons.
These used to be the first social event of every young girl and boy.
Not even socialism could forbid dances.
There were only small changes from the times before the
Communist regime.

Girl's dresses were not so fancy and pretty because no one had
money for material. Sundays dresses had to be enough.
The boys wore various suits, not the classical black ones.

In the past the student's mothers were the chaperons at every lesson.
Now the mothers had to stay home.
There were no chaperons.

Still, the dancing survived socialism and I learned to dance.

With it came my first real ball.
My mother was excited about sewing my first evening gown. And for this special event the mothers were allowed to be chaperons.
My mother was very happy.

Life was sometimes exciting without regard to socialism.

I really do not know where I found the energy for everything that I did during those times.
In the middle of the first year, I was second in my class and at the end of my first year, the first.
I was as happy as a fish in water.

I did not care much about communist propaganda.
I had other things to do.

During the summer break, we were once again reminded of the misery of our surroundings.

Our English teacher and her boy-friend tried to escape to the West.
They decided to swim across the Danube, a strong border river, with heavy cargo ships going up and down.

How desperate and brave would a person have to be to jump to such malicious and deep waters.
With every stroke closer to freedom.
With every breath closer to the dream.

She managed it through the bullets.

He did not.

With mixed feelings I entered the last year of high school.

However fate had a surprise ready for me.
I broke my leg when I jumped from the rings during class; I was just a fraction of a second late.

It was not a simple fracture, so I had to have surgery.

The surgeon was young, handsome and open to everything new and revolutionary for this time. He asked my father to consent to a new procedure and my father agreed.

My broken ankle was screwed to the bone back and then the leg was put in a cast. I was a *guinea pig,* but a happy one.
Against the prognoses of other doctors, both legs were identical in length.
At least this was all right.

There was still uncertainty about my ability to ski again.
I was told to wait a few years and then try.

The doctors underestimated me and my strong will to ski.
Exactly one year later, with swollen ankle laced in a ski boot, I was on the ski slopes again.
I was determined to take part in competitions in the near future.
It took me another two months, and I reached this goal, too.

The broken leg brought me other problems besides the cast, crutches and cane.
High school graduation was in sight.

Since I could not walk, I could not take part in lessons.

I was forced to do my school work at home.

My friends helped me as much as they could.
My schoolmate sent me copy of her class notes, another one
helped me with my homework. It was very tiring.
But we all managed it and I was successful.

I took the first semester finals in the principal's office.
There I sat behind the desk with my leg placed on a chair.
The teachers came in with the tests, one after another, for two
whole days.
Then I was through.
I was qualified for the last semester, the most important one.

Slowly everything started looking up.

After two months I could go to school again.
I walked on my own two legs and used only a cane; what progress.

My father took my heavy school bag on his bicycle to school every
morning and in the afternoon back home again. So I could walk
slowly.
I needed 45 minutes to go one way.
But I was so happy to walk again that nothing could change my
cheerful mood.

Six months later, a second surgery was necessary to remove the
screw.
The family and friends were helpful again.

The time of graduation came near.

Even before graduation I racked my brain with the question, "What I
would like to do after I finish high school?"
Or better yet, "What am I going to be allowed to do?"

The principal invited my parents in for a talk about my study.
He told them briefly, that it would be difficult because of my political

profile.
I had to forget all the universities with humanities and the
universities that were full of applications.
What was left, then?
To find a university that was half empty.
One that had little interest for most people.

My parents were shattered by the news.
They were so proud of me and the great job I did the last two years.

But the Party was still watchful.

Finally my teachers helped me.
We were able to find a university that was, in fact, almost empty.
A small university in a small city of Podebrady, a branch of
the Technical University of Prague, with only one course; the
Radiolocation engineering.

Soon I found that the Prague University offered a specialty that I
would enjoy.
Radio, TV, and Film engineering.

In these times, nobody knew what would happen the next day.
Not to mention next year.
'Maybe a transfer to Prague would be possible,' I secretly thought.

That was all I allowed myself to think about.
It was a waste of time to think too much.

I was realistic.
I knew that I may not have had any chance to go study, so I had to
take what was available.
Not to think too much.
Not to dream too much.
But to make the best of the situation I was in.

At the end, everything worked out well.

I graduated successfully from my high school.
The University accepted my application.

After the summer break in 1955, I went to Podebrady.

Chapter 7

The car is fast, indeed.
It tears along the road at the speed of 30 miles per hour.

The boy behind the wheel enjoys it.
A left curve and then immediately a right one, flat stretch and another curves.
He laughs loud with pleasure.
But not for long.

Out of the blue, he hears a siren and then sees a police car.
A hand signals him to stop.

The boy responds swiftly and steps on the brakes.

A policeman gets out and slowly walks to the window of the boy's car.
"Can I see your driver's license, young man?"
Oh, no...

He suddenly awakes with sweat on the forehead and looks around in confused state of mind.
Finally, he understands and heaves sigh of relief.

Thank heavens!
It was just a dream.

The war was over in Podebrady.

Frantisek began to repair prewar cars that had to be ready to drive immediately.
They had to be good enough for now.

Everybody was eager to have a car but the market was empty.

Vera Stanek

There were no new cars available.
Because there was no money and no time to produce cars.
The post-war nation needed more important things, like food and homes.The only solution was to repair the old ones.
Frantisek was very busy.

Frank was happy about the end of war for another reason.
Whenever Frank attempted to drive a car, his father told him, "After the war."
Now the war was over.
And Frank knew that his father would hold to his word.

The first lesson behind the wheel was scheduled on September 1st, 1945.
13-year-old Frank was behind the wheel.
22-year-old Lada sat next to him.
"Make a mistake and I will slap you," were the first words Lada spoke.

However, it did not matter to Frank.

He had watched his father's hands for many years.
He knew exactly what to do.
Put a key in the ignition.
Step on the clutch.
Engage the first gear.
Accelerate.
Go!

Now he repeated it in his brain and put the car in the motion.
He drove by himself.
With ears red from concentration and with his head in the clouds.
His first drive, his big dream came true!

There were only a few cars on the streets and the traffic flowed smoothly without any traffic jams.
There were just a few policemen in charge of the traffic.

The rules were a little different then and so were the cars.

It was in a small country in Europe.
After the war.

The freedom brought opportunities you didn't have before.
Just choose one.
Work hard to fulfill your dreams and believe in yourself.
This was the new thinking.

After exile in England, two men, a doctor and a professor, came back home.
They came with a brilliant idea and the vision how to do it.
They wanted to build in the city of Podebrady a high school in the same style as in England.
A boarding school.

Together with the city authorities they worked hard and with unflagging energy.
Finally their vision became a reality.

The new boarding school was located in an old castle in the middle of the town. The castle belonged to one of the mighty Czech kings of 13th century.
To King George of Podebrady.

Now the castle awoke to new life.

The classes were next to the birth-room of the king.
Soon the entire castle rang with new sounds.
On one hand of students' voices and their laughter, on the other hand with the serious voices of the professors .
Even the king would have been happy there!

A coincidence brought Frank to study there.

The school did not have enough students and so the local students were asked to join them.
Frank's parents decided to use the opportunity and sent their son to the boarding school.

Frank was eager to be a student of this different school.
He was proud to have a uniform and a cap with the school emblem on it as a mark that he was a member of this school.

But what he liked most was the style and the knowledge of all his teachers. Something really special at that time.

It was a pleasure to be educated there.
The Russian language was taught by a Russian professor, the English language by an English professor from Scotland.
The mathematics was lectured by a resolute, but fair professor.
And history by a professor with the knowledge of world events, not just the Czech past.

Everyone was a unique personality.

The school board did a great job by putting together the best of the best.
Soon the school was the best in entire county.
It was a privilege to be a student there.

The school laid great emphasis on knowledge of compulsory subjects, but not just this. The education there included many different activities.

One of the most important was sport.
More sport during the year gave the students a balance between a healthy mind and healthy body.
Frank loved athletics.

An old soccer field by the river Labe was given to Frank's athletic

club by the city authorities.
The students built a small stadium with lanes for sprints, a jumping pit, and even a shot-put ring.
With excellent conditions came excellent results.

One of Frank's teammates held first place in the Republic in shot-put. Frank's own record in high jump ranked him among the first ten in the Republic.
Then there were all the competitions with other schools.
Every member of the team performed by using every ounce of energy to win.
What an exciting life they had!

And what was the best?
That they were a team.
Friends.

Aside from sports, the school supported other activities.

At the celebration of St. George, on April 24th, followed an annual tradition.

The day began with swimming in the cold river Labe.
In April, the water was terribly cold.
It was just a few strokes for the most brave; students and professors under the leadership of the strict mathematics professor.

The day continued with celebration worthy of this special event.

In the afternoon, there was a theater performance in the castle yard.
Every year another performance of classical Czech writers.
The director was Milos Forman, who was in these times a student of the school.
Nobody knew then that he would become one of the best.
In another time.

Vera Stanek

In another world.

The time at the boarding school was wonderful.
Some of the best years in Frank's teens.

Only they did not last long.

The year 1948 began, and with it the February coup.
Soon there were radical changes not only in politics, but in
everyday life.

Frantisek knew he did not have much time left.
It was necessary to react without hesitation. Every day counted if
you were going to survive or lose everything.

Together with his former friends in Prague, Frantisek found a
solution. They all hoped it would help them to survive the first
Communist *cleansing*.
The idea was simple.
The men founded a car cooperative.
Their car repair shops merged.
They were no longer individual owners, rather members of a
cooperative.

The Communists left them in peace, at least for now.
But for how long?

Nobody knew the answer.
Not even Frantisek.

The changes reached Frank's school, too.

The English professor, the Scotswoman Meira, left first and was
substituted by a Czech teacher. Naturally, the lessons were no
longer the same.

Over time, other professors left, mostly for political reasons.

Soon there were problems.

One Monday morning, Frank's class met in the castle yard.
Who likes to go to school on Mondays? Nobody.
All the fourteen students came to the same conclusion.
Especially with regard to the terrible group of today's subjects, like math, chemistry and history.

After a short discussion they decided to go home.
Just like that.

Frank went to his father's workshop.
In these times Frank was already building his own sport car and spent every free minute in the workshop.
Today he was happy to use the free time to improve his new engine.

However his happiness was not permanent.

At 11:00 a.m., his father appeared at the door.
"Why are you not in school?" Frantisek asked.
"Oh, the lessons were canceled today," Frank lied .
"Beat it! And quickly! You and your classmates are in big trouble. The class professor called," Frantisek told his son.

In a moment, Frank disappeared.

In school he joined his classmates, fearful, but curious about what would happen now.

The principal came in.
"Boys, what you did is unforgivable," he told them.
"Yesterday was a national shift. Your behavior today was classified as a political provocation. You will be questioned about it."

Vera Stanek

The boys were desperate.
How could they forget?

The national shift was an action declared by the Party many times a
year. On certain Sundays, you had to go and work for the republic;
with no pay.
You had to clean the streets.
You had to pick up the trash in the parks, or cut trees, ...
In school, you had to clean the windows or paint the classrooms,
organize laboratories, or... mostly manual work.

Of course, everybody was observed by watchful Party members.
You could get *minus point* if you stayed at home.

Now this happened to Frank's class.
What could be more terrible than a provocation?

The students were questioned by a group of professors for the
entire day and finally at the evening were sent home.
Was it provocation or just a boyish prank?
The situation was very serious.

"What would tomorrow bring?" the students asked themselves.

Next day in school, the principal came in again.
"Boys, there is just one solution to save you from being expelled
from the school. All of you will sign the application to the Youth
Organization. Now!"
They did it.

All of them filled the application to the Party organization for young
people.
All of them accepted the worst grade for conduct in the school
report.

The story had no happy ending, but in some ways it was important
for the boys.

To understand that life had changed.
Freedom was gone, and new regime was holding you on the leash,
a very short one, in fact.

The message was to play by the rules.
Think before you act.
Be aware of consequences.
Obey if you want to survive.

They were old enough to understand.

Life in the boarding school changed dramatically.

One by one the professors were dismissed.
They were replaced with another group, the enthusiastic Party
members.
The spirit of the boarding school disappeared.

Frank was close to being finished, his graduation was in sight.

On June 13th, 1950, was his "D" day.
He was prepared to show the commissioners that he knew his
material.
Frank appeared before them wearing a high buttoned jacket.
His blue shirt with the sign of the Young Organization on breast
pocket was almost not visible.
All of the students had to wear it.

Frank graduated with success.
He was convincing and excellent.
But would it be enough for an acceptance to the University in
Prague?
What will the Party say?

Prior to the graduation, Frank filled out the application to the

University.
His class professor told him to leave some parts open.
"I will fill it in myself at the right moment," he told Frank.

After the graduation the professor took Frank aside.
He decided to tell Frank what actually happened behind the closed door.

The head of the commission was a woman; a dedicated Party member.
When the commission was about to decide Frank's application to the University she told the others, "Did you see his hands ? These are not the hands of a bourgeois boy, these are the hands of a working class person."

And that's how Frank got the permission to go study.

How could it happen ?

Frank worked diligently on his car and it was not very clean work. The traces of oil penetrated his hands and not even an intense washing with soap and water could clean them completely.

After the summer break Frank started his study.
The spirit of the almost 600-year-old University changed, just like everything else.

The attendance was mandatory.
At the beginning of every lesson you had to sign an attendance list. And there were another changes, only some years before absolutely unthinkable.

Selected young Party members were sent to the University, and smart non-communist students had to take care of them.
It was obvious, that the Party members did not go to the University because they were smart.

They went there because they were Party members.
That's what counted.

Frank received his assignment.
To take care of three of *his* students, in math and descriptive
geometry. It was not just hard work, it was completely hopeless.

Fortunately, most of them failed already during the first year. They
all were transferred to the military academy where they were
welcome.
What was left behind was a bitter memory.

Frank found out after about 20 years, when for the first time he put
his hands on his own personal file.

Every person in Czechoslovakia had a personal file.
The file was collected by the Party members around your house,
from the street you lived on, the school, and mostly from your
working place.
It went with you your entire life, from kindergarten to the grave.

Some people's files were thick as a book.
About what they said or did not say, what they had or had not done.
In it was every person's life in a nutshell.

It was a secret file and nobody was allowed to see it.
It was just for the eyes of Party officials.
For the people that decided if you got a job, went to school or
received a bonus.
For the group of chosen, but not for you.

However, sometimes there was an opportunity to look into it.
But secretly, of course.

Surprisingly, this happened to Frank.
Somebody let him take a look, but only for half an hour, not more.
Frank decided on a place, where he would be not interrupted. He

closed himself in a restroom and read.

He saw things he did not know about himself but others seemed to know.
Like a statement from a cleaning lady.
A testimony from a housekeeper and neighbors.
Even a declaration from one of his students from the University.
This eager Party member wrote about him, "He helped me very much, but I felt his bourgeois background on every step."

This is how the world pays you back.

Or just the Communists?

After the first year, Frank was free from his students.
He sighed with a relief. He needed some time for himself.
During the week, he lived in a small apartment together with a roommate. He took classes at the University and did the homework.
But weekends belonged just to him.
Then he drove home to Podebrady and worked on his car.

Step by step the car began to have a form.

A small, low, silver sports car.
Made with Frank's hands, done on the basis of his own ideas.

Only Frank could put into words the sensation of the first drive.

He sat behind the wheel of a car he knew to the last bolt.
He stepped on the gas pedal and the car shot out like a rocket.
Frank smiled.
Speed! The car need more speed.
He pressed the gas pedal down.

In this moment the Earth stopped its rotation.
Frank's feeling was flooded with nothing else but an absolute happiness.

Forgotten were the hours of hard work.
Forgotten were tired and sometimes wounded hands.
Forgotten were the black walls of workshop instead of blue sky.
Forgotten was the smell of gas instead the smell of roses.

Frank finished the car in his third year at the University.
As expected, he began immediately to plan a second one.

Only this time it would be something special; a race car, and he
himself would be behind the wheel!
This was quite clear to Frank, already.
He had plans and ideas.

But he underestimated the Communists and their influence on the
life of every person.

Frank never finished this car, because everything changed.
It remained only a dream.

Frank had other dreams, and one of them came true.
He could study with the faculty of car engineering, his old love and
his passion.

Frank was completely absorbed in the books of car design, engine
construction, car technology. He was eager to know, to understand
what he did not know, yet.
It was his life and it was everything he had wanted.

He was satisfied with it and nothing could change it.
Nothing.
Not even military training.

The military training began in the second year of Frank's study.
One whole day a week.

In the beginning it was easy.

How to put a gas mask on your face.
How to turn to the left and to the right.
How to march and sing, take the gun apart and march and sing again.

The first year of military training ended with five weeks of training camp.
They lived in tents, trained hard and ate excellent food.
During this time the Party built a strong army, an army with discipline and order.

The goal of the training camp was simple.
Improve fitness and military discipline.

During the day was a training on the meadow.
Run!
March and sing!
Crawl!
Hurry over obstacles!

With every day of training the students changed.
Eventually their breathing became easier and their legs stronger.
The bodies suddenly had muscles. The spoiled city boys became men (most of them).

The training continued with undiminished intensity, day and night.
Every other night, there was a night drill.
March and sing!
Run!

"Attack the gamekeeper's lodge nearby," was the command one day. "The enemy is there!"

Frank's group quickly disappeared into the dark forest.
It was difficult because the forest was dense. The branches of the trees lashed in their faces and the only light was the dim shine of the moon.

The group advanced slowly and quietly.

Frank was anxious.
There was a thought in the back of his mind.
But he just could not remember it, no matter how hard he tried.
He continued along with the group going deeper and deeper into the forest.
'Very soon we would attack the lodge,' he was thinking.

"Use your brain, Frank," he told himself.

At once he put the fragments of his thought together.
He remembered.
The fence, of course, what else!
All of them knew about it.
They had been there many times during daytime, but they all forgot about it. Before Frank could react, the group was running forwards with a "hurrah" to attack the lodge.

"Stop!" shouted Frank, but nobody paid any attention to him.

Frank stopped and tried to see through the dark.

It happened exactly how he had imagined it.
The men slammed into the fence and all of them were knocked down to the ground, one after another. It looked as if an invisible hand smashed them like troublesome insects.

Frank could not help himself and began to laugh from his whole heart.
It was a laugh of amusement, loud and long-lasting.

This was the end of the night attack.

This time they didn't win but maybe tomorrow would be better.
Tomorrow is another training day.

The young men learned quickly.
They learned to obey and to subordinate to the discipline.
Be prepared to fight.
Be smart.
Do not forget, an enemy must be defeated.
Anytime and anywhere.
At the meadows or in the forest... day and night.
They all changed.

The five weeks flowed by like water in the river, and the new young men drove home.

Frank took a train.

When he reached the transfer station, he found out that his second train had already left.
What to do? An easy decision.
"March the ten miles, but do not sing today!" Frank ordered himself.
With a case in his hand and light footsteps, he marched.
It was nothing compared to the military gear.

With this training, Frank's military career did not end.

After the graduation from the University, another training was planned.

Only this time it was more serious.
Frank drove a real tank!
For the first and last time in his life.
What an excitement!
And not only did he drive the tank, but he even took part in an actual fight with gunfire.
He survived.

Now he was prepared for higher tasks.
He was promoted and became an officer.

Additional training was waiting for him in the future.
But it was just training.
Unlike most Czech men he did not have to join the military service
and serve this mandatory two years in the army.
He had completed his military training at the University and could
go directly from school to work.

In November 1954, Frank graduated by defending his thesis before
the examiners.
He became a mechanical engineer.

It meant another fulfilled dream and another step to the future.
A rose or gray colored one?
Nobody knew the answer.

The graduation ceremony was in a concert hall.
Frank's parents and Grandmother Anna were very proud of him.
Anna had told Frank many times, "I have only one wish in my life.
To see you as an engineer."
Now her wish had come true.

On this day, they all forgot their own worries.
At least for these few hours of celebration.

There were changes not only in Frank's life, but in the life of his
family.

In 1953, the Communists lost their patience with Frantisek and his
cooperative.
As a first step, they took all of his employees away.
The Party ordered them to a nearby tractor station where the
Collective Farm needed their machinery repaired.

Frantisek held on.
He continued repairing the cars together with his two brothers.

Still in his own company, but not knowing how much longer could they survive.
The answer was *in the stars.*

But all of them knew that the day would come when this small repair shop would cease to exist.
It would come soon and the Communists would take it for themselves.
Everything was only a question of time.

The three brothers held on for another year and then the day came.
The pride of Frantisek was nationalized.
The shop that Frantisek had built for almost 30 years changed owners.
It did not belong to Frantisek anymore.
It belonged now to the people.

Frank's mother Bozena tried to appeal this decision, but to no avail.
The decision was final.

Frantisek was ordered to work in a car repair shop in Podebrady.
There *the people* were already the owner.
His former shop got a new manager, new employees. Frantisek could watch them from the window of his apartment.
It was all that was left to him.

When Frank graduated from the University, his father's shop did not exist anymore.
With this changed situation, Frantisek lost more than his shop.
He lost his dream about the future of his own son.

It was not just a dream, since Frantisek had an exact idea about it.
He explained it many times to Frank:
"My father was a small farmer.
I am a tradesman.
You have to be an engineer.

Because the family should move up.

When you graduate, I do not want to see you for five years.
You have to go and see the world.
You have to collect experiences.
When you come back, you can choose between my company or build your own.
In any case I will help you."

But his dream, his idea could not come true.
The first part had been realized and Frank was an engineer, but that was all.
There was no longer the possibility to see the world.
There was no Frantisek's company anymore.
Frank was left on his own.

As everything, it was not easy.

The Party made decisions about your entire life.
Now they were to decide where Frank would be most useful.
To the people, how else.

Not what he wished.
Not what he was able to do.
But what the Party wanted.
Period.

Now the Party wanted him in a bus company outside of Prague.
Frank was dissatisfied.
He had to go away from Prague and from his apartment, from the few friends he had, from the girls!

He knew that the time had arrived, when he alone had to take the initiative in his own hands.

First he began a search for job.

Soon he found a promising position in a development institute, in Prague.
They were interested in him, but what to do with the Party order?
To change it, that was the problem.

Frank decided to drive to the bus company with an intention to visit the most important person, the personnel officer.
Only when Frank arrived, the personnel officer was not available.
"He is at Party political training today," the secretary told Frank
What to do now?

It was necessary to react and react quickly.

'Maybe it would not be bad to have a small talk with the secretary,'
thought Frank, and soon he found that this was a brilliant idea.
He assumed that secretaries knew about everything if they were good enough. This one was, surely, one of the best.

She told Frank that his job order had not been closed yet.
There was still some hesitation, because the company was not quite sure if they should take him or not .

'Great,' thought Frank. 'It is exactly what I need!'

He talked to the secretary so long until he persuaded her that he would solve this situation himself. He told her about the possibility he had for another job and promised not be a problem for the bus company.
Naturally, he would take care of everything.
Especially change of the job-order in the Department of Engineering

To Frank's great surprise, the secretary gave him his papers.

Now it was necessary to deal with the Department, but he believed that his stroke of good luck would hold on.

Frank went to the Department of Engineering.
He explained his problem with the bus company and pointed out their indifference to him. At the same time he showed his concern not to be a burden on them.
And he highlighted his initiative in search for another job.

Quite nervous, he waited the response of the official.

The official put the job order in a typewriter and asked, "What's the name of the new company?" Then he crossed out the name of the bus company and wrote the name of the development institute.
It was so easy!

Frank could not believe his luck.
All the sorrow, all the problems vanished in the air in the twinkling of an eye.
With a smile on the face and the changed job-order in his pocket, Frank left the Department.

The future looked rosy.
At least for now.

On January 2nd, 1955, Frank started his job in Prague.

Sometimes you just have to be lucky.
Nothing else.

Chapter 8

I am standing at the railway station on the platform number five, waiting for a train to Podebrady.
I am leaving home with a feeling I will not come back.

Everything I own is in the two big suitcases at my feet.

I am not alone.
My father is with me.
We do not speak.
Everything that was necessary has already been said.

In the distance the train is already visible.
It hoots loudly, brakes and slowly arrives at the platform where it stops.
I am lucky to find a free seat.
Otherwise I would have to stand all the way.
I put the suitcases in the net above the seats and quickly leave to give a hug to my father.

He is still standing on the platform.

When I embrace him, I see tears in his eyes.
Or is it just a speck of dust?
No, it is not.

He knows it, too.
He knows I will not come back.
In this moment he is just about to lose me.

'Does he remember the time we have spend together?' strikes me suddenly.
I am sure he does.

But he doesn't say, "Do not go!"

*He knows that children have to leave home to find their own lives.
It is a law of a mankind.*

I have tears in my eyes, too.

*With them I say goodbye.
To the family.
To home.
To my childhood.*

*The train is leaving with me.
My father's figure is smaller and smaller until it disappears
completely.*

I am alone.

I came to Podebrady in the last days of August 1955, with pockets
full of money.
How could I have pockets full of money?
It was easy, I had earned it.

During the last summer break I worked hard and long to earn it,
because I needed it.
I needed it to pay for the books, for a room to live in, for food.
My parents didn't have money to give me.
It was a poor time for our family again.

So I went to work.

But this time it was different than the years before.
No picking hops.
No planting saplings.
No harvesting.

I needed big money!

To make it, I went to work in a sand opencast mine.
The work was terrible, but the money I made was great.

I pushed the cars full of sand on the tracks.
When some of the tracks crossed, it was necessary to turn the cars
on a turning-point. This was the most difficult work, because the
cars were very heavy.
Sometimes I had to clench my teeth to hold on.

But the vision of big money was stronger.
And so was I.

What was almost unbearable at the beginning slowly began to
change. I was less and less tired and worked more efficiently.
And I had time yet to joke with my fellow workers, mostly other
women.
After six weeks, I brought home a small fortune.
I had more money than my father!

I was satisfied with myself.
During the same time, my mother worked hard, to put together a
wardrobe for me; a few skirts, shirts and slacks.
One coat for the spring and one coat for the winter, but that was all.
There was no money in our family for anything else.
This was already too much.

'The two coats I would probably wear the whole time at the
University,' I thought. But secretly I hoped to be wrong.
Only I was not.
It took five and half years, until my first salary, when I bought a new
winter coat.

After I left for the University my mother went to work.
She was not able to live in such conditions anymore.
The family was poor as church mice.
My sister was already a big girl and she could stay by herself,

occasionally.

The little money my mother brought home was a big help.

Mother found a job she liked.
I think she was just sorry she had not taken this step a long time ago. She worked in huge textile store in Prerov as a sales person. Again she touched silk, lace, wool, and cotton, something she had loved so much in the past.

Immediately she began training for her new job, and very soon she passed all examinations with honors as the oldest person ever to do so.
My mother was simply good.

But what was more important, she was happy again.

Salaries of both of my parents were insufficient to pay for the University. I applied for a grant that I did not have to pay back, and I got it.

On this occasion I made a vow to myself.
I would go through the University and not once ask my parents for money.
I held the promise.

It was just a question of planning, although it was sometimes hard to endure. But it was possible.

I found a room in Podebrady and I moved in together with a roommate. It saved some money and it was nice not to be alone.
I liked her very much and we got along very well.
We took classes together, we did our homework together, we helped each other.
We had great time.

I did not have a lot of time to think about home.
I had too much to do.

The University was located in a castle.
Yes, you guessed right. It was the same castle where Frank had
once attended the boarding school.

The classes were hard, at least for me.
Until then I had not been interested in engineering, particularly not
in classes such as math and descriptive geometry.
But now I had to learn them, if I wanted to get through the
University and be successful.
So I worked hard.

I solved hundreds of math problems, working on them every day.
I was sure, that the best solution to my problems was to train the
brain. And I was right.

After the first semester I was at the top of the class.

But not just classes were my life.

Immediately, I joined the ski club at the University.
That I was the only woman among 20 men was something I had
gotten used to already.
Because if you are at the technical University, it is normal.

I went to a trainer's school high in the mountains and it was
wonderful.
However the greatest thing for me was that my broken leg held out.
I was very pleased with myself.

Only two months later and I took part in a cross-country skiing
contest. I fulfilled my wish of skiing again, and my leg survived this
time, as well.

Another love stayed alive.
I joined the theater group in the city of Podebrady and acted again
with a group of people I loved and respected very much.

My life in Podebrady was full of work and joy.

What more could I want?

Once a month, I took the train to visit my parents in Prerov.
It was not so easy.

It took about 5 hours for 200 miles, especially in the winter.

By the time the train arrived to Podebrady from Prague, it was
already packed.
People were sitting even in the corridor on their suitcases or on
newspapers on the floor, some of them next to the toilet.
It was bad, and not just because of people.

Many times, the heating system was frozen and so were the
passengers. The only way to survive this trip was to stay in your
coat, with a shawl wrapped around your head and with gloves on
your hands.

But everybody wanted to go.

It did not matter which train I took, it was always the same.
I knew that my father would be waiting for me at the railway station,
and my nervous mother would be expecting me at home.
She would fear that something terrible had happened to me every
time I was late.

But taking this train was the only way home.
There was nothing I could do about it.
Just be patient, nothing more.

I liked Podebrady .
I began to feel good at the University and I liked all of my activities.

But, I did not see my future there.
I came to the conclusion to change the University.
I had to try the Radio, TV and Film engineering specialty at the University in Prague.
I had to try.

I asked about a transfer, filled out all the necessary papers and waited for a decision.
To my big surprise the answer was, yes.
What great news.

I finished the first year successfully.
I quit my room and said goodbye to the many friends I had made and to Podebrady.
It had been a good and interesting year for me, but I was not sad to leave.

A new life was waiting for me after the summer break.
To tell the truth, I looked forward to living in Prague.

My second year at the University began and everything was different.

First, I was assigned to the dormitory.
There were five girls in one room and although from the same University and from the same year, it was devastating.
Because you could find one girl with the similar interests.
But not five.

So the life was full of struggle for sometimes unimportant things like wet stockings on a chair, the radio playing too loud for someone doing homework, or the non existent closet space.

Vera Stanek

There were other differences, too.

In Podebrady, we were like a big family.
Here in Prague, it was a "factory of producing engineers en masse,"
as we often called it.
Nine women and three hundred men.

I was unhappy.
My grades fell, but somehow I managed to stay without flunking the
tests. It was hard, but I was stubborn, and I still hoped that it would
be possible for me to study the specialty, I decided to go after.

Life in Prague was not so bad.

There were theaters, movies, concerts and everything I loved.
All these events were reasonable priced, and I could afford to go
see them. There were times, when I knew all the repertoire of a
particular theater.
I was a season-ticket holder.
I went regularly to symphonic concerts.
I was informed about many cultural events in the city.

I did not forget my old love and went skiing again.
Sometimes with the Ski Club of the University, sometimes by
myself.

I didn't need much.
A bed and the possibility to cook the soup I had for dinner every
day; I did not have money for anything else.

I had found a chalet in the mountains with a young couple as the
property managers.
In exchange for a bed, I helped in the evenings in the kitchen.
They repaid me with kindness and friendship.
I continued to stay with them for the next 25 years every time I went
skiing, later with my whole family.

We became more then friends.
We were like a family.

Only once during my days at University I went to visit another
mountain area and was happy to survive.

Everything seemed harmless at the beginning.

My father gave me a ticket for a skiing vacation to a nice mountain
hotel by the name Lucni Hotel.
A very generous gift, indeed. The hotel was not one of the cheapest
ones. It was a big surprise for me.
Such a nice place!
"Where did father find the money for it?" I asked, first myself and
then him.

The answer was plain.
My father described it to me in a letter as a *wonder of the century.*
He had changed jobs and the Party did not protest.
He worked now in a factory that produced optical appliances
like binoculars, telescopes, and cameras. He was an excellent
machinist with skills he had learned during the war.
Now he could use them in this factory.

He blended into the crowd of 200 people until he retired.
For the next 25 years.

I knew this hotel, but just from the outside.
It stood on a plateau, high in the mountains with a great view at the
peaks nearby.

The only way to get there was a four-hour walk from the nearest
village. But that didn't bother me.
I was in a good shape and used to the mountains.

I was very excited!

I took a bus from Prague to the nearby village.
A man with a horse sled was waiting at the bus stop, exactly as the travel agency had promised.

It was not just me going on vacation.
Three young people got off the bus with me.
One girl and two boys, just a little older than I, with the same destination. We agreed to go together and I was pleased not to be alone on this difficult hike.
The village already had 50 inches of fresh snow .

"How much of it will be on the way?" I asked our man with the sled.
"Not too much," was the answer.

I had some doubts about this statement, but I did not think about it further.

The man took our baggage, and we put the skis on our shoulders.
Maybe we could use them, at least partly, we thought.

At 2:00 p.m. we hit the road.
We chatted happily and laughed.
We were young and we were on vacation.

They were two chalets on the way we had to pass: Richtrovka, the first and Vyrovka, the second.
All of us knew the way so it seemed no problem at all.

But the sky clouded up, and the first snow flakes fell quietly to the ground. We felt them on our faces, they covered us with a white layer.
The conditions got worse; then we felt the first whiff of a wind.
What to do?
We had not even passed the first chalet yet!

So we quickened our pace.

In about 20 minutes we reached Richtrovka.

The man with the sled told us, "I am not going any further!" and disappeared into the chalet.
After a short discussion, we decided to stay there, also, until it stopped snowing.

We did not know very much about this chalet .
We just knew, that the chalet was a vacation place of the Ministry of Education.

Very cautiously, we opened the door.
The dining room was already packed with children between 12 and 15 years old and their teachers.
The smell of wet clothing and sweat hung in the air.
After a while we found out that these kids were from a school in Prague. As a reward for their accomplishments in school they received a one-week ski vacation at Lucni Hotel.
Now they were looking for shelter, just as we were.

The property manager came into the room.
He made crystal-clear to the teachers that he did not want them in his chalet. Not in this room, not elsewhere.

Desperate, the teachers called a ski patrol.
The men arrived soon and decided to go with the children to the Lucni Hotel, despite the weather and the growing darkness.
They organized everything very quickly and all of them left.

What would happen to us?

We asked the manager for shelter, for the night.
"You can stay, " came the prompt answer. "But remember, I have no bed and no food for you."
'Go to hell,' I thought, 'I will make it to Lucni Hotel, if necessary on

all fours.'

But this time, I was alone with this decision.
My new pals wanted to stay.
So we separated.

I left quickly, because I wanted to catch the school children ahead
of me.

I needed only about 10 minutes before I reached the end of the line
they formed.
I remained there together with one man of the patrol team.
We went step by step in snow that was knee deep.

The movements became automatic.
"Follow in the footsteps of the person in front of you," we were
advised, "move slowly but constantly."
Easy to say, but hard to do.
The kids were city kids, most of them not fit at all and with
inadequate clothing.
Some of them were in the mountains for the first time.
What to do with them?

We persuaded them to keep walking.
Not to sit in the snow and relax, like some of them tried to do.
"Just one minute, please," they begged.
But we remained insistent.
"Move, move, do not sit, keep going!!!"

I knew the danger as did the patrol.
We knew what would happen.
If you sit in the snow, you close your eyes and you relax.
It is so nice and so peaceful, but... you freeze to the death!
The white death comes in this way, slowly and in silence.

So, please, do not sit, keep going!

We talked to them.
We threatened and dragged them.
"Just a few more steps, please. You can rest later," we persuaded them to continue going.
It was not easy for them nor for us.

At some point I left my skis in the snow, under a fir.
I did not care what would happen with them. I needed to have my hands free for the kids.

Eventually, we reached the second point of the trail, the chalet Vyrovka. It was just a small wooden cabin after a fire had destroyed the original hut.
However we were thankful to find a roof over our heads!
At least for a few minutes no snow.
No pleas," Please, keep going!"

The cabin was small and the possibility to be inside was restricted.
We had to stand one next to another, like sardines in a can.
The people in the cabin, just three men, were great. They were forest workers in the summer and rescue servicemen in the winter.

Now they made tea for all of us.
It was the best that they just could do for us in this moment.
A mug with hot tea worked miracles!

I have to confess.
First, I put my fingers into the tea to warm them, and then I drank the tea. Believe me, it was the most delicious cup of tea in my life.

The only problem was that our mission was not finished yet, because we were not at the end of our journey.
We had about two third of the long way behind us, but still enough to go.
It was necessary to get out into the snow again.

The snow was still falling.

The night was a little windy but that was all.
It was already about 7:00 p.m.

This time, I was at the head of the group, directly behind the first patrol man.
Other adults took care of the tired kids.

Those at the head worked out the way for the rest of the group.
It was harder than before, because the layer of snow was much deeper here.
We sank into it up to our hips now.

Time stopped for me.
I just put my foot in the footstep of the man before me, not really seeing anything.
Maybe more feeling, like an animal in danger.

We reached the highest point of the whole trail, just a small peak.
Suddenly, a blast of wind leant against us with an amazing strength.
"Go on all fours," the patrol man shouted.
I shouted the same to the person behind me and sank on my knees and hands.

We went on all fours maybe a few feet.
Maybe a few yards.
But they seemed like miles to me.

Once over the top we could stand again and continue.

Suddenly I heard something.
At first I thought it was an illusion, but it was not.
It was real.

It was a siren that was operated from the hotel.
The people there wanted to let us know that we were near. They wanted to show us the way and mobilize the last remainder of strength in us.

The will to survive.

I have to be honest and admit that I did not think anymore about the kids, I fought for myself.
I was 19 years old and I wanted to live.
Should I be ashamed?

I got to the hotel on all fours as the fourth person that crossed the treshold at 9:00 p.m. I was completely exhausted.

I was given another tea, some food and a room with a bed.
But before I fell into it, I went to the hotel entrance, to check on the children. I wanted to know what had happened with the group.
There were many people gathered near the door, prepared to help.
"We will do everything that is in our power," they told me.
They really did.

This group of volunteers from the hotel helped the kids to finish the way. They picked up the ones that could not walk anymore and collapsed in the snow.
They put them on sleds and brought them to the hotel.
Two doctors, visitors of the hotel, were waiting for them to give them first aid.

I did not stay long.
I was too tired just to stand there.

The following morning I woke up.

I opened my eyes and immediately looked out of the window.
All I could see was *white darkness,* a wall of still falling snow.
So I fell back to bed again and decided to stay there.
But soon I was on my feet.
I was too curious about what happened with the kids that I could not sleep.

Vera Stanek

I descended the stairs to the dining room, but it was empty.
No kids at all.
"What happened?" I asked the waiter that brought big can of hot coffee to me.

The news I got was frightening.

Up until 11.00 p.m., the volunteers and rescue teams worked hard to bring the kids to the hotel. Half of them with frostbite on their faces, hands or feet.
That nobody was injured seriously was a miracle.

I am sure the kids have not forgotten this day all their life long.

The weather remained the same throughout the day.
I was at the hotel, but where were my skis and baggage?
Surprisingly it did not seem important to me.
First I needed to feel better again.
"Relax," I ordered myself, "everything will be fine tomorrow."

When I opened my eyes the third day, I could not believe it.

The sky was blue.
The sun slowly emerged from behind one of the peaks.
Everything was white and glittered in the first beams of light.
How breathtaking!
Exactly how I imagined it would be.

I sprang from the bed.
Enough of laziness, I am here for skiing!

I ate my breakfast quickly and got on the way to find my possessions. It was not as easy as I thought it would be.
The way in this fresh, deep snow was difficult, so I continued very slowly.
But in this weather, it was no problem at all.

The man with sled I met near the chalet Vyrovka.
My baggage was there.

Now all I needed was to find my skis.
But where? I did not have a clue.
I knew, it had to be a little further down the trail so I continued. It was easier for me to go now since I could orient myself after the traces of the sled.

However it was necessary to leave the path and search systematically. So I submerged myself in the deep snow and began searching in rows from and to the path.
Finally I found the skis, stacked in the snow under one of the firs.

Now the world was all right again.
The ski vacation could begin.
Wonderful!

Soon I met my three buddies from the bus.
They were miserable and exhausted.
They had spent two nights on wooden benches in the chalet

Richtrovka with little food that was sold to them for outrageous prices.

The rest of the vacation was like a dream.
Every day the same picture of blue sky and sunshine.
Excellent skiing, and my new friends.

The week passed by quickly and I returned to Prague.

Afterwards I went to visit my parents.
But I did not talk about my harrowing experience.
I talked about the blue sky.
I didn't want them to worry.

Vera Stanek

At the University, an entirely nasty fight for the specialization began.
From the third year on, the classes were split.

I do not know how I got the place.
But I was accepted into the Radio, TV and Film engineering
specialization.
My dream had come true.
Along with two girls and 16 boys.

The classes were much more interesting, and soon my results
improved.
At the end of the year, I got more money in my monthly grant.
Because I was good, I got a grant for honors students.
A whole 150 Krones per month.

This was the reason that I allowed myself a small luxury.
I bought fabric for a new dress and my mother sewed it.
I was *brand new* after long time.

There were other changes for the better.

I found fun in the school and in the classes, because we all formed
a team.
We spent most of the time together, both in and after school; we did
some crazy or even stupid things.
However we were young and we were sure that life belonged to us.

Our classes were in different buildings of the old University.
In rooms that were several centuries old, with thick walls and small
windows, which made them terribly cold.
Especially in the winter.

Then we tried to heat the room.
There was an old coal oven, possibly from the time of the war.
We brought coal from the dark cellar full of spider nets, and then we
lit the fire.
Sometimes, thick smoke was the only result.

It meant we sat in our coats and opened the windows to ventilate the room.

But sometimes we were successful.

In that case, the oven radiated warmth, and we cooked tea in a big can and ate *dog* cookies.
No, not pet food.
They just tasted so bad. Only the cookies were cheap and we did not have money for something better.
It was food and it was warm.

We studied together and we celebrated every end of the semester with weird events. All together again.

We went to the movies and saw not just one, but three pictures in a row. And what movies!
We went to watch Soviet films, because we wanted to be alone.

Does it not make sense?
That's because you do not know the socialism of these times.

The movie theaters were empty.
Who would go to see Soviet movies full of working class and propaganda?
Maybe in the winter a few retirees.
If they did not have enough coal to heat their rooms, they attended these movies.
But that was all.

So we knew that nobody would disturb us.
We sat in the last row, and we did everything that was forbidden.
We ate and drank, we chatted and told jokes, we laughed at every scene on the screen.
We needed to let off steam and it was almost the only place we could do so.

It was mad but we did not care.
Another semester was behind us and the life seemed to be wonderful.

Not for everyone.

Some students were fired from the University.
They showed their sympathy with the Hungary Revolution in 1956, a revolution for more freedom and humanity.
However the guardians of socialism were watchful.

The Revolution was suppressed.
Only the students who talked louder than was appropriate had to leave.

Our group stayed intact.
We did not talk about politics.
Maybe we were smart, or just lucky?

We just wanted a little happiness.
Or was it too much to want to listen to Beatles or dance rock'n'roll?
Both of them were forbidden!
It was the "rotten music and lifestyle of the West."

Keep away from it if you want to stay at the University!

But there were groups in Prague that met secretly.
To listen and to dance.

I was invited.

I came.
I heard.
I saw.
I participated.

It was great!

For a few evenings I was able to forget the Soviet and popular
Party songs.
To forget that I was the future of socialism.
To forget the Party propaganda and the miserable life we all lived.
I just wanted to forget!

Do you find it crazy?
Then you are right.

Only it was socialism, you know.

The next year, our living conditions improved.
We were no longer juniors so we were put into another dormitory.
Not five girls together, only three.
Two Czech girls and one foreign student.

I lived with Jana and a Chinese girl named Wu Tiu Zun. My former
roommates lived with a girl from Korea.

This Asian girls were extremely hard-working.
To fail at the University would be terribly humiliating because
they would "lose face." They memorized everything because the
language problems were enormous.
But they worked very hard and most of them succeeded.

The only problem was with the girl from Korea.
She began to talk to us and tried to be like us.
At night, by the light of a bed lamp, she sewed dresses for herself
in the same style like we had. During the day she did not have time,
she had to study then.

She was so beautiful in her new dresses!

She fell in love with one of the male students from Korea.
They were the nicest couple I had ever seen.

But there were problems nobody understood.

She was asked to go to the Korean embassy.
There she was told that she had become too westernized and that she had lost the connection to her own people.
She had been under observation for a long time already.
Without hesitation she was sent back to Korea.

Her boyfriend was pardoned after he publicly gave her up during a meeting of young Korean Communists.
He conceded his mistake of having loved her.

The love story was over.

All of us girls survived the University.
Probably because we were a good team.

During the summer breaks we paddled on Vltava, the river that flows through Prague.

We began at the spring and went down the stream.
The river was clean.
Its water sparkled in the sun with every blow of the paddle into the water.
We drove through narrow openings in small dams.
We enjoyed the beauty of campfires at night.
We loved sleeping in tents on the meadows, with the river singing a lullaby.

On the way we also visited old castles placed high on the cliffs like eagle nests.

If you closed your eyes, you could see them.
The armies of soldiers in armor with spears in their hands, storming to occupy the fortress. But in vain.

Because the landlord knew where to build his residence.
The stream under the cliffs was strong and malicious, sometimes dangerous.

If you held your breath, you could hear the river sing endless songs.
Songs of water running through small gorges and jumping from one stone to another in waves shimmering in the sun.
Songs of meadows and birds.
Later, the stream became a river.
Then you could hear songs about the majestic history of Czech kings while passing by the castles.

Our river Vltava!
How we loved it!

After two weeks, our trip ended in Prague.
We hoped to go again the following year, and the year after that.
And we did.

But the Party decided to build one of the "Constructions of Socialism," a dam, on our river Vltava.

When we came the following year, everything had changed.
In *our* places were machines, the excavators dug ruthlessly into the earth, and convoy of trucks transported it to another place.
There were no birds and no meadows anymore.
Just dust everywhere.

We sat in dirty grass and cried.
We loved this river.
It spoke to us in a language nobody could understand.
Now they had hurt it!
They destroyed the water ways our ancestors had known and enjoyed in the same way we did.
For it, we cried.

Our trip to Prague was not very pleasant that year.

And as if the heaven knew our sorrows, it rained in streams for the remainder of the journey.

Still, we tried again the third year.
But we did not have fun anymore.

Additional dams came later on.
New factories were built on the banks with outlets of waste water into the river.
The river is dying, now.
It sings the last requiem for the dead.

My classes at the University continued.
In the summer break, before fourth year, we had to do a practical training at radio stations, TV studios and the only film studio in Prague.

The film studio was my destination.
I was very excited.
I wanted to see how the illusion with the name FILM was made.

I was assigned to sound research.
The offices of this department were next to the stages.
The hallways were full of people in costumes, with wigs on their heads and make-up on their faces.
It was a very special world.
Magic.
I loved it.

Suddenly I knew what I wanted to do.
I wanted to work there.
And I was willing to do everything for it, almost everything.

From the time of my practical training I began to go there one day a week.
It was the day when boys of our group had their military training.

Then we, girls, were free.
I worked in sound research on different projects and sometimes more than just one day, if necessary. Occasionally all night if the project was due.
I worked with no pay.
But I was glad to be there.
That was all I wanted.

My classes slowly ended.
I wrote a dissertation and successfully defended it.

Five and half years at the University were over.
I was an electrical engineer.

Our graduation was very festive.
After some years of disregard it returned in the old manner to the old historical places with the old glory.

The big event took place in a palace.

The palace was some centuries old and had been excellent renovated. The walls and floors were built of stone, now almost black with the age.
The auditorium was furnished with wooden benches. There were seats for graduates and their families.
It was a very imposing place.

The graduates themselves were imposing.
The men were dressed in black suits, the young women wore black dresses.

Nine women and one hundred eighty men were left from the three hundred that had started.

The entire graduation was precise.
The representatives of the University sat on the high stage.

The chancellor, the vice-chancellor, the dean and a group of professors.
The dignitaries were dressed in long red capes with stoat fur on the hem, as was the beadle, that lead the ceremony.
It was fascinating and majestic!

Then the speeches, and then the biggest moment.
My name was called by the beadle.
The chancellor congratulated me and handed me the diploma.
My parents were terribly proud of me.
My mother cried.

I was 22 and a half years old and I had the diploma in my pocket.

I also had a job contract with the film studio.

I took the initiative and asked about a job in sound research at the personnel department at the studio.
To my great surprise, they agreed to open a job contract for a development engineer, with my own name.
Could you believe it?

In addition, the Party did not protest, which was a small miracle.

The last step was to reach an agreement with the Ministry of Culture.
After some days of waiting for the decision came a letter.
"In accordance with the regulations....." and with permission to my job order.

I could not believe that everything went so smoothly.

Fortune smiled on me this time.
I accomplished what I had wanted so much.
To work at the film studio in Prague.

From January 2nd, 1960, it was a reality.
Not a dream.

Chapter 9

It is a gray winter day.
Cold and windy.
Bare branches of trees bend in gusts of wind.
It is chilly outside.

Frank's family gathered in Podebrady.
To say goodbye to Anna.

The stroke surprised her as she was working, unexpected, with full force.
She was brought to a hospital, but it was too late.
She died.

Frank is standing by her grave with flowers in his hands.
He lays them slowly on the piled-up earth and with tears in the eyes he silently whispers, "Goodbye Anna, goodbye mother !"

He did not have time to tell her more.
And now she is gone.

But she will stay in Frank's heart forever.
Because that's where we keep the people that we love, alive.

In our hearts and in our memories.

Frank had only been at his job for two weeks when Anna died.
When he asked for a day off to go to her funeral, the personnel officer turned down his request with "No, she was only your grandmother."
But Frank disobeyed and left saying, "She was my real mother, I simply have to go."
And he went.

The director passed it over in silence.
He was a trustworthy Party member, but not a bad man.
He had been a lathe operator in the past, now he was Frank's boss.
The boss of the development institute for carburetors, where the Party needed him.

The institute was located in an old house, a few steps under street level. The test room, Frank's empire, was on the ground floor, and so was the workshop.

Frank was put under the supervision of an old and experienced engineer.
Their sole work was to build a carburetor of their own design.
If they succeeded, then the current license would be canceled and the government would save money.

It seemed as a great idea.

Frank was excited with this assignment and completely engrossed himself in his job.
With great enthusiasm he finished up the test room.
He put all the necessary equipment in it, so the tests could begin.

But first they had to build the carburetor.

The entire process began with an idea.
It was discussed with all team members, and then drawn on paper.
Afterwards the new design was taken into the workshop to the skilled hands of the mechanics. They made the prototype, tested in the test room and in driving tests with cars and motorcycles.

It was exciting to be part of the team.

Frank loved his job.
He was not just good, he was excellent at it.
Soon he was promoted to the head of the car carburetor division and was extremely contented.

But he forgot that the Party was still watching.

Now the time was ripe for inviting Frank to the Party.
Because the Party needed young and smart people.
Smart engineers.

Frank received the application to the Party.
The personnel officer in person put it in front of Frank with the words, "You are young and smart. Forget your father and come with us. You will go upwards like a rocket."

Frank was surprised and terrified at the same time.
'What should I do?' he asked himself, 'why me?'

He sat behind his desk.
The application had the Party insignia, a hammer and a sickle, at the top of the page.
Then followed all the information about the applicant; first name, last name, etc.
Frank looked at it.
In his mind he saw himself writing his first name, Frank....
'No, no! I can't! I can't put my name under this symbol,' a thought crossed his mind.
For once he knew it beyond all possible doubt.
He could not do it.

He had known it before but tried not to think about it too much because he hoped that the Party would never ask him.
But now they were asking!

Time to make decision, Frank.
Choose!
Career and an easy life, or never-ending struggle.

Choose, Frank!
Now!

He chose.
He did not fill out the application.
He took it back to the personnel officer saying, "I am sorry, but I am not interested in politics."
The personnel officer nodded, as if he understood, but probably he didn't. Only a fool would refuse an offer to be a Party member, to belong to the privileged.

So Frank stayed in his position without further promotion, and he knew why.
He had just paid the price for the peace of mind.
He paid the price for his conviction.

However he did not have time to think about it too much.
Frank was busy and life continued.

Then in 1956, the Revolution in Hungary broke out.
Hungary was also under a socialistic regime, and in serious economical crisis.
In a nationwide revolution the people demanded changes.

The government decided otherwise and called for military assistance. The Soviet comrades rushed to help and they suppressed the revolution at the embryo stage.

The Party in Czechoslovakia was still powerful.

Now it was time to show it.
To show their strength to all people.

Since some people may have had similar ideas and would like to follow Hungary.
It was necessary to stop these thoughts and stop them immediately.
The political screenings began.

What were these political screenings?

The Party formed committees of Party members that decided now about you, about your fate, about your future.
It happened in all workplaces, at Universities, everywhere.

Every person was questioned by the committee.
What do you think about the revolution in Hungary?
What are your feelings on influence of the Party?
What do you think about the Soviet army?
Explain your relationship to the Soviet Union!
Tell us...
Just to name a few of the questions.

You had to answer in accordance with the Party line.
Or at least close to the line.

Then your answers were evaluated by the committee members, and the result was written in your personnel file.

If your answers were appropriate, you won.
You were allowed stay in your work place, where you could be useful to the Party.
If your answers were not good enough, you lost.
Then you were transferred to another job, sometimes to another city, but still useful to the Party, of course.

And you were watched on every step.
Your behavior.
Your friends.
Your dates.

You did not know when but you knew why.
You were not reliable and that was it.

This screening action changed Frank's institute, like many other companies.

There were personnel changes in the higher ranks.

Frank's supervisor had to go away and was exchanged with a new man, a good race driver but a bad engineer.
Nobody knew if he was a member of the Secret Police or not; what remained were just speculations and insecurity.
In any case, you had to be careful.

The personnel officer also disappeared, allegedly for *political weakness.* The test station got new blood, a young engineer with the Party supporting him.
He should strength the political consciousness in the institute.
The conditions worsened.

Frank was told simply, "You can stay."
A small victory, at least for today.

However not everybody was so lucky as Frank was.
His mother Bozena failed.

After Frantisek's company was nationalized, she found a job as an accountant in a construction firm.
Now she was fired because she was considered untrustworthy.

What was worse, she could not find another job.
The *black mark* in her personnel file, to be a wife of a former capitalist, closed all the doors, and she did not have the keys to open them.

One whole year she kept trying until she found a job in a small village, five miles from her home,
She became the only sales person in a small grocery store.
But she was very happy to find this job.

Because the times had changed.

She and Frantisek used to have enough money, but that was a long time ago.
When the Communists came, it was worse, but still relatively good.
Until the day when Frantisek's repair shop was nationalized.

These changes had a big impact on their personal life.
Now it was a necessity for both of them to work, to have money just to live.

Frantisek was still working in Podebrady.
In his mind's eye only one question, 'How much longer are they going to let me work?'
He was old now, but he had no right to get a pension.
He had once been a *burgeois,* not a member of the working class.

The time of political screenings sped his decision.
He knew he needed help.

A well known physician had cured Frantisek from a disorder of the blood cells for a long time already.
Now he used it as a good reason to put Frantisek on disability.
The physician arranged it and Frantisek received a pension.
He was free from political screening.
He was free from the Party.
Lucky Frantisek.

But Frantisek's pension was too small and so Bozena had to work.
She was eager to work, because she had worked her whole life long and was happy when she was working.
Lucky Bozena.

The personnel changes in Frank's institute were just the beginning.
The structure of the entire industry was modified.
Companies of similar interests were united in a big conglomerate.

This was the reason why Frank's institute was totally restructured and with it came new and higher tasks.

It meant for Frank's team to work not only on carburetors.
To their plan was added the technical development of mopeds.

Frank was busy.
He still worked on *his* carburetors for cars and racing cars.
He took part in the development of a range of carburetors, sold to some socialist countries and to Australia.

Besides, Frank found another pleasure.
He did tune-ups for race car engines so they had more power and more speed to win!

Life was full of excitement, and Frank enjoyed it.
He enjoyed driving with the best Czech race driver, Pavelka.

One day, a Russian delegation was announced.
The boss was excited about the opportunity to show the race car and to boast about the development.
Frank and Pavelka had the privilege to demonstrate it.

Everything was ready.

Frank, Pavelka, and three of the Russians got into the car on the test loop of the institute.
Pavelka accelerated and shortly was at 70 to 80 miles per hour.
Then he made a sharp turn with a skid to the right and another to the left. And with a another skid around the gas station he drove back where the superiors were standing.

Already before the car stopped, the doors opened, and the Russians sprang out.
Their faces were white.
Their eyes nearly out of their sockets.
Their hands on their stomachs.

Not a big success?
On the contrary.

It was very big success.

Pavelka told it to Frank exactly, "They will not come again."
And he was right.

In 1958, Frank got a new fellow worker.
An interesting man in every aspect.
An engineer, a Russian with a very colorful life, named Zarzecky.

Zarzecky was born as an only child to a ship doctor.
He spent his childhood on a Czar ship, crossing the oceans until
the October Revolution in Russia, in 1917.
Then he was put ashore in France by his father, studied and
became an engineer.

After the war, he was sent to Czechoslovakia to build a carburetor
company.
There he fell in love with a Czech woman and they married.

When the communists took over, they tried to escape.
Only they were caught and put in jail, *just* for 15 years, to become
sober.

But he was an excellent technician.
While in jail, he made some proposals for improvement.
As a reward for it he was set free after only a half of his sentence
was completed.
His wife remained behind the bars.

Frank's boss had known him from the old times and appreciated his
expertise. Now he offered him a job.
So Zarzecky appeared in the institute, and Frank had a competitor.

The competitor was a nice older man with a head full of know-how
about carburetors. And Frank was smart enough to see his chance
to learn more from him.

Soon the two men were a good team.
They worked together.
They discussed the ideas.
They complemented each other.
Zarzecky was a man of class.

There were not many of them around Frank.

The chief engineer had come the closest.

The chief engineer was a hard worker.
He worked about 20 hours a day, sleeping mostly in the car when a driver took him on business trips.
Not a very easy man to work for because he demanded the same from his people and for most of them, it was a problem.

One day Frank was asked to join him on business trip.
A company in Moravia had a carburetor problem to solve.

Frank knew about this problem.
He himself made an effort to find the solution. He searched for it in books and journals and was surprised to find it in one of his Russian books.

Frank intended to take some steps to confirm the results.
But he had no time to do it, because he was already on the way to the company.

There both men tested the wrong carburetor.
Frank suggested adding one small hole, using the idea he read about in the Russian book.
But the chief refused it.

Disappointed Frank returned to the hotel and to the room he shared with the chief. He went directly to the bed and fell asleep; the day was long enough.

Suddenly Frank awoke with the feeling he could not breathe.
In a confusion he looked around and saw that the room was full of
smoke. 'Fire' was his first thought.
He sprang quickly from the bed and tried vainly to recall in his mind
where the extinguisher hung.
But before he could move, he froze.

Behind the table sat the chief.
His ashtray was full of cigarette remains.
He lifted his head from a paper, looked at Frank and told him, "You
were right. This one small hole is the solution! Now I know it!"

Why all of sudden?
Because he solved it mathematically, working effortlessly during the
night.

A new day dawned, morning was near, so the two men returned to
the company.
They drilled the hole, then did a test and the result was first-rate.
Everything was fine, just fine.

It was time to go home.

One problem was solved, another was already waiting.
Only they did not know that not just one but many problems are
near.

And much more serious than a hole in a carburetor.

A big turn was waiting for all of them.

The director left and a new one came; a Party member who else?
His first action was to fire the chief engineer.
His second was the decision to move the institute outside of
Prague, to the factory that produced the carburetors.

Development to the production, was a new trend, declared by the

Vera Stanek

Party. That was it.

The situation in Frank's institute was chaotic.

Of 130 employees only three left Prague.
The rest remained, looking desperately for jobs in other companies.
Frank began to look around for a new job.

But the new boss surprised him.

He gathered about 20 of the best people of the *old* company
and with them he built another institute; a research center for
motorcycles and bikes.
He asked Frank to take a new position as chief of a laboratory with
an interesting task; to find the right method for testing motorcycles
and bikes.
Just one method for all companies so the results could be
comparable.

Good idea, indeed.

Frank thought about it for a short time and then agreed.

The new research center moved to another part of Prague and that
was the only big change.

Soon Frank was completely absorbed in his work once again.

He was almost overrun with many another assignments waiting for
him.
Work out the standards for testing and develop and realize all
essential devices for it. Work together with the University to develop
rotary engine, etc.
These were only a few of the most important tasks.

It seemed, that everything worked out fine for Frank .
There was only small problem.

The way to his new job took too long.
Frank had to use different trams and busses to go almost through half of Prague.
'Enough is enough,' Frank told himself one day.
He began to search for a better and shorter way.
This was now his number one priority.

He started to use different ways until he found what he was looking for. A shortcut with less people and less traffic.
Frank was very pleased with himself.
Using this way would save him lots of time!

Frank lived in the same apartment as when he was a student, only he did not have a roommate anymore.
The apartment was placed on a hill above the river Vltava with a wonderful view around.

The new way Frank discovered was so easy!

Just down the hill, walking or running.
Then a short way around the tram station and through an underpass to the river.
There Frank took the ferry.
A simple boat, in reality, moving by help of rope and pulley, that was hooked on a cable, stretched between the banks of river.
There was only one ferryman at the helm.

Frank began to use his new way in winter, in January 1962.
It was not problem, because the ferryman held its way ice free.
It didn't matter to Frank that it was bitter cold.
The ferry ride lasted only a couple of minutes.

But winter passed and spring was on the way.
Nature woke up from winter sleep to a new life.

One day Frank watched the ferry, coming from opposite side the

river. A new person was on the board, a young lady.
He had not seen her before.

She was in her middle of twenties.
Tall and slim, with brown short hair and warm brown eyes.
When Frank turned around he saw it straight away.
Her legs were a work of art.
"Wow!" Frank let slip a remark in low voice from his lips.

'She is probably married to some rich person.'
'Not a chance for me,' Frank thought each day.

Why is that, Frank?
The answer was easy.
Every day the woman wore a different dress, something so unusual for these times.

She looked dapper, but that was not all.
She was somehow alive. Her look and her style told the people, "I am here and I love the life! What about you?"

Frank liked what he saw.

Every day he tried to be on time to see her, to catch her passing smile.
That was all.
Nothing more.

Frank knew, there was a problem.
He was too shy to establish contact in the presence of others.
Moreover, he was sure she was not interested in him.
Why should she ?

Not even a new discovery changed his mind.
He looked thoroughly on her left hand, but didn't find the wedding ring.
Frank didn't change his attitude.

'Maybe she does not wear a ring. Who knows?'

And this little smile was probably just part of her.
Nothing special.
Not for him.

Slowly it became more important for him to see her every day.
Frank believed that his entire day would be nicer if he just caught a glimpse of her.
He watched for her but that was all he allowed himself to do.

What a disappointment for him when she disappeared!
Once she was not there.
One day, no problem, it could happen.
Wrong timing.

But there was the second, then the third day, and she was still not on the ferry.
Not this little smile on her lips.
Not her eyes.
Nothing.

Frank was sure he would not see her again.
'That was it,' he told himself, 'What a shame.'

He still took this route, but he did not look forward to it.
To him it was just a way for work, nothing else.

A whole week passed by.
Frank did not hurry these days; one ferry sooner or later, it did not matter anymore.

One day, he walked through the underpass and suddenly he saw her. Was it a vision or reality? No, no, there she was, walking slowly with the help of a cane.

Oh no, what happened to her?

Frank put all of his courage together.
He stopped, smiled at her and broke the silence with, "Hi!"
"Hi!" she answered, smiled back and stopped walking.
Frank boldly continued, "What happened to you?"
"Oh, I just sprained my ankle," she answered, still smiling.

"Then, get well soon, bye," were Frank's last words.
The last ones, indeed.
His courage was gone.
"Bye," she answered with the smile on her lips.

Frank had the feeling that he had seen how her eyes sparked.
'Maybe she enjoyed this conversation, after all,' he thought but was
not utterly convinced.
He turned on his heels.

They continued in their ways, both alone.

However something changed.
From that moment Frank greeted her at almost every morning and
they smiled at each other until...
Until everything changed, again.

Frank began to go on business trips that went on for days,
sometimes even a whole week. The project of testing reached the
phase when he had to go.

Normally that was not a problem.
Now, it was, at least a small problem.
Frank was conscious that he would not see her for some time, or
maybe forever.
He was unsure what would happen later, but he did not want to
think about it now.
So he simply disappeared from the ferry and was not bold enough
to tell her.
There was no goodbye.

She was only someone nice, but still a stranger.
Frank would forget her.
Her face would slowly slip off of his mind definitely.
Life goes on.

Life continued without changes until August 5th.

Frank's mother Bozena called,
"Please, come home I need your help. My car stopped going."
Frank was used to going home to help his mother with her car.
Her car was 15 years old and Frank's hands were needed more
often now.

Without hesitation he drove home to Podebrady.

There he quickly dressed in his boxer shorts, his popular clothing
for work.
Grandmother Anna sewed them for him from an old German flag.
It was the only red material available in a time, when Frank needed
red shorts for his athletic competitions.
Now the shorts were faded but perfect for the work.

Frank went to the workshop, the only one that remained in the
family from better times.
He knew this car by heart.
He could repair it with his eyes closed or in the dark of night.

Frank began systematically.
He put the car on the jack and laid himself under the car.
Then he took the broken part out, dismantled and repaired it .
It was not easy this time.

Mother brought him lunch, later a snack.
The evening was near.

Suddenly he heard voices.

Afterwards, the door of the workshop opened and Frank's cousin Milena was standing in the door.
"Hi, Frank, how are you? Did you see my husband, Mirek?" she asked him.
Then she continued talking to somebody behind her, "Vera, please, meet my cousin Frank!"

Frank looked up and froze.
Before him stood the young lady from the ferry.

Smiling.

Chapter 10

The view from my room is breathtaking.
The river Vltava, my love, meanders through the valley like silver
snake.
Above the river rise high the hills of Barrandov.
My future destination.

Up the stream is visible an outline of another project of socialism.
A new bridge, the "Bridge of Intelligence."

Built by the lawyers.
The unreliable.

Built by the engineers.
The unreliable.

Built by the university professors.
The unreliable.

"Mr. engineer, would you, please, pass a brick to me?"
" With pleasure, Mr. Professor!"

They built the bridge in about 10 years.

You, maybe, do not understand.

Because you did not live in socialism.

Before I could start my job I had to solve a problem, a hard one.
I had to find a roof above my head; a place to live.

It was not easy to find a place in Prague to live, especially if you
were from another city. Free market of lodgings or apartments did
not exist.

Vera Stanek

Everything was just a question of luck, good friends or coincidence.

I was desperate and did not know what to do.

I began to ask for lodging to almost everybody I knew or met.
Strangers and friends without exception.
And I believed in a fate.

Finally, one of my friends helped me.
He persuaded his aunt to take me in as a lodger in her great villa placed on a slope above the river Vltava.
Just opposite my work place.

I had all the luck.
A room just for me!

It didn't matter to me that the room was small and high under the roof. It didn't bother me at all to have only a water tap with cold water in a small niche with washbowl and a toilet one floor down.
Nothing mattered.
I had my own bed and place I called home.

I overcame all the difficulties and could start work.

In this moment I had everything I wanted from life.
A job.
A room.

And in addition to that, a cloudy future.

In January 1961, I began to work in the greatest film studio in Czechoslovakia named Barrandov.
I worked as an engineer in sound research; my task was to develop different devices for sound recording.

Barrandov stood on a hill, surrounded by villas of the rich, famous,

and beautiful.
The rich and famous were devoted Party members and they were able to pay the beautiful.
It was quite simple.

I had a long and not exactly easy way to go to work.
Two trams and a bus to reach the top of the hill.
Sometimes I skipped the bus and walked around the villas, or I walked directly through meadows.
They were full with flowers in summertime.

I liked to be at Barrandov.

But very soon I found, I did not like my job very much because it was boring.

I liked to be with people.
However, now I was hidden in small room and worked on some projects, alone.
Then the job itself was a stereotype.
One project after another but just on paper, never realized.
The task was fulfilled and that was enough.

In socialism you often work just to fulfill the plan because this is decisive.
It does not matter how good or bad your work really is.
You are paid equally without regard as to the results.

I needed balance to a job that did not satisfy me.

I joined a theatrical group of young and enthusiastic people.
Evenings we rehearsed the scenes often until late at night; during the day we all worked.
On weekends we acted in surrounding villages of Prague for the joy of the play, not for money.
I was happy to be part of them, and I enjoyed it very much.

Vera Stanek

My life was full of excitement.
For many reasons.

One day we trained how to survive an atom bomb explosion if the
imperialists were to attack socialism.
We had to be prepared on everything.
The imperialistic enemy was around the corner.

Men were trained in military action.
But what would the women do?
The company decided with political consciousness that every
woman at Barrandov had to go through training.
Period.

At the appointed day all of the women of Barrandov, including me,
met outside Studio A.
It was one of those summer days with blue skies, sunshine and
really hot.

Our leaders choose an interesting place for the training .
A western village, built in the area of Barrandov directly behind the
studios.
Then it was undeveloped. Still a piece of nature, with rocks and
sparse vegetation around.

Many film studios from Western Europe shot their Westerns there.
They leased the whole village.
Wooden houses, even bank, post office, and saloon.
It was cheaper for them than building their own Western village.

We went to our training place.
We received gas-masks and were ordered to put the masks on our
faces and hide in some of houses around the village.
Later we changed hide-outs and actually had great fun.

But only until we removed the masks.

Then our laugh changed to horror.
Our faces were red with a rash, a reaction to the chemicals used for impregnation of the masks.
It was just too hot this day.

Some women were brought into the emergency hospital.
The rest of us got the day off.
"Go home and wash your face with soap," was the only advice.
But it was long process to be lovely to look at again.

However our training was successfully finished.
We were prepared.

From my first salary I bought a new winter coat and for spring another one.
After five and half years of study with a limited amount of money to spend I had to change everything.
From underwear to shoes.

My mother helped again, like in old times and sewed brand new dresses for me.
She was still very good.

In summer I fulfilled another dream of mine.

I went to see the ocean for the first time in my life.
I traveled to Bulgaria to see the Black See, which is not black but an azure blue.
I was overwhelmed.
It did not matter to me, that the way there lasted two days and three nights. I did not have enough money for air travel so I traveled by train and that was tiring.

My salary as an engineer was laughable, much lower than the wage of a laborer.
I was not working class, that was it.

Anyway, I saved enough because I knew how.
I had lot of practice.

My enthusiasm for my job slowly fell.
I was positive that I needed a change.

An idea gradually formed in my mind until I knew what I wanted to do.
I had wanted to make sound recording by film and be the first woman in Czechoslovakia to do this job.
Until now only men did this job, but I was convinced I could manage it. It was necessary to choose the right tactic on how to reach this goal.
That was all.

Slowly, I began to work on a *project* of mine.

After the work I visited sound professionals.
I watched them at their work and talked to them.
I set rules for the entire way to reach my goal and rule number one was, they had to know me.

It was necessary to be smart and patient.
Despite all my character, I was patient.

Almost unbelievable, but true.

In the spring of 1962, I found another way to go to work.
Short, with less people and less traffic.
I took ferry across the Vltava river.

It was so easy for me that I wondered why I did not use it long time ago.
I walked to the ferry just about 10 minutes down the road, then
I sailed on a ferry to another bank and without hurry walked to

Barrandov.

It was comfortable.
Moreover, the way was wonderful.

Especially in the mornings.
The ferry slowly emerged from a haze.
First you could see only the silhouette of people, later you
recognized the faces.
It was like in a fairy tale.
Dream or reality?

It was real!
And the face I looked for was real too.
Because...

From the opposite side came the ferry with a man on board.
He had curly blond hair, was tall, and handsome.
And he was there almost every day at the same time I was.

He just looked at me with his deep blue eyes.
Nothing more.
Not a greeting, not a sign of interest in me.
Nothing.
However he was there.

'A shy knight,' was my first thought.
'This is not the kind of man for me,' the second one.

Anyway I used to see him almost every day in the morning but his
interest in me didn't change. He stared at me and that was all.

After some weeks there was a little progress, to be honest.
He slightly smiled at me and I smiled back.
My shy knight.

Then I sprained my ankle.

Vera Stanek

I jumped from a tram before it stopped on the station. At the
hospital the leg was put in a cast and I had to stay at home.
I held on for a few days but it was boring.
So I decided to go to work.
Slowly and with a cane I dragged myself along the way.

My knight was not on the ferry.
Actually, why should he be?
'Maybe he took another way,' I thought. Really I was not that
interested in him.

Then it happened.

At the moment I had walked through the underpass I saw him.
He was on his way to the ferry and little by little he approached me.

Not knowing how to behave, I slowed down and finally, after his
"Hi," I stopped.
But that was not all; he continued and even asked what happened
to me.
After a short exchange of a few words, he wished me well.
What a big surprise!
My knight could speak!
Wow!

From this moment something changed.
He greeted me every time he was on the ferry.
Only it did not last long.
Suddenly he was not there and I wondered why, what happened to
him. But I could only guess.

'That was all,' I thought, 'Why should I be worry when I did not know
him?'

Maybe he was just a dream.
A vision that vanished into thin air.

On August 5th, I took an invitation from an old friend of mine,
Milena, to her home in Podebrady.
I knew her from my study there.
She was a secretary at the University, and we stayed in touch all
the years.
Now I went to visit her and her husband Mirek.

I looked forward to seeing her.
We had so much to talk about; books, movies, theaters, news from
our workplaces and all our joys and worries.

This time was not an exception.

We sat in the kitchen and talked, laughed and cooked.
The smell of fresh kolaches filled the air, the pork was roasted in
the oven, the potatoes were cooked on the range.
Our dinner was almost ready.

Only Milena's husband Mirek was not there.
He escaped to the workshop to work on his *projects.*
He was not interested in our *women problems,* and to tell the truth
we did not miss him.
Only now he was due for dinner.
Where could he be?

Milena and I went to the workshop to look for him.

Milena opened the door and talked to someone in the workshop.
I curiously glanced into the room.
There, just in red shorts, stood a man, with oil on his face and dirty
hands.
I could not believe my eyes.

My shy knight!!

Vera Stanek

"Vera, please, meet my cousin Frank, " Milena introduced him to me.
Smiling at him, I said: "Hello Frank, nice to meet you. I am Vera."

Fate intervened.

We were both at the right time on the right place.

Chapter 11

It's Monday morning.

Normally I do not like Monday mornings.
Since I have to work another five days until another weekend.
But not today.

Today I am looking forward to going to work in the expectation of seeing Frank.
I feel, no, I know I will meet him.

I am very excited.
I need more time today to choose the right dress, to do my hair, to put make-up, to look often in the mirror...
Moreover, I am very impatient.
To be on my way is the only thing I am able to think about.

But the time goes so slowly!
I look at my watch every minute, but the minute hand moves without increasing its pace.
Tick, tock, tick, tock...
Only my heart is thumping with velocity of light.

Finally, the time when I normally leave the house for work arrives.

But today I do not walk, I run to the ferry.
No, no, I walk on air.

Yes, I was right.
He is already on my side of river.

A shy knight no more.

Everything was special.

rank drove me to Barrandov on a motorcycle and for once it did not matter to us that it took longer than with ferry. The longer the better. After my work hours he waited for me and we drove outside Prague.

We sat on a shore by the dam and talked.
We drove to the meadows and talked.
We drove to the forests and talked.

There was so much we wanted to talk about.

We were everything but alike in so many ways.

It did not take long and we found that we were in love.
We knew exactly what we wanted, now and in the future.
We wanted to be together; not occasionally, not sometime in the future, but immediately.

Only there was a problem we did not know how to solve.
I could not bring Frank to my room.
He could not bring me to his room.
Forbidden.

I asked my landlady, if Frank could...but the answer was exactly as I expected. "No."
To make it absolutely clear a few weeks later she gave me the notice of my eviction.
Now I didn't have a roof over my head anymore.
I did have not a place to stay.

As a last alternative I considered sleeping in my office at Barrandov. I knew that such thoughts were insane, but I did not know what to do.

So I went to the personnel office of Barrandov.
I talked to the official about my problem and asked for help.
A miracle happened!

They had a place that was used as a storage room or in emergency as a temporary accommodation.
This room was now empty.

I hurried to see it as soon as possible.

It was very scruffy there, indeed.

The room was in the courtyard gallery house.
In a parterre, with an entrance door just two steps from the yard.
Inside was a water tap with cold water and that was it. No bathroom, no toilet.
The only toilet was on the corridor and I had to share it with five other families.

But for me it was a heaven.
I had a room just for me, what a luxury!
I didn't depend on a mercy of a landlady.
I could almost not believe in my luck.

I moved quickly into this room before somebody could change their mind. Soon afterwards Frank moved in with me.
Now we were together!

Shortly after we moved into this place we got a visit from my relatives from West Germany.
My cousin Lisa's husband came to see Prague together with his friends. They surprised us one day in our room and they were very terrified.
They told to us, "Not a beggar will live by us like you live. And you are two engineers!"

They did not understand.
How could they?
They didn't have our experience.
They didn't know what it is to live in socialism, but we knew.

Frank and I were absolutely identical in our political views and that was very important for our future.

Yes, you could be different in your personalities.
Extrovert versus introvert.
Shy versus bold.
Blond versus dark.
But hardly a devoted Party member could be together with non-loyal one.
So you had to know the political views of your partner even before you started a serious relationship.

In socialism you had other priorities.
It was important what you did, where you lived, what you wanted from life.
But most important was your political profile.
In this respect Frank and I had no problems.

Of course we had another problems waiting to be sorted out.

One of them, how to be together, was solved by moving to this room. Not many young people were so lucky as we were.

Mostly young couples moved into one of their parents' home or apartment. If they were fortunate enough they could have one room just for themselves.
For how long?
Sometimes for twenty years, sometimes longer.
Nobody knew exactly.

There was a long waiting period for your own flat in Prague, if you were on the list of applicants for a state-owned flat.
To build your own house privately was not practicable due to lack of money and building sites.
There was no free market of parcels, surely not for ordinary people.
Although everything *belonged* to them.

If you were smart enough you could find other possibilities.
You could buy a cooperative flat.
But you had to have had enough money and time to wait some years.
Or you could get a company apartment.
But you had to be lucky and work in a company that had the opportunity, and money, to build houses for their own people.

So you see why we were so lucky?
We had a place to be together.
To talk.
To dream.
About another life in the future, where we could do everything we wanted to do.

Because we had a dream.
Maybe it was more than a dream. It was a vision, obsession, hope...
A conviction that the time was near when the socialism would fall apart.

It was already fifteen years from the coup and the people were unhappy and especially tired.
What if they united and rebelled against the Communist government?
What if this revolt succeed?

Sometimes a wonder happens, why not now?
But wonders happen not so often.

Only we did not know it.
We were too young.
We had too little experience with socialism.
We forgot to look into history.
We were just two young dreamers and nothing more.

So we had a plan of what we would do when a change happened,

when Frantisek got his former possessions back.
Naturally, we assumed that Frank would follow in his father's footsteps.

Frank would open a car shop, that was obvious.
He would sell new cars, maybe repair the old ones, build a gas station that included small food market.
Our life would be completely different.

We would build a house by small pond in a garden, directly behind the station.
We already drew this house.
We planned every room, window, door.
I knew what my kitchen would be like; white kitchen cabinets, big refrigerator and absolutely modern appliances.

Do you think it is crazy?

Maybe, yes, if you do not know what it is to dream.

We kept this ideas alive for another two years until we stopped believing that there would be any change of the political system in Czechoslovakia.
Until we understood that it would remain a dream.
A nice one, but only a dream.

The reality was different.
But nice too.
Why?

Because we married.

On one rainy December day we said "I do" to each other in a small wedding company of only three people next to us.

In socialism the wedding ritual had a form of a civil marriage ceremony.

An official, you didn't know, talked to you not about your love, your
responsibility to each other or your fulfilled dreams.
He talked about political consciousness to raise your children in
spirit of socialism.
It was not easy to stay calm in this moment.

We found this ceremony as an essential step.
It had nothing to do with our love or with our dreams.
For us it was only paper, no more.
Nothing changed.

But yes, something changed.
I was pregnant.

We were so happy and so unsure about the future.
How can we bring a child to this room?
How long could I stay at home after the birth of our child?

The immense problems of all mothers in socialism.

A man was not able to support his family.
Generally salaries were so low that it was a necessity for the
woman to go work and bring home some money.

Hard times for a family began with the birth of a child.
What to do with a child?
That was the problem.

The common practice was simple.
A four-month-old child went to the day nursery.
Often very early, at 6:00 a.m., and stayed there until about 5:00
p.m.

For the mother remained the question, "Would the child recognize
me after a while or not?"

What would follow next?

Vera Stanek

A nursery school from age three with the same school routine.
At age seven the child started elementary school with children care
after the classes and with the same routine.
Nothing changed.

Every day care or school was under socialistic education and that
was the worse.
Love the Party!
Love the Soviet Union!
Tell us what your parents say at home!

How could you explain to a child to say in school something
different from what was said at home?
You could not.

Later got the child a key on a string around the neck.
It was the mark that the child was old enough to go home after
classes. To go to a flat that was empty, with nobody there who
would give a hug and say, "Hi, I missed you so much."
With nobody to talk.
With nobody to laugh.
The child stayed alone, enclosed in four walls of the flat.
Waiting for a mother who would come home at evening, tired from
her work.
With her head full of concern what to cook for dinner, how to help
with child's homework or if would be necessary to do laundry.

That was all we didn't want for our child.

But we didn't know what to do.
We had no idea.

We just believed, we would somehow manage it when the time
came.

Our daughter, Eva, was born on August 15th, 1963.

On a very special day.
The day when the first woman astronaut, Valentine Tereskovova, visited Prague.
Valentine was the hero, celebrated by press, radio, TV and went on a parade through the city.
She was a lucky woman.

I was not.

The radio in the delivery room was on full volume.
It blared, with no interruption, the songs of the Soviet Army, the songs of Young Communists of Soviet Union and hurrah!...together with commentary of this event.
It was terrible.

But not one nurse helped me.
They just let me lay there and wait until the time was ready.

So our daughter was born by the beat of drums in honor of Valentine.
Thanks heaven she was not damaged for life.

After Eva was born, we three moved to Podebrady, to Frank's parent house.
To one room of their big apartment.
For once we were like millions of other young parents in all the communist countries. We had no other place to go and our room in Prague was not appropriate for a small child.
The move seemed to be the only way out we had.

It was better to be in Podebrady.
The apartment was bright and airy. A big garden behind the house was, at least in our opinion, the best that a small child could have.
Moreover there was still the possibility to go for walk to Podebrady, to the green parks of spa resort.

Little by little we had problems with Frank's parents.

The well known problems between the young and old.
Between the generations living together in a small place.

After nine months we gave up and came back to Prague to our old
room, although we didn't know how to live there with a small child.
But we did not have another choice.

There we were at least alone.
I could walk with Eva every day to the river Vltava.
There we could enjoy the grass and sometimes flowers on the
meadows nearby.
Slip away from our small, dark and unfriendly room.

The river was still my love, but a past one.
I had another life now.
Sometimes it felt as a century had separated me from the life with
and on this river.

Frank changed jobs again.
In a fight of power his boss lost and with him the whole institute was
shut down.
That was a common practice of socialism.

Finally, Frank found a job in a small group that analyzed bike
production with the help of mathematical methods.
It was not too interesting, but it was a job.
And the people around him were nice.

I prepared myself to go back to work at Barrandov.
I could only take one year free to raise my child, and this year was
slowly approaching the end.
There were not more dreams about the sound recording job in my
mind. I knew I had to stay in research, because I had a family now.
It was not about just me.

The times changed and I changed, too.

Before I went to work, Frank and I decided to visit my relatives.
We decided to go to West Germany.

To realize it was not easy, but we were used to overcoming difficulties.
The relatives had to send us an invitation in writing, with a very important sentence, "We are responsible for all expenses connected with the visit."
Why?
Because we could bring only 10 Deutsche Mark, not more.
There was not enough hard currency for private trips in socialism.

Our small daughter, Eva, had to stay in Czechoslovakia.
She was the guaranty that we would come back.

We agreed with this requirement.

To our surprise we got the permission to go.
Actually, no one knew before if the answer would be yes or no.
Maybe the responsible person just did not sleep well and you didn't get it.

So we put Eva in a care of my mother in Prerov and went.
We had to.
We had to see it with our own eyes.
The rotten capitalism.

I could describe the entire visit with one word: shock.

Everything began on the border.

We came by train.
My cousin Lisa, daughter of Uncle Franzi, waited for us together with the whole family, Uncle Franzi include.
We were put into a Mercedes and driven to their home in a small

city in Bavaria, Kulmbach, only about 50 miles from the Czech border.

We were overwhelmed.

How clean were the houses.
How nice they looked with window sills full of flowers and small gardens at the front.

And the fields!
One green with grass.
The second one yellow with grain.
All of them with a mark that someone cared.
It was so different and so unusual for us, people from behind the *Iron Curtain*.
We forgot already what it is a clean house or one field!

Because in socialism there were not separate fields.

There were never-ending pieces of land, where the grain was grown.
The fields were taken from the owner.
The boundaries were plowed up.
It was no longer your field, it belonged to the people now.
Only the people did not care too much.

Now we experienced it in a country that lost the war, but now was wealthy again.
You could see it on every step if you just looked around.
The people were well dressed, the children looked so nice and happy.
What a gap between them and us.

We were the poor relatives, again.
Nineteen years after war.
Sixteen years of socialism.

My mother sewed new dresses for me, but I was still the poor
Cinderella.
Frank had a new suit, trousers and some brand new shirts.
But he was still the poor husband of mine.
We ourselves were aware of these differences, but we were lucky
to be there.

Our relatives and their families were nice to us.

My cousin Lisa married a wealthy man.
He was an owner of transportation company that was in the family
over 80 years.
They had a nice house above the garages of big trucks.
They had a large circle of friends.
They looked so happy and contented.

Frank and I were like *Alice in Wonderland.*

The first day Lisa asked me what I would like for her to buy me.
I answered, "Please, buy me one orange."
She did not understand that for me it was something special,
something I could not buy in socialism every day.
Maybe only few times at Christmas, and if I had the opportunity to
buy oranges now, then I would give them to Eva.

From now on I ate many oranges.
Lisa placed them on kitchen table on a plate and I could have them
anytime I wanted. I felt very spoiled.

Frank and I walked throughout the city.

We found a market with every quantity of vegetables and fruits.
Everything was so fresh, colorful, and clean that we could almost
not believe it was possible.
Then we found a church, burned to the ground in medieval times by
a Czech religious sect. Another conclusive piece of evidence that
our nations lived for centuries together as a neighbor, friends or

enemies.
There was so much for us to see and to experience.

Such as joining the family for a Beer Festival.

It took place every year in summer, in the city Kulmbach.
At every corner on the main square stood a big barrel of beer. Four of them exactly; one for each different brewery in the city.
On this special weekend people gathered there.
They sat down at long wooden tables, drank beer, and ate every amount of food.
They talked and laughed.
They were happy to be together.

The children took part in the festivities, also.
They marched in a parade in fancy dresses and with balloons on a string in their hands. At the end they released the balloons with a message to the children in the neighborhood, in Czechoslovakia.
The mayor told it in his speech.
"Hello children in Czechoslovakia. We have a celebration today. We send our balloons to you. Celebrate with us!"

It was really a speech of the capitalistic enemy!
The enemy that would put a nuclear bomb on Czechoslovakia at the first opportunity.
That was told us many times.

It is mad, isn't it?

Only, we felt like we were in seventh heaven.
In our mind began the germination of the idea to be free again.
To be a human being, not a slave of socialism.
To be free like those people there for the rest of life.

Unfortunately, we were without Eva.
So we put the thought away and enjoyed the visit.

We went to Ingolstadt to visit Aunt Trudy.
She and Uncle Erich were pleased with their life there and by no
means poor.
There we met another cousins of mine.
Almost the entire family was together except for my mother.

Our time passed by and it was necessary to leave Germany and go
back.
To Eva.
To our room.
To socialism.

Our relatives brought us back to the border.
We said goodbye, not knowing if there would be another possibility
to see each other.
It was quite sad.

The train from West Germany to Prague arrived to our border
station. It was already full of people.
So the railway officials decided to add some new wagons.

The group of people waiting together with us to go by this train was
immediatelly surrounded by the customs.
Czech customs with stoned faces, with suspicious eyes and dogs
with sharp teeth on leashes.

We knew we were in another world again.
In a world of the harsh reality of socialism.

In a short time the new wagons were connected, and we were
asked to board.
We entered the wagon, but we could not believe our eyes.
What we saw was a shock.
Only a different one this time.
The wagon was dirty.

Vera Stanek

On benches lay a layer of black dust, the windows were opaque.
The whole car smelled of urine.

We stood there not knowing what to do.
We knew exactly what we would like to do, that was turn and run
back. But it was not only too late, but there was Eva, our little
daughter, waiting for us.
There was no way out.

We stood there, awake from a dream.
As always it was necessary to set the priority, to save our best
dresses first.
We began cleaning of the dirt from seats with handkerchiefs, but it
was not a good idea.
So we covered the seats with plastic bags.

We knew that it would be better to use newspaper or magazines for
the cleaning, if we had any.
But this could be not put in a practice.
Under the pretext of capitalistic propaganda was forbidden to bring
newspapers and magazines from West to Czechoslovakia.

Finally, we survived the journey.
We picked up Eva from my parents and came back to our room in
Prague.

Life slipped to the old routine.

First we went to a grocery store to buy some food.
We found milk and bread and then I asked about vegetables.
A dirty lady put a bunch of carrots together with chunks of earth still
on them on the scale. Then she flung them in a newspaper and put
that into my shopping bag.

At this moment I lost control.

I put everything on the counter and escaped from the store, crying uncontrollably.
I have had before my eyes the market in Kulmbach with clean vegetables, and clean people with smiles on their faces.

And in this very moment I promised myself to do everything to bring Eva away from this country.
I was aware of the impossibility to do it in this moment.
But one day, I swore to myself, we would manage it.
We have to wait on the right moment and until then be patient.

Soon afterwards I went back to my job.

Against all my bad dreams it was more horrible than I imagined.
For almost thirteen hours every day I was away from home, away from Eva.

Until now we solved at least one problem.
What to do with Eva in the hours I was at work.

We found a lady, a former nurse, who was now at home with her three boys.
Two boys were in school, the last one was still a baby.
This *Aunt* took now care of Eva.

I was very grateful to her.
She loved Eva very much and I did not need to worry.

There was only a small problem.
This lady lived in another district of Prague and our problem was, how to bring Eva to her apartment.
This time Frank took the initiative.

Every morning he put Eva into a buggy and walked with her more than one hour through the dirty streets of Prague.
It was a long way to bring Eva to the aunt.

Vera Stanek

Frank had to start this journey already before 6:00 a.m.
We did not have a car and at that time of the morning the trams
were full of sleepy and unfriendly people.
Frank tried to go by tram, but only one time.
Then he decided to walk.

We held on for one month.
Then everything changed.

Through a coincidence we could buy an apartment in one of the
new settlements that sprang up like mushrooms in suburbs of
Prague.
The opportunity was excellent, and we seized it immediately.

We bought an apartment with two bedrooms and our own toilet and
bathroom.
It didn't matter to us that this settlement was built by criminals.
It was our first home and we were very happy.
Nothing more.

It didn't bother us that the apartments had many defects.

It was impossible to close the doors in kitchen cabinets, because
the hinges were screwed in the wrong place.
The corners of the walls in the kitchen were knocked away,
because one worker turned there with a ladder on his back.
The glass around the balcony was cracked.
Our nice living room was three inches higher on one side than on
the opposite one.
That all was not a problem for us.

The streets were not finished yet.
When we moved, we drove and then walked through mud.
But nothing could change our spirit.

Our apartment was placed on the best side of the settlement.

We had a view of the pond and meadows.
Something unbelievable in Prague!

The best part was the route to Eva's aunt was shorter now.

With big enthusiasm we began to improve our flat.
We had something to do; a sense, a goal that we could concentrate
on.

We did not forget what we wanted, we remained patient.
A visit to West required a waiting period of two or three years, so
we could not try anything right now.
Meanwhile we waited, improved and furnished our apartment.

We fixed our attention on many big and small projects.

A walk-in closet was one of the first accomplishments.
Next we furnished a room for Eva, where she could play and stay.
We covered the uneven walls of our living room with wood paneling
and built benches whose cushions could be turned into a bed in
minutes.
Later Frank designed a net in a shape of a parabola to divide our
living from the dinning room.

We carried out our ideas with no regard to difficulties.

The materials we scraped together by hunting for them through the
entire city every minute we could spare.
But we enjoyed our new hobby.

Next to the big ones we had many small projects, too.
For example to decorate our hallway with wallpaper.
To our surprise it was not an easy work.

One Saturday afternoon we started our project.

After we measured the wall, we cut the wallpaper and with a thick

brush we spread the glue on its reverse side.
We managed it to our satisfaction.
Next Frank put the stepladder in the middle of hallway. Carefully he stepped on the first rung and pressed the glued wallpaper to the ceiling with his hands
I stood next to him, prepared to fulfill every wish he could ever have.

At last Frank succeeded and the wallpaper held in place.
Only our joy of the first achievement did not last long. Little by little the wallpaper slipped from the ceiling, until it fell directly on Frank's head.
In a moment my dear husband was wrapped in wet glued foil.

I reacted immediately but probably not appropriate.
I began to laugh with all my heart.
The tears of joy welled up in my eyes and I could not stop.

Frank got furious.
"Stop laughing and help me," he shouted and began to rip off the wallpaper from his head.
He stood there with the glue that dripped bit by bit from his hair, face and hands, and with the wallpaper, torn in pieces, by his foot.

After we discussed the possibility of divorce, we calmed down.
Then we put new piece of the wallpaper on the ceiling.
Finally we did great job and had fun.

Almost at the same time I changed jobs.
I could not hold on with my work at Barrandov and with Eva, together.

An interesting job was offered to me and I did not think about it too long.

I began to teach at a technical college to have more time for Eva.

After half a year, I was transferred to another type of school. The same technical college but for the evening and external classes. Now I had even more time for Eva.

My students were different now.
Not teenagers, but workers.
They worked predominantly from 6:00 a.m. to 2:00 p.m., mostly in factories.
Then they took part on our classes.
Three times per week.
Four to five hours every time.
Five years.

If they passed through final examination, they got a Certificate of Education.
I took my hat off to them.

The students were between eighteen and fifty-five years old, in a time of big changes.
They got married.
They divorced.
Had children.
Had or didn't have an apartment of their own.
Mostly they were lucky to have only one room for themselves.

They were happy or not, with big and small problems, but for sure with a life that was everything but easy.

Sometimes they hid the Certificate.
Since finishing at school their status changed.
From blue-collar they became white-collar workers and it meant having less money because they were no longer of the working class.

Do you understand this?
Probably not.
You have to believe me.

Vera Stanek

I loved this job.

Frank also changed his job.

The Party interfered like many times before.
Frank's small group was shut down and the job was put outside
Prague. This decision was only confirmation of common knowledge.
Nothing was secure in socialism.
You had to be prepared on immense changes.

Frank found a job in a Research Institute for Transportation and
began to work on a projects about road accidents.
He was very happy to find a job with cars, his old love, again.
Because nothing could change his relationship to them. Not even
the best paid job was good enough if it was not a job with cars.

Our life stabilized.

We had a nice apartment.
We had jobs we liked.
We had a daughter we adored.
Except we missed something very important to us: freedom.

So we decided to escape.

We got in touch with our relatives to get an invitation for all of us.
To our great surprise our relatives refused to write it. They feared
that we could stay in West and that they would be responsible for
us. After their viewpoint, we belonged to Czechoslovakia because
wo woro Czechs.
Period.

History repeated itself.
After the war the Czechs evacuated them to Germany with the

same viewpoint. Why should they think different now?
Why should they understand our dreams of freedom?

We were terribly disappointed.

How could they did this to us?
What would we do now?
We were desperate.

Before we could develop another plan, the course of events moved
in a new direction. We met Eberhard, the boy-friend of my little
sister Eva.

My sister, Eva, lived at this time in Prague.
She studied at the Economical University and visited us often.

On one of her visit she introduced us to her new friend, Eberhard.
He was a university student from West Germany.
Exactly said, he was a lawyer before a doctorate degree, who wrote
his dissertation paper about East Block law.
It was a pleasure to talk to him, discuss people habits and politics
of many countries he visited and we knew only from books.

Other visits followed and soon we became good friends.

After some time we mentioned our plans to leave Czechoslovakia.
Eberhard promised, without hesitation, to help us.
Immediately he wrote the invitation we needed, and to our surprise
we got permission.
All three of us.

At first we thought that maybe my sister, Eva, would like to come
with us. But later she changed her mind and decided not to go.
We didn't persuade her to go.

We began to prepare ourselves and made some arrangements.
Eberhard took our diploma and birthday certificates with him when

he left for Germany one week before us.

Before we left we went to visit my parents in Prerov.
We thought it would be the last visit for some time.

When my parents asked about our plans for vacation we did not want to lie.
We told them about our plans to visit West Germany, but we gave them only an approximate answer.

We did not know how terrible mistake it was.

My mother began to lament, "You will not come back. I know you. I will not see you again," and she cried hysterically.
We were shocked and remained absolutely silent.
In this situation we assumed it was better not to say anything.
We knew that my mother would not understand, because in her view we had everything.
Nice apartment.
Jobs.
Great child.

She did not ask, not just one time, "Are you happy?"
She was sure, she knew best what was good for us and what was not.
Maybe it is common thinking of all mothers, but maybe not.
Anyway, we did not want to discuss our intentions with her or with my father either.

We came back from this visit with mixed feelings.

We did not know the most fatal thing that happened next week.
My sister came to visit my parents, together with her girl-friend.
We did not know many another events.
All of them happened the last week.

When we knew them, it was already too late.

The day of our departure arrived.

On July 5th, 1967, we took the bus to Bayreuth in West Germany, convinced that we would not come back.

The trip began smoothly.

The way was pleasant.
We came near to the border.

The bus made the last stop.

Chapter 12

I am in a jail, behind the bars.

I keep my mind only on one thought: I have to go out, to go home.
Someone waits on me, I am sure of it, only I do not remember who.

I shake the bars.
However they hold.

Why do I not just unlock them?
I have a key in my hand.

The problem is, I can not put the key into the key hole.
I tried it at least hundred times but every attempt fails because I can not hit the hole.
I cry out of despair.
I shout at the top of my voice, "Let me go, pleaaaase!"

Then I wake up.
My dream.
So often now that I stopped counting.

My nightmare.

We were at home again, in our apartment in Prague.
They brought us there sometimes in the night yet, directly from the border.

We were back at home and we still asked ourselves, 'What will happen with us?'
We did not know. The following days would show it, certainly.

The next day they came again and took Frank away.
To a place we knew just from talking as a place for investigation

of political crimes. A place very well known and feared as the last place you would like to be.
Who were they?
The Secret Police.

I was crazy with fear.
I did not know if I would see Frank again.
And if yes, then when? Tomorrow, in some days, or years?

I tried to behave as usual.
I cooked for Eva, went with her for walks like we would do it on a normal day.
But it was not a normal day!
I was paralyzed with horror, my mind stopped working properly.

The time passed slowly, but still, I watched the minute hand on my watch.
From minutes were hours.
From hours almost all day... and still nothing.
No Frank.
No call.

The uncertainty was unbearable.

The evening approached.
Like a programmed machine I prepared dinner for Eva and put her to bed. Then I took a seat by the kitchen table with view of the meadow, sat down and waited.
The dusk fell.

The people enjoyed the nice evening outside.
They played ball with children, they laughed and had a fun.
How could they laugh when I am so unhappy?
How could they?

Then I had heard an elevator halt at our floor.
The door of the elevator opened, and I heard steps that stopped by

our door.
My heart began to throb quickly.
I knew that the next minute would be crucial.

And really.
Someone put the key to the key hole.
Frank!

I jumped from the chair and opened the door to the hallway.
Frank stood there, with head bent, without movement.
Then he looked in my eyes and said simple, "I admitted everything."

"Why Frank, why?" I cried.
I hugged him and I did not want to release him.

Slowly we went to the dark kitchen and sat at the table.
Frank began to tell me what happened.

At the beginning he talked about the vacation and about the
intention to visit relatives and nothing more.
Then he repeated it, again and again.
Until they showed him a statement with an exact description of our
plans, with details even, signed by my sister Eva.

This statement broke Frank down and he gave up.
Finally he admitted everything; it was senseless to deny anything.
They knew about our every step some days before our departure,
because we were put under surveillance.

Now we should pay for our intention to betray the socialism.
We were told to be prepared for a trial.

However first we got an order to write to Eberhard to send our
diploma and birth certificates back.
We did it without hesitation.

Vera Stanek

We were very surprised when our papers were given back to us by the police.
In vain we tried to find a sense in this action.
We racked our brains over only one question; why from police and why not from Eberhard himself?

We got answer from Eberhard.
He wrote two letters to us where he assured us of his friendship and his intention to help us anytime we needed him.
But we did not know under which condition he wrote them.

Did he work with them or was it just coincidence?

We did not know and we would not know.
It would stay the biggest mystery of our lives.

They were times we could find him, but we did not.
Why?
Maybe we were hurt too much.
And we still are.

We could only try to erase from our mind everything and everybody from those times.

In the fall we went to a court.

We were sentenced after Soviet law for, "preparation of an attempt to leave the Republic."
Why Soviet you would, maybe, ask, why not Czech law?
Because the Czech law has the, "preparation of an attempt" only by a capital crime and that was not our case.
We had passports.
We had permission to go.
It was only an attempt.

So the judge helped himself with Soviet law.

We had to be punished!
Moreover we were told, that nothing would happen to us if we were laborers.
Our problem was, we were engineers.

We were sentenced to six months in jail with the probation for two years.
Our passports were confiscated and we were told clearly, "You will not go together to the West during your whole life. Do you understand?"

We understood.

Later we found that it was not only my sister who testified against us.

First it was my mother.
She talked about her fear, we could escape, with a friend of my sister Eva, when the girls visited our parents in Prerov.
My mother didn't care if this person was trustworthy or not.

The girl was engaged to a university professor, a class professor of my sister.
He was a member of theSecret Police.
It was he who organized it all, including the statement my sister Eva signed.

What happened then?

Sister Eva finished the University without interruption.
Her former study problems were wipe away.

I did not speak to her for seven years.
I could not.
When I heard her voice I could not answer.
I just had a big lump in my throat and I did not emit one word.

Sister Eva's girl-friend married and went off to West Germany.
What an irony!

And the professor?
He died.
Next year.
He was 40 years old.

Very slowly we began to live again.
It was tiring to live with a hole in our heart that did not want to heal.
We needed time, trusting the wisdom that *time is a great healer.*
We had to be patient, believe in ourselves and not hurry.

We were not in hurry.
We had no reason to hurry.
We had to live our life as if nothing happened.

To our surprise we were not fired from our jobs although we were
certain it would happen.

We were invited to a discussion with our bosses.
They both finally decided that we could stay in our positions.
"Yes, of course it was a mistake, but it would not happen again!"
Surely not, this we knew.

Maybe this mild treatment from our employers was an omen of
something in the air.

Early in 1968, big changes were in view.

First in our family.
Because I was pregnant again.

Second in Czechoslovakia.

Because of changes in the Party.
After years of struggle a moderate wing, under the leadership
of Dubcek, came to power with a brand new idea: to build a
"socialism with human face."

The changes began slowly and cautiously.
The people did not believe in changes.
They did not believe the Party would bring something new and
better.
Not after 20 years of experience.

But the journalist were no longer patient.
Now they knew they had to act to awake the nation from years of
long sleep.

Everything began with the "Literary News" and its journalists.
They wrote a letter to well known officials under the name "2000
words."
This letter was signed by actors, intellectuals, people on the street
... including Frank.

What they actually wanted?
What did we want, an all Czech nation?

We wanted more freedom.
We wanted release of political prisoners.
We wanted connection to the world.
We did not want censured press.

And we wanted democracy, no socialism.
The separation of Party and Government.
An elected president, not appointed by the Party.

Spring was on the way.

Prague Spring came, and everything was in blossom.
Both nature and people blossomed.

Vera Stanek

The trees, lifeless and leafless until now were budding.
The people on the streets lifted up their heads and began breathe
freely.

After the spring came the hot summer and not just because of
weather, but politically.

The people wanted more.
The events escalated.
The Party lost control.

It was the time we were waiting for.
Frank and I were alive again.
How we needed it!

Was it maybe fate that prevented us from going away?
Did we get a chance to be free by staying at home?
Was the price for it too high or too less?

We didn't think about it too much, we lived it.
We enjoyed it with enormous pleasure despite my problems in
pregnancy and the necessity to stay at home, away from school
and my students.
The life was exciting again.

With the same excitement we waited for our child to be born in just
couple of months.

Then there was August 21st, 1968.
Another summer day was waiting on us, but...

It was an early morning.
I slept peacefully until it came to my consciousness that somebody
tried to awake me, delicate but persistent.
Finally I opened the eyes.
By my bedside stood Frank, completely dressed to go to work.
He repeated just a few words.

"Vera, please, wake up. The Russian army is here. Please, wake up...."

At first I did not understand.
Russian Army?
Here?

Still half asleep I asked, "What do they want?"
Frank answered, "They are here to save us before contrarevolution."
Still it made no sense to me.

"Which one?" I asked, without understanding the whole situation.
But slowly, by reason of ninth months of my pregnancy, I rose from bed.

Frank was already back in our living room.
He was holding our TV antenna in his hand. He circled round and round to place it in the right direction to catch the picture and sound of the temporary TV station.
The national TV didn't broadcast, the transmitter was off.

Eventually we managed it, together.

The announcer, a woman, sat before camera.
With no make-up and with circles under the eyes, almost not recognizable compared only to some hours before.
She was always so pretty and neat, but now she aged considerably over night.
But it was not normal day, and it was not a normal situation.

We were keen to know what happened.
Any information we got was worth a piece of gold.

The news was horrible.
Worse than we could only imagine it.

Vera Stanek

During the night the Russian Army crossed the borders together
with many *brothers* armies of the Eastern Block.
They came to save the socialism and to stop the democratic
process in Czechoslovakia.
Allegedly some loyal Party members asked for help, and our mighty
allies and friends rushed to assist them.

In these hours the tanks were on the way to Prague.

The people began to build barricades to stop the tanks on their way
into the city.
Street names and building numbers were removed so that nobody
could be found and punished.
The country had enough experience with the aftermath of such
events.
Almost an entire nation connected to one goal: to stop the intrusion.

Frank decided not to go work and stay with me at home.
He was not sure how I would manage this situation alone.

We spent some hours before the TV and then we came to the
conclusion, that we had to react on this extraordinary event.
Life went on; we had to eat and go on with our everyday duties.

Our refrigerator was nearly empty.
The grocery was just 10 minutes of walking away, and I made my
rounds there every day.
On the one hand to stay in motion because of my pregnancy and
on the other because Eva needed this small walk as well.

Today we made our rounds together.
Through the street and around the corner... suddenly we stopped in
astonishment.
Before the grocery was a line of about one hundred people with the
same idea as ours, to accumulate some supply of food.
To survive, in case something happened.

Slowly we continued to the end of the line.

But already by getting closer I was stopped.
Almost the whole crowd parted to make way for me.
The people guided my way through with words like "Lady go directly to the door," or "It is out of the question for you to stand in the line" or...

Moved to tears I hesitantly approached the door of the grocery.

For a long time it did not happen, that a strager was so good to me and now so many people at once. Smiling, they began to push me to the door.
There was another shock waiting on me.

One of the sales persons came running with a chair in hands.
She asked me to sit down, and then she continued, "If you tell me what you want I will put it together and bring it to you."
'No, it could be no true! I am dreaming!' were my only thoughts.
But it was true.
Believe me.

The sales person gathered all the items from my shopping list and put them in shopping bags.
We went home with only one feeling, how good the people were.
At least today.

In the meantime Russian tanks reached downtown Prague.

There were struggles for Radio and TV stations.
The Russian Army opened gunfire.
Part of the National Museum was completely destroyed.
The Main Square was a mess with remains of barricades and partly devastated houses nearby.

First people died, hit by the bullets of our *liberators.*

Vera Stanek

A paradox.

23 years before the Russian Army brought the freedom from the war and an annexation to Hitler.

Now they were here to annex us back to the socialistic block.

Why did everybody want to have us under their thumb?

Was it because we were so small a nation?

Were we so strategically a benefit?

Why, we asked ourselves at least hundred times?

At the beginning we believed that somebody would come to help, that the world would not let this happen.

But the whole world just watched!

Nobody helped!

Why, we asked ourselves again?

We should understand that the world was divided on domains of interest, and we had the misfortune to belong to the Russian one.

We had bad luck, that was all.

Only in the first hours or maybe days we did not think.

We just felt.

And our hearts told us that the world let us down.

But our greatest tragedy was that we lost the hope for a better future, for us and for our children as well.

We were closed again behind the *Iron Curtain*.

In a big jail watched by the Soviet Army and their tanks and artillery.

They stayed in our country for the sake of socialism.

The Army was everywhere.

A machine gun nest was just short way from our home.

The anti-aircraft guns were even in the hospital I needed to go for

delivery when the child was ready.
I didn't know where I would go when this happened.

I was told to wait.
There was still the possibility they would clear the hospital and
leave. In an emergency I had to find another hospital in the middle
of the city, where the Army was not present.

They did not leave *my* hospital.
It was necessary to go for my delivery to a small hospital that Frank
found before, whose staff promised to take care of me, if...

Our son David was born on September 10th, 1968.

Earlier than we thought.

Chapter 13

Everything is gray.

Gray is our life.
Because we have not the hope that something would change.

Gray are our days.
Because we see not the future. Neither for us, nor our children.

Gray are the streets.
Because they are full of gray people. People that do not smile.

Gray are our hearts.
Because we lost a chance to be free.

Why we live?

Because of our children.

There have been changes.
In our family, in the Republic also.
We had two children, five-year-old Eva, and new born David.
The Republic had new guests, the Russian Army.

The Russian Army was present in Czechoslovakia to watch our behavior, since we had to stay devoted to socialism and to the Soviet Union.
The nation was brought back to the socialistic reality.
People hung their heads again.
The smile on the faces disappeared.
Their wings, prepared to fly, were clipped yet before they could start.

We had other priorities and hopes.
So different from ones we had only months before.

Now we could just believe that *they* would not find Frank's signature
under the "2000 words." If they could not find it, then he could be
not persecuted.
Or lose his job.
Or maybe more.

Welcome socialism.
We are back again.

Another political screening was waiting on everyone.
It was necessary to eliminate the people that were too active in
Prague Spring.
The Party needed only the true ones that remained steady and
didn't yield to temptation.
These were now rewarded with higher positions.
With better jobs.
With more money.

Frank went through political screening with few scratches.

He could stay in his job and it was good for him.
In these times he was the head of small group of five people that
tested import cars.
He loved his job.
He loved his people.
Although he could not say the same about the management of the
company.

But his joy was taken from him and it was not good.
At his second job Frank became an expert witness for traffic
accidents in court.
To tell the truth, we could use the money he earned.
This job survived our escape attempt, but not this screening.

Frank was miserable about this situation since he loved this job.
During the years he worked out an excellent reputation with his
knowledge and capability.
Now the Party had forbidden him to continue.
He was not loyal enough to be present in court.

Ultimately he was told, "If you think you can go after another job
then forget it.
We will not allow it. Is it clear?"

The screening was over.

Behind remained Frank, closed in a cage, with two children to take
care of.
The only way out for us was for me to go work earlier than we
assumed it would be necessary.
We simply needed the money.
So I went back to the school after only six months and taught again.
I worked ten hours a week, but I brought home a wage and it was
better than nothing.

Moreover, we could organize our schedule in a way, that we
managed the care of our children alone.
Through the day I was at home and took care for both of them.
I cooked, went with them for a walk and went to work in the
evenings, after Frank came home from his job.
It worked out quite well.

Our life would have been stagnant if we had not Eva.
However with her we had to stay alert all the time.
Eva was only five, but eager to learn, eager to know, with
permanent curiosity about things and events and with zillions of
questions.

Sometimes we had problems with how to answer her.

What would you answer a child that asked you,
" If 5x5 = 25 and
  if 6x6 = 36 why is not
    7x7 = 47 ?"

We were speechless.
We tried vainly to give her the right answer that she would find
sufficient to understand her big math problem.

Soon we found she could read.
We did not know if we should be happy or not.
The teachers in school preferred not to be confronted with children
that already read.
There was a principle that children should not learn to read until
their first class of elementary school. Not even in pre-school care.
So we were not sure what would happen to Eva in the first class.
We could only rely in a mercy from the class teacher.

In reality Eva began to learn reading earlier, even before David was
born.

She had spent afternoons with her new *Aunt.*
This lady had a granddaughter in the first class of elementary
school and the girl began to learn reading.
Our two years younger daughter learned to read together with her.

We found it out when Eva began to make strange remarks.
"We should be at home soon. Look we passed the drugstore
already."
Or reacted on a trams jam with the words, "Something happened.
Not one tram number 2. Only lots of numbers 11."

We began to be suspicious.
Can she really read or is it just an excellent memory?
She could read.

We capitulated and bought her first book, later the second one and then more.

Before she went to the school she read ten books by herself. She counted them very precisely.

Frank reacted in unusual way.
He brought Eva a new *play.*
He began to teach Eva the English language from a textbook for children. The book was full of pictures of animals and things of everyday life, complete with words and short sentences.

Frank thought the best way for her is to put her brain to work.
So we did.

In the fall of 1969, we tried to put Eva to school.
But it proved not to be as easy as we assumed it would be.

She was born in the last days of August, but still within the deadline to enroll her for school this year.
This was good.

Only there was one problem.
Eva did not attend kindergarten.
The school officials thought, this would be a big disadvantage for her. We were told that, "She would probably lag behind."
'Politically, sure, but that would be all,' we thought, but we did not say anything.

To our huge relief they took her.

The first day of school we went for a talk to Eva's class teacher.
We informed her about the fact that Eva could already read and count.
Anxiously we waited for her reaction.
She was great. She assured us she would manage it and we

should calm down.

Soon we found how really brilliant she was.
This teacher brought Eva her books to keep her busy during
lessons, while she taught the other children to read.
What was more important, Eva was happy at school.

We were right.
Eva had never problems at school.

It was our business to keep Eva busy outside of school.
We tried to find different ways to do it.

One of them we chose, was to give her an interest in sports.
At the very least those we knew and loved.

In winter we started to teach her how to ski.
The winters were long and surprisingly full of snow in these years.

Eva started her first steps on skis on our meadow, on a short and
gentle slope.
We taught her how to go down and not crash to the ground.
And if she did crash, then without breaking her legs.
Later Eva made turns among trees and began to enjoy it very
much.

So we took her to real mountains when she was barely six years
old.
There she could use all the experience of practicing in our meadow.
Eva was good, indeed.

We did not neglect David either.
We put him on ski when he was two-years-old and despite his age
he was soon a passionate skier too.

We all had lots of fun!

In the spring and fall we took the children for long walks to forests, hills, and meadows.

The summer time was dedicated to just one activity.
We taught both children to swim.
Thanks to my job I had two full months vacation.
So we three spent most of the days at wonderful swimming pool among craggy slopes in a suburb of Prague.

It was another benefit of my job.
Good for me but better for the children.

I was still at the school and I still loved to teach.
I liked the people around me, the colleagues and the students in the same way.
Maybe because we were not a normal school.

As a result of political screening our group was mixed.

Many teachers from colleges in Prague were found unreliable to teach children.
Some resigned the Communist Party in the Prague Spring. Some resigned after the Russian Army occupied the Republic as a protest.
To do so was a big mistake.

They were punished by transferring them to our school.
There they could not have a negative impact on inexperienced children.
There they taught the working class.
And nothing and nobody could influence working class!
This you should know, already.

Soon we formed a team.
We accepted each other and tried to bring lots of knowledge to our

students.
We were a team of intellectual personalities.

We had a great time together.
We discussed topics such as how to teach better, how to help our students to study, how to respect each other....
It was not a job.
It was a mission.

In our spare time we had so much fun!
Among the teachers and among the students as well.

To keep this job I agreed to go back to university for postgraduate study for classes essential for teaching, like pedagogy, sociology, history, teacher's personality, etc.
So I sat behind the university bench once again and took classes.
In my spare free time I studied and passed examinations.

After two years I finished with success.
I was now officially a "professor for college education."
I had a paper for it.

Still, I often thought about the words of my former old experienced colleague.
He told me once, "My dear, you are a teacher or you are not.
Because you have it in your blood or you haven't, and no university could change it!"

Frank worked at his former institute on a new project.
He was named as the head of a team that was assigned with a national task, to build first test station of seat belts in the entire Eastern Block.
An important task.

It was a big challenge for Frank.
With enormous energy he threw himself into this job.

He made proposals on how it should be done, found a place where it should be done, and he began carry out his ideas.
However everything was a problem.

Materials, devices, machinery... where to find them?
Almost nothing was available locally.
To look abroad was a waste of time because of lack of foreign currency.
So Frank began to crisscross through the Republic, hunting for everything that he could use.
He was sure he could manage it.

He began a long way in search of simple or complicated parts.
With talking and persuasion, sometimes with bribes and promises, Frank was tireless and persistent.
He was not sorry for the time he spent on the road, for all the hours of overtime he devoted to his work, for the problems he had to solve to fulfill his project.

Finally Frank succeeded.

After one year of hard work his dream came true.
His other *child,* his test station for crash tests, was ready.

It seemed so simple.
Human figure, made of special material, a foam, was put on a seat and fastened to the seat belt.
The seat was a part of the trolley, pulled to the start position by help of a gummy rope, in the same way as stretching a sling.
Then the seat was released and the trolley crashed into a concrete block. A speed-shot camera recorded it all.
That was it.

Our life stabilized.
But we were unhappy.
The settlement got on our nerves.

Why?

We had, for once, a feeling that we were only numbers and not people.
We felt like we were swallowed by the crowd of thousands people around us in a monotony that we found unbearable.
The weariness of life in a settlement.

You wake up.
You go to work.
You come home at evening.
You go sleep.
At the same time as your neighbor next door.
As the entire house.
As the whole street.

That was the reason for our effort to change it.

The only solution to our problem was to look for an apartment exchange. We did not give ourselves too much hope for this.
Who would like to change an apartment in city for an apartment in one of the settlements?

To our great surprise we found an exchange relatively soon.
And what an extraordinary one!
We found a big apartment directly in the middle of Prague, just five minutes from the Old City Hall, on one of the nicest streets in all Prague.

The house was a part of old Jewish houses, built in 1907, with the statue of King George in a fight with dragon on a front corner.
The staircase had a wrought iron banister and on every floor of this six-storied house was a window with lead glass.
Every window with a different mosaic of colors.
Every window with a different motive.

The apartment itself was a jewel!
There were two big bedrooms, hallway, kitchen, a small room,
formerly for a maid, and bathroom and toilet.
The living room was enormous; the ceiling was about 11 feet high,
decorated with stucco ornaments around the chandeliers.
A marvelous work of a former handyman!

The apartment had only one disadvantage.
It was used in last two years by an eighty year old grandmother and
her sixteen year old granddaughter.
They left it dirty and neglected.

But the people wanted the exchange and that was important for us.

Moreover the people wanted our apartment on the settlement like
we created it.
With all the furniture and all the changes.
Just how they saw it at their first visit.

We agreed without hesitation.

If we were absolutely excited with our first apartment then it was
nothing to compare it with our excitement now!
We had a dream apartment.
In a dream house.
On a dream place in Prague.

With great enthusiasm we began to change it to fit our imagination.
Our idea was quite simple; to follow the spirit of the house and
apartment.

We were prepared to build and create something special what
would be a picture of our know-how, our skills, and our feelings for
this marvelous house.

We were looking for a sense of life, again.

Vera Stanek

Not just surviving, but living the life we had without regard of dreams and desires.
Live in the present and look, maybe, ahead, but carefully.
And live it in the best way possible.

So we started again in the summer of 1971.

We organized one room for our kids and that was it.
Everything else was open for ideas, for discussions and later for realization.

Project number one was a realization of a central heating system. It was necessary to heat the big rooms when the summer ended.
Then we continued with a new tile floor, made kitchen cabinets, and more.
But everything took so long!

The biggest problem was not the work, but to find materials for our plans, despite our experience from the furnishing the apartment at the settlement.

In socialism you could not buy what you want.
You had to buy what was available.

For example, imagine you need number six screws.
But they are not on the market and so you begin to hunt for them.
You try it overall but you are not lucky.
Why?
Because this year you can find only number eight screws .

Why?
Thanks to a planned economy someone planned only number eight screws for this year.

What you would do then?
The answer is easy.

You would buy number eight screws, put them in your storage and wait.

Next year when you may need them, they would not be available. Next year you could probably buy only number ten screws, after another decision of the planned economy.

So you accumulate in your storage things you could need sometimes in future. Only you do not know when or how much.
What you know precisely is simple.
You have to be prepared for everything.

This experience we gained very soon.
With this knowledge we went on transforming our dreams into a reality.

The way was long and hard.
Because in a certain sense we were, and still are, perfectionists.

To follow the style of the house, Frank began to study the art of stucco
He created big frames with stucco on the walls, using his hands and his know-how. Onto frames we glued fabric, a brocade.
We purchased an old, antique furniture, that completed the decorated walls.

We bought beautiful bedroom furniture, through an inheritance sale, from the beginning of the last century.
It was a gem; wooden leaves on the headboard of the bed and marble plates on bedside tables.
But the most wonderful piece my father bought us in Prerov.
It was a chest of drawers from about 1826, a real bargain.
It was a marvelous piece.
With smooth curved doors.
A headboard with an angel head.
The legs in the form of lion claws.
We were so excited!

Vera Stanek

I have seen in my life many wonderful pieces of furniture in many
countries of the world, but this was the nicest piece ever.

One Saturday morning we went, like almost every week, to the
hardware store nearby our house, to look for what we could buy.
But this time we had no luck.
There was nothing that we could use.
Frustrated we left the store.

On opposite side of the store we noticed an open door of a gallery.
We entered and slowly continued through the rooms, looking at all
the paintings
on the walls.
Suddenly we stopped.
A painting thrilled us.
So simple and lovely!
A woman figure in a profile with a mirror in her hand and a small
table next to her.

We wanted it so much, but we didn't have the money.

After a short hesitation we decided to buy it on monthly installment.
Not one day in our life did we feel sorry that we bought this painting,
although it took seven years to pay for it in full .

So you see how it was in socialism?
You went to buy screws, and you come home with a painting!

Not bad, is it?

We built this apartment for eleven years!
Finally it was a jewel, done to our imagination and dreams.
But do not believe we had an eleven years of holidays and a sack
full of money!

No, no, it was just a hobby!

On weekdays we worked.
On weekends we were creative.
That was it.

Our life in this new apartment brought many changes to the whole family.

First of all was necessary to put Eva in a new school.
Thanks heaven her school was only ten minutes away from our house, in an area of the city with light traffic.
Soon Eva was happy in school again; she found new friends and her new class teacher was not only excellent, but male.

Do you not understand?

In socialism school was the domain of women.
The flexible hours were almost an ideal working place for women with children.
A man as a class teacher was something special.
And if he was humorous and child-loving, then more rare.
He was adored by children.
He was adored by parents in the same way.

Eva was a lucky girl.
Only she did not let us breathe.

One day she came with an idea.
She would like to learn to sing.
We agreed. Why not?

We took Eva to a music schools in our neighborhood.
We were told that to sing, playing a music instrument was inevitable.

"And Eva what do you want to play?" was the question of the teacher.
With her head down she told him in a low voice, "A piano."

That was it! A piano!
Only we were not in a possession of a piano.
So we had no choice but to buy one. Only Eva had to be patient.
And she was.

The first month of her piano playing lessons was special.
Frank made a piano for her from a big strip of paper.
On it he painted a black and white keyboard, and Eva practiced on this *piano* every day.

During next month we bought her an old piano.
It was not a very good instrument but surely better then her *paper piano.* It was for us not easy to fulfill her wishes, because we had no money for a new one.

We were looking to find other ways to purchase a better piano.
Finally we found it.
We leased a piano through a cultural organization.
And it was not a piano, it was an instrument of dreams.

Eva enjoyed it for eight years, and it took her another 15 years until she found a similar one.

So began the piano career of Eva.
Like many other things she did, she did it excellently.
She played piano at concerts at her music school and took part at an international competition.
Of course, she continued in her singing lessons as well.

With our moving to the city, David's life had changed, too.
First he got another *Aunt.*
With her he discovered parks close to our home, walked the narrow lanes of the old city or played with other children on the

playgrounds.
This lady took care of David while I was at work and Frank was not at home from his work, yet.

Crossing the threshold of our apartment, Frank got busy.

Eva did her home work and played piano.
She was independent enough to fulfill her duties alone without Frank's help.
But David was the center of continuos attention.

In the evening prepared Frank dinner for them all.

Sometimes, when my lessons at school took longer, I found the children already sleeping when I came home.
It was the price for staying at home in the morning and working afternoons and evenings.

Everything has it's own price.

Our children did not require a kindergarten or another child care.
They were not exposed to socialistic education and propaganda.
This was the reason why we organized our life in this style despite the disadvantage of it for Frank and me.

It was the price we paid for a peace of mind.
We knew it.

We tried to spend more time together on weekends and twice a year on holidays.

We scheduled our holidays for winter and summer time, during school breaks.

Every December 25th, we boarded a bus and went skiing.
To the same place and to the same people I knew from my skiing

times at the university. All of us were older now and had children, but our friendship held for all the years.

We spent a week there, sometimes longer, and it was good for all of us.
The children improved their skiing.
Soon they were so skilled on the skis like walking.
Frank and I were happy for having the opportunity to ski as well, because we both loved this white sport with our whole heart.
It did not please us that with every year the lines for ski lifts extended, and we mostly only waited in lines. Sometimes one hour in a line for 10 minutes of skiing.
But we were on holiday.
We breathed fresh air, and when we were lucky, the sun in the sky smiled on us.

At evenings we played the cards; all four of us.
We were passionate players.
We laughed, argued, were excited.
We ate cookies and drank tea.
We felt happy.

In summer it was a little difficult.
We wanted to travel to foreign countries, but at the beginning of seventies we still did have not our passports.

We had only one possibility to travel abroad.
To go for trips with the travel agency to the countries of the Eastern Block, such as Romania, Bulgaria, etc.
Then a list of participants was enough and we didn't need our passports.

So we tried it.

We made our first trip with Eva by going to Romania and the next one by going to Bulgaria, with both children.

But there were many problems.

Since we didn't have money for a plane we could travel only by train. It turned out to be a horrible experience.
We needed two full days for one way and that with David, who was only four.
It was unbearable.

Yes, we enjoyed the stay there.
Warm sea, nice weather, good food... that was the good part of the holiday.

Eva improved swimming in the sea and diving in the waves gave her great pleasure. She was our big girl already and could find enough opportunities to entertain herself.
In and out of the sea.

David was happiest when creating sand castles on the beach.
Although he tried to swim in the pool and later at the sea with the help of air "sleeves" holding him above the water.

But he was a little scared.
Especially at the beginning.

One day he was prepared to jump into the pool.
But he suddenly stopped, turned to Frank standing nearby and in a low voice told him, "Papa I fear to jump. Could you push me into water?"
Frank fulfilled his wish and waited for what happen next.
After a while David rose to the surface.
With a smiling face he called, "It was great, Papa, could you push me again?"

By the end of our holidays the pushing was not necessary.
David got along in the water very well and jumped without help.

It was a pity.

Neither David, nor Eva could improve their skills at the sea.
After a truly horrible trip home on the train, we decided not to go on such trip with children again.
It was simply not possible.

So we remained at home, in Czechoslovakia.
It had it's own benefits.

At least we no longer felt like criminals, requiring *special treatment.*
And it happened every time we crossed the border.
We were the only people that were controlled by customs and marked off on a special paper.

It did not matter at all that we were reprieved in 1968 by a new president
We remained criminals.
That was it.

In the future we traveled only in the Republic.

We discovered the caves and streams of Slovakia.
We camped by the ponds of south Bohemia.
We swam in the sandy lakes in Moravia.
It was more comfortable and easier to go there, and we loved it too.

For a change we took the children to the mountains for hiking.
We tried to bring them love of nature. We taught them endurance, tenacity and understanding of their own ability to manage different situation.
We thought they could use it all later in life.

In these brief moments we enjoyed the nature and our togetherness.
We lived for our children.

We did not know what the future would bring; everything was so cloudy.
But we could show the children our love in many different ways.
Like to try to make them happy all year long.
Not just during family holidays.

We tried to encourage their interest.

We had enough experience with Eva, her piano and singing.
Now we concentrated our efforts on David.

What to do with him?

Before he attended the elementary school he began to play violin.
We thought, 'If Eva is so good then maybe it is in the family,' and we tried to prove it with David playing the violin.

David started to take lessons.
With more or less success he continued his education in violin.
He held on for about three years.
It could be not said about him that he was a passionate player, and it seemed to us that he was happier, when he finally quit.

David was different than Eva and we accepted it.

As an example of his difference from Eva I have to mention his reluctance to go to school.

His birthday was just 10 days from the deadline to enroll in elementary school. There was still the opportunity to let him go to school earlier.
So we asked school officers about all necessary steps we would have to take.
We were told that David would have to be tested by commissioners to see if he was underdeveloped or not, because he didn't attend

Vera Stanek

kindergarten.

In this moment we were furious.
We should not have to prove that our son is not an idiot.

So we gave him a gift.

We did not take him to the tests and we let him stay another year at home. We assumed that he was obviously not mature enough.
That prolonging his childhood by one year would be just right for him.
And it was.

After one year was David ready to go to school; he looked forward to learn reading and counting.
He was eager to prove he was a "big boy."

Moreover, it was not necessary to take any tests.

But we still racked our brain how to fill his free time.

We were sure that a boy more than a girl needs to be involved in sports. Because during his *silly years* as a teenage boy, he would need to be busy.
So busy, that he would have no time to think about getting into mischief.

What to do with David then?
Until now his joy in sport was limited to skiing and swimming.
But it was too little. These were only seasonal sports, dependent on exact conditions like enough snow in winter or nice weather in summer.
Both sports were more or less just hobbies.

It was necessary to find something different.
Something what he could do all year long and in Prague.

Like every boy in Czechoslovakia he wanted to play soccer.
But we did not know where to go and whom to ask for information.

Small clubs did have not an interest in young players.
And in good and bigger clubs David had no chance at all.
It was just for the privileged and for their friends.
We were neither the one nor the second.

By coincidence, we gained important knowledge.
A tennis club near our home would be opening a tennis school for
children age seven and eight.
David was almost eight, so maybe still in the right age.
In any case we had to try it!

David was keen to take part in the qualification tests.
Though he was not too agile or hefty, he went and tried everything.
This was the reason they took him, together with 31 other children.

The tennis school had a strategy.

For the first year they took 32 children and put them on a training
program.
Girls and boys learned to use wooden rackets and learned skills
with the ball.
By the end of the first year the children took some tests.
The results were carefully considered.
Sixteen of them, without required results, were asked to leave.

The remaining group was put through a second year of training,
only everything was more serious.
The children learned to play real tennis and were lead to gain
stamina.
The qualification at the end of the second year decided their future.
Eight of them had to leave the club.

The third year was the last year of this school.

The eight children were trained the entire year almost to the verge of their limits.
Then the last selection, and four children remained in the club as a member of a team, that was supposed to represented the club in competitions, tournaments, etc.
David was among them.

Those three years were hard, for David and for Frank as well.
Fortunately Eva was old enough to take care of herself.

Frank was very busy looking after David.
David was too young to go alone through the streets of a city like Prague. It was necessary to escort him to the club hall and back, mostly because the training was scheduled in late afternoon or evening hours.
So Frank and David visited tennis school together.

After three years they were both excellent.
David by playing tennis and Frank in the theory of tennis play.

Apart from it, Frank was there when David needed him.
It happened occasionally, even if not often.
David was first a schoolboy, and sometimes he had just too little time to do his homework and simultaneously play tennis.
Then it was urgent to set priorities.

What to do for example with a civic education?
This class of empty socialistic phrases?
In this moment Frank rushed to help David.

While David trained in the hall, Frank was writing his reports in a style like David would have written it.
Frank was without doubt an extra class.
The teacher was overwhelmed with *David's* work and almost moved to tears.
Once she told to children, "Remember David when you are adults.

David would be an excellent Member of Parliament. Vote for him!"

Because of circumstances, David lost his big opportunity to pursue a career in a socialistic country.
But he won something else.

That's the way thing are.

In the meantime our life continued with some changes.

On one sunny summer day Frantisek died.
He was in poor health for a whole year and after spine surgery he had problems with walking. He had to stay in bed for most the hours of the day.
Pneumonia killed him.

You know, I still think about Frantisek as the most generous man I ever met.
He was a man of high caliber!
What a shame you could not meet him, because then you would love him too.

Frank changed jobs; how many times already?
I do not know, I stopped counting.

Only this time he had to be careful and smart.
Do not forget what was told him at the last political screening.
"No change!"
So Frank had to find the right way out.

Even in socialism there were ways to leave a company despite their strong opposition to it. Like winning a competition elsewhere.
And this knowledge brought Frank to the following action.

He talked to the new employer about his problem.

The employer instantly advertised the post for a control engineer, Frank announced his intention for the job, and finally he gained the post in a open competition.
Now there was not a chance of stopping him.
They had to let him go.

Frank came to the Institute for Road and City Traffic.
His task was to prepare rules for technical control of vehicles.
He started to work on this task, but before he could bring it to the end, everything changed.

The Ministry of Traffic gave this Institute the responsibility of testing seat belts.

Frank was excited.
His *child* would come to him again.
How great!

The bosses decided that Frank would build a new test station!
Frank walked on air.

Equipped with the know-how from the first one, he began to build his second test station with big enthusiasm and skill.
He built not a copy, but a new, more modern station on the suburb of Prague.

It did not take long and Frank's new *child* was ready to prove its quality.
It was decided that this station would be in charge for testing seat belts for countries of the entire East Block.

So Frank began to travel.
To East Germany, Hungary, but mostly to Estonia that was still a part of the Soviet Union.
He got a "company passport," that he could use only for business trips.
Later we used this opportunity and asked for our old passports.

After 9 years, in 1976, we finally got them back.

I was still at the school and taught.
There were not big changes.
Just the students changed and that was all.

But we started a brand new tradition.
My friend and I sat once with a glass of wine and during our talk an idea slowly formed in our mind.
We decided to organize for our graduated students a big and very festive ball.

We got the desired *green light.*

We rented the most famous dance hall in all of Prague.

The hall was placed on a small island in the middle of the river Vltava and connected with the street by wooden bridge.
In this famous hall, more then hundred years ago, Czech patriots danced polkas, waltzes, and all national dances.
In this hall, decorated with gold ornaments, marble steps and stained glass, were organized the most wonderful balls ever.

Now it would be the place of the ball of our graduates.

We managed our first ball.
With a polonaise and a festive parade of all our graduates and their class professors and with dancing all night long until past midnight.

It was such big success that it was unanimously decided to make it a school tradition.

We organized altogether, ten balls.
Then we went our separate ways, and that was the end of this tradition.

I was busy and I did not have free time.

First I worked.
And in the time I didn't work and the children were in school, I hunted all over the downtown.
In socialism there is not difference if you need screws or vegetables or books.
Because you have to hunt for them in different stores.

The only exemption were books.

Every Thursday at 9:00 a.m. came new books on the market; the titles were known already a week before.
If it was something you would like to have, then you had to come early and wait by the store doors until the store opened.
The first people came usually before 7:00 a.m., but I know a case when people had waited all night long.
Why?

There were some rules about edition of books in socialism.

Political books were brought out in huge editions, because the people should improve their minds about socialism.
But bestsellers were published only in small editions.
For one bookstore only about twenty books were available and about 200 people who hoped to get them, me included.

I joined the crowd very often and tried to be among the first twenty people.
So I stood in a line for two hours, sometimes more.
But believe me. It was the best line I ever stood in. Maybe it was the reason I stood there so often. The people talked to each other, not a common habit in socialism, mostly about books and their view on the subject.
Some older people brought small chairs and sat on the sidewalk.

The only problem was bad weather like rain or frost.
Because then we all suffered.

Only one time was there an incident.
I stood in a line before the publishing house this time, because
there was better opportunity to nab today's book, a bestseller from
the West.
For this we were in a greater crowd then normally.

Suddenly police on horses appeared and waving truncheons went
for us.
It took only couple of minutes and there was not line at all.
It was hard, indeed.
We were peaceful people.
We did not want to fight.
We did nothing against the regime.
We just loved the books.

To be honest it was the only line I stood in.

Everything else I tried to manage by choosing many different
varieties.
Especially for food or clothing I was an expert.
I had to be.

In the meantime Eva finished at elementary school.
Nine years without problems; now we had one.
What to do with her.

She was excellent in everything she touched, and we did not know
what would be the best for her to do.

We connected our efforts to find the solution with Eva's class
teacher.
We discovered that an Institute for Education worked out tests to
help children to decide about schools or jobs.

Frank and I shouted with joy and right away let Eva go through the tests.
Our joy lasted only a few days.
Then we got the results.

We were told that her results were absolutely remarkable.
She could do whatever she liked.
It was wonderful, we were proud of her, only it did not help us, that was the problem.

After a long hesitation we finally decided to let her study another three years at the high school.
We hoped, that by then we, and she probably too, would be able to choose the right university.

Who knew what would happen in three years?

To celebrate the graduation of elementary school, Eva, at age of fourteen, made her first travel abroad to East Berlin to visit our friend Karin.

This was the start of one of Eva's big loves, traveling.
After the first trip followed another countries.
Estonia in Russia and her first touch with West, in West Berlin.

The more Eva traveled, the more her thirst for knowledge increased.
She wanted to understand the people, to communicate with them in their own language, to read about the countries she visited in the language of the country.
Eva began to learn foreign languages.

Today she knows about eight of them, written and spoken.

Meantime, David played tennis and went to school.

It was not as easy, as he thought it would be, being a member of tennis team.
The club wanted results and that meant to play tournaments.
Not one or two but lots of them.

First he had to play all-Prague Club tournaments in mixed teams with Frank as a team leader.
Second he had to play for himself, because his remaining in the club depended on the amount of points he got by playing tournaments in different places in the Republic.

A nomadic life for David and Frank had started.

Almost every weekend they were at another place.
The tournaments had only different names, but the sleeping in dormitory and the only available food, sausages, were the same.

We found this situation intolerable and made a decisive step to change it.

We bought our first car.

Not that we were immobile until then.
Thanks to Frank's job we could use his test cars for weekends very often.
Until now we did not feel the need to own a car.
But now a test car was too small for Frank and David. They needed a car where two people could have enough room to sleep.

Frank bought an older, used car of Czech production, once a car for government members.

The car was not in very good shape, but we did have not money for a new one.
Moreover we could use Frank's skill for repairs; he was still excellent. With the help of glass fabric and resin he patched up all

rusty places from chassis to bumper.
Then he put on coats of paint and soon the car looked like brand new.

Frank and David began to travel.
The car was a transport vehicle and bedroom.
When David grew to a taller boy, they bought a tent and slept there.
Both of them had untiring energy in managing this lifestyle.

But it was hard.
Sometimes, mostly toward the end of season, it was just too much of tennis.

Surprisingly, David held on and became a regular member of the tennis team.
The best year in his tennis career was 1980.
David climbed up on a ranking list to the third place in Prague.
He was strong physically, he had already enough know-how how to play tennis, and his tennis career looked promising.

But sometimes life make turns when no one expect them.

Toward the end of the tennis season problems began.
David could not hold his tennis match to the end.
He was unable to breathe, his head was swimming, and he had to forfeit the game.
It was alarming.

We took David to the doctor and the result was devastating.
We were told that David had asthma, and if he wanted to play tennis he had to take special injections, but before the season started.
This year there was nothing we could do.
We had to wait until next year.

We were terribly sorry.

However it was not in our power to help him or make his life easier.
They were times when David had no problems, and we hoped that
everything would be all right.
But another day came and his old problems were back.

We waited anxiously for next year.
By spring David and I visited a specialist.

To our horror he told us, "You know, to be effective for the season it
has to be done in winter. You are too late."
Absolutely desperate I asked him, "What should we do with David
now?"
The doctor said, "Wait until next year."

There was nobody to help.
We had to wait another year.

Meanwhile...

Despite serious worries with David, we had no time to lament.
There were other problems; with Eva.

The time passed quickly by, and suddenly we found ourselves
before the old well known question, "What to do with Eva?"

She was only a short way from high school graduation.
She was all the time the best in class with many different interests
in addition to school, but no plans for the future.

Yes, she wanted to study.
However she did not know what.
We took the list of all universities in Prague in hand and began to
discuss the opportunities.

Of course, there were still our *minus points,* because both Frank
and I were not Party members. That was still decisive.

In addition, there was a much more serious problem; our status as engineers.
Under this classification we did not belong in the category *working class* parents.
It was crazy.

The problems repeated themselves without change; first Frank, then I, now Eva.

Socialism was still at power on the basis of old practices.

After some undecided time we all three came, suprisingly, to one conclusion. Eva would try to enroll in Charles University to study environmental protection.
Finally we were all in agreement.

Eva graduated with honors in June 1981.

After entrance examination to the university, we waited with tension for the results. A letter with the rejection brought us before the problem how to respond.
This time we were absolutely sure that we had to do something that would help her.
There was no doubt for the reason of the rejection, because both of us have had enough experience.

First, we wrote the appeal against the decision.
Second, we came to conclusion that we need help and decided to pay for this help. Corruption was quite common among the officials with no regard of the level of offices they sat in.

The grapevine told us that for medical study you had to bring a key to a car if you wanted your non-communists child to study.
Thanks heaven Eva did not want to study medicine.

I called an old friend, working at the Ministry of Education, and asked him for help.

He organized a meeting between me and a person with influence on this matter.
As a *thank you* for the help we presented this person a gift box with fine food, wines, and an envelop with...

Eva's appeal was accepted.
She was signed up at the university.

It was the first and the last bribery in our life, but we were sure that Eva deserved it.

In last months at high school Eva joined a chorus.
The entire group was prepared for a trip to Switzerland and Germany.
They were sorry for Eva but she had to stay at home. She was new and did not know the repertoire.
Anyway, the whole paperwork was closed.

To earn some money, Eva worked during summer break by picking hops outside Prague.
In the evenings, when thre group entertained themselves with music and play, she disappeared outside to the empty fields, and sang.
She had managed to learn all the repertoire of the chorus.
She hoped that something could happen and if she was prepared, then she would go on this trip.

Eva was stubborn.
I do not know who she inherited it from?

You would probably not believe me, but something really happened.

A soprano, Eva's voice, got sick and the spot was suddenly free.
For Eva.

In September Eva took part on the trip of her chorus, and it was her fate.

In Switzerland their group met with a friendship chorus from Balwill, a small village near the city Lucerne, for a festive dinner.
Eva spent the whole evening talking with a young man, named Hans, sitting next her. They both continued talking the next day.
But that was all.

They said goodbye and promised to write to each other.
The chorus went to Germany and then home.

Eva had studied at university and stayed in touch with her new friend in Switzerland.
To our great surprise he came suddenly in November to Prague, to visit her.

The first day she took him for a trip through the city and spent most of her free time with him.
On the second day she came home about 10:00 p.m, her normal time.
By this time Frank and a I were already in bed.
We were reading before sleep.

Eva knocked on the door of our bedroom and entered.
With a questioning look we waited for what she had to tell us.
She did not let us wait too long and came directly to the point.
"He would like to marry me," she informed us briefly and waited on our reaction.

I began to laugh.
I do not know why but I could not stop.
"Stop laughing, this is very serious," urged Frank.
After some time I succeeded and calmed down.
Not until then was I able to think again.

First we talked to her.
We tried to explain her that a marriage is not play, that it is a responsibility for both partners.
Then we argued with her about the reality, that they did not know each other enough to go directly for a marriage.
We asked her to think and start to know him better before she made this decision.

She had opposed with the reason that she could not get to know him better because the officials in charge would not let her go to Switzerland.
We had no an argument against it.
We knew, she was right.

We tried to appeal to her intellect and talked and talked, but nothing changed.

Eva decided to marry him.
She decided to go away from socialistic Czechoslovakia.

On April 17th, 1982, Eva married Hans at the Old City Hall.

Nobody and nothing could stop her.

Chapter 14

We are sitting around a round table.
Eleven people; the whole wedding company

Directly opposite of me sit Eva and Hans.

I could almost not recognize my own daughter.
She beams with happiness.
I have not seen her to be so happy before.

And I wish her from my whole heart that it stays with her.
The happiness.
The love.

I do not know if she is aware what changes brings her this today's,
"I do."

The future would show it, for sure.

But it would be her life now.
She should live it like she wants and not like I would like.
It is all her responsibility.
And joy too.

Good luck, Eva.

Be strong.
Be happy.
Be fair to yourself and to others.
Love and be beloved.

You deserve it.

Because you are still our daughter.

It was not so easy to marry a Swiss citizen and moreover to want to go to live with him.

No honeymoon at all.
Hans left after three days later for home, and Eva stayed in Prague.
She had to deal with all the necessary papers for leaving the Czechoslovakia.
A heap of them.

After she successfully finished her first year, Eva quit the university and began to gather stamps.
Oh no, not like a hobby!
But to fulfill all the necessities for release from the Republic.
And it was hard work, because Eva wanted too much.

First, she wanted to leave Czechoslovakia and emigrate to Switzerland, officially.
Second, she did not want to keep her Czech citizenship.
With the marriage to Hans she obtained, in those times practicable, the Swiss citizenship.
She did not want to complicate her new life with her Czech past.

So the heap of papers was bigger and the amount of stamps too.

What was most tiring was the harsh reality that some of the papers had limited validity. So a good sequence was of big importance.

Only Eva had to act with many different officers.
Local and civil.
Men and women.
Able and unable.
Sometimes she could just not go through with it.
Somebody promised to do this and didn't and the whole sequence fell to pieces. It was essential to begin from the first step again.

But somehow she managed it all in about three months.

Then there remained just two *simple* steps.
First, it was necessary to pay for permission to leave
Czechoslovakia and it was not exactly cheap.
What was left us? Nothing. To pay for it and not think about the
similarity with paying the freedom for a slave.
Now we bought out Eva.
What a difference?

The second step was a not very pleasant one.
Eva had to pay customs duty on all her things she took with her to
Switzerland.

We called the customs officer, and he came to our home.
Slowly and thoroughly he went through her prepared cases, back
and forth,
counting her pants, blouses, bras...
After he finished his control, he closed all the cases, sealed them,
and wrote statement. Then he named the last amount.
We paid it without asking for what.

Afterwards we found that we paid a duty for Eva's wedding ring,
given to her by Hans on their wedding's day.
But we did not protest.
We already forgot what the word *protest* means.

In August Hans came to Prague for Eva, and this time it was final.
The sealed cases were put into his car, we gave them a hug and
said goodbye.

For once Eva was not there.
Her room was empty.
Nobody laughed, nobody played piano, nothing.

It was hard.
Much more harder than I thought it would be.
And not just for me but for the whole family.

Frank, as on each occasion, closed his feeling to his heart.
He did not say a word.

David was disturbed.
His teacher told us that he changed; he was insecure and unhappy,
and we did not know how to help him.
David needed time to get used to being an only child with no
siblings and no company.

We were happy he had his tennis friends and his responsibility to
the team.
We were sure it helped to bring him a smile and happiness to his
face and heart again.

About a month after Eva left for Switzerland we got a letter from the
university.
It was addressed to Eva and had informed her, that she had an
obligation to come for help to pick potatoes.
The socialistic farmers needed her.

I called the university.
I told them that Eva quit the university, now lived in Switzerland and
therefore is not available for this higher task.
To my surprise they did not understand immediatelly and it took me
longer to explain, until they finally got it.
I did not know why, but probably not so many students from the
university leave Czechoslovakia for Switzerland and are not able
for picking potatoes.

In the end I was happy.
Eva did have not to go to pick potatoes.
At least one problem was successfully carried out.

There were another problems to take care for in our family.
I could not mourn for Eva too much.

Our school was to be closed down.

A new point of view by the school officials prevailed against the old opinion.
A separate school for working class students was preferred no more. All the students and professors would be put under the new management of the day college for kids.

The rooms of this school were afternoon and evening empty, so we could teach our students there. It saved money for a house and principal.

There was, maybe, something more in the plan.

We, professors at the evening school, were not more separated in our own school. We were transferred to a day college.
Many colleagues from the day school took some of our classes and it meant that the teaching staffs were mixed
It was for us a catastrophe, because we didn't know them.
We did not have the knowledge about their enthusiasm and their collaboration with the Party.

The strong team, we once were, was broken.
We were unsure and suspicious to everybody.

Well done - Party!

We were not more the same people alike as in the sixteen years before.
Slowly we had stopped all the activities we used to do in past.
Not more celebrations.
Not more the balls.
Not more togetherness.

We came to the school, taught our lessons and aterwards we slipped off to home.

Suddenly we were like millions of other people in Czechoslovakia.
The socialism fell on us with undiminished power.

We lost the trust to each other and our enthusiasm.
The gray days caught up with us and the hopelessness struck us in full.
It was the end of an exception we once were.

Frank was right.
He told me many times how lucky I have been with such a team.
He had missed what I had and almost envied me the condition in our school.

Only I didn't think about it too much, I took it for granted.
How stupid I was and how naive.
One decision, one change, and everything was different.

I thought about leaving the school, but finally I was not sure if it helped to solve my problem. Probably it would be the same at another day school.
However even with the whole misery, I still loved to teach the adults and not children.
So I remained.

That all was just a part of our sorrow.

We had asked Eva in Switzerland to find help for David's asthma.
She had consulted a doctor and sent David special injections that should bring him relief for a whole season.

The injections were really expensive, even to Swiss conditions.
We appreciated it very much.
Finally a help for David!

We did not need to beg the Czech *specialists* and rely on their mercy.

I took the injections and David to our doctor at the health center and asked for a shot from our supply.
"I can not do it, " I was told, "I need to check if the injections are the right ones."
All right, we had still enough time and could wait.

After some time we began to get a little nervous.
Under some excuses we changed doctors, but to our uneasiness the situation repeated. It was alarming.
So we visited a well-known doctor of one of the few friends we had.
We were lucky, indeed, because he told us the truth.

Still we were shattered by the reality.

The doctor told us, "Nobody in Czechoslovakia would give David the shot. This foreign injections are not on the lists of products we are allowed to use.
There is nobody who would take the risk."
Period.

We were desperate.
Nobody could help him.
By waiting on opinion of the doctors, we wasted time for possible Czech treatment for this year.

Eva spent her money vainly.
It was like she threw them out of the window.

After I cried some days, I threw the Swiss injections in a garbage can. It seemed to me to be an appropriate place for them.
I wanted to have them out of my view, because I needed to find balance in my life again.

But something in myself changed.
I remembered my promise, given to Eva in the past, to bring her, once, to the free world.

Vera Stanek

Now I swore it to David.

Perhaps, it was the right time.

The experience with David shook Frank in the same way.

The discussion as to how to organize our second attempt to escape
was put on our agenda.
We agreed to ask for permission to go visit Eva, and then we
intended to stay in Switzerland.

There were a few rules we determined for the whole process.
Not one word to anybody.
Not one word about this subject at home.
It was absolutely essential to be very cautious.

We were quite sure that a bug would be put in our apartment the
moment we would present our request about the trip to Switzerland.
So we talked about it only on busy streets, doing the shopping on
Saturday mornings.

You probably think we were paranoid and, maybe, you are right.
But you still have to have it before your eyes; our unsuccessful
attempt of fifteen years ago.
So do not pass judgment on us.

The rule of not saying a word to anybody included David as well.

In spring of 1983, we filled the request for a visit to Switzerland.
We had not too much hope that we would all be permitted.

Frank mentioned it only carelessly on his work place and was
surprised with a reaction of one of his colleagues.

The man told him, "Don't be stupid and try it. I have a theory about
the work of responsible officials. You know I am sure they drink in

the worktime and then work under the influence of alcohol in the following way.
They take a half of the requests and stamp it; these are the people who are allowed to go abroad.
The other half is thrown off into waste basket; these people do not go.
If you are lucky you would be in the first group. "

And he went on.
"Look, my wife is a doctor and until now she took part on many conferences in the West. But last time she was not allowed to go. I assumed, she was probably in the second group."

Frank just shortly laughed, but the words did not let him sleep.

Finally, we filled out the necessary papers and added the invitation from Eva.
As expected with the promise of taking care about our well being.
The waiting time had started.

We were terribly nervous, although it was necessary to stay calm and go about our everyday lives without change.
To behave as nothing would happen if the answer would be "No."
It was not easy to hold on.

We could not to relieve ourselves by talking about it.
We have had too many another sorrows.

Here was David still suffering with breathing.
He graduated from elementary school and more or less tried to play tennis.
We filed an application for him to enroll in high school.
We were very wary to do as if everything was in accordance with normality.
Our behavior and our habits must be not changed.

Vera Stanek

It was only myself, who did something that was not normal for our family.

Secretly, behind Frank's back, I went to a travel agency.
I made reservations for a one week holidays in Yugoslavia for one person only.
I chose a place near to Italian border.
Why?
Because I was sure that one member of our family had to stay at home as a guarantee that the two others would come back.

And I do not know why, but I thought it would be me.

So I made a plan B.
If it would really happen, and I would not get the permission for the trip the Switzerland then I would go to Yugoslavia and hope that Eva would come to bring me through the border.
First to Italy, and then to Switzerland.
The controls were not so strict on these borders.
And if she came with a Swiss number plate then maybe...

I know it was insane.
Only it was a time when we were just a little step away from insanity.

I was unhappy in school.
Frank had no plans for the future; his work was done, and nobody knew what would happen next.
David fought with asthma.

That was not all.

The Czech nation began a *free fall* to the ground.

Everybody was corrupt.
The main subject of most jobs was drinking alcohol and only in a spare time working.

The morale of the nation was failing.
The streets were dirty and from the houses fell the plaster on sidewalk, where hundreds of feet crushed it to little pieces and spread it overall.

Where were all the cultural values of a nation, that was once on the top of Europe?
They passed from sight, they just melted away.

Do you understand then why we were so desperate to go away?

Only I do not know if you could imagine it.

Because you do not know what it was to live 35 years in socialism like we did.
What is was to live with a hope in the heart that once would everything change.
To believe and wait for a miracle that didn't come.
To grow older and find, that there was nothing to be proud of.
To live a life that ruined all the good quality you, at one time, had.

What was left then?

We did not know if something respectable was still in us, since we had not known the standards. How we could estimate and compare ourselves?
We had not a clue.

Moreover, we were not sure if we could change, yet.
Maybe we were not more able.
Maybe we were too much marked with socialism.
Maybe we were too old to start again.

But hey!
We were not only ones, there was David!
If we were too old and unable to start again, what about him?
Should we let him grow into the same misery we grew into?

Vera Stanek

To let him bend his back for the rest of his life?
No, and no again!

He had a right to be free if just for one reason.
Because he is our son.

All these black thoughts disappeared the moment we opened the
envelope from the government office.

It was written very shortly to us that our request was accepted and
WE, ALL THREE, could now take the formal steps for getting the
Swiss visa.

We just could not believe it!
It was not possible!
We got it!

We had to apply the brakes on our emotions and did try to be not
too optimistic.

It was only the first step.
What if they stopped us on the border?
But why should they?
We would not be so stupid this time.

Everything would be exactly after the rules; not one Swiss Frank
more, not our birthdays and school certificates, nothing.
We would go only to visit Eva, and after our permit for vacation
expired, we would come back.
Our entire behavior should prove our intention.

We stood a line for Swiss visa, for about four hours.
We stood a line for German transit visa, another three hours.
But we didn't care.

Meanwhile we lived our life like nothing happened.

Only one day I canceled my trip to Yugoslavia and hoped that nobody knew about it.

I went through graduation of my students like every year.
I was interested to know my schedule for next year.
I was interested in all the changes necessary for the classes, include all political training that was now more intensive than ever.

Then I told my colleagues, "See you in two months," and we all went for school holidays.

Frank went to East Germany for his usual business trip and fixed the next meeting immediately after the holidays.

David finished elementary school and was accepted for high school.
He was still clueless about the real reason of our trip to Switzerland and looked forward to seeing Eva and Switzerland as well.
It was his first visit to the West.
So he was quite excited about the trip.

He played tennis with mixed results.
Sometimes he was in good shape and without breathing problems; then he finished the tournament.
Sometimes he was not all right; then he was forced to give up.
We were already used to it.

The day of our departure came near with only one weekend left.
We scheduled our departure for Monday.

David played his last tournament before we left for vacation in Prague, so it was not necessary to travel.

Like every time Frank was with David.
To stretch his legs Frank made a loop around the tennis courts.
At one place he caught a stranger, watching the playing boys and girls through an opening in the fence.

The two men opened up a conversation.
After a while the stranger asked Frank if he, by a coincidence, knew about someone who would like to sell a violin. But not too expensive.
He, the stranger would be very interested in it.

Frank thought just some seconds and told him, "Look, if you are really interested then I can bring you a violin of mine. If you would like it, we could talk about the price. What do you say?"

The men agreed to meet tomorrow morning at the same place.

Frank came home exited.

You know if you plan to escape you have say goodbye to many things you love. It is interesting, that you find, there are many of them.
You could not take them with you, because with your decision you have to *close the door* behind you and look not back.

It is not easy, believe me.
And if you are already older like we were, then it is harder.

More then leaving the things are the thought of who would now have them.

Since you know what would happen.

All your possessions would be nationalized, and everything that you had would be taken away. Some other person would own things that belonged to you and were part of your life.
Maybe this, absolutely unknown person to you, would love them, maybe not.
Somebody would put your book or a piece of furniture in the garbage, exactly the piece you loved and what you once stroked with your hand in admiration.

Everything like this goes through your head and your heart is heavy.

But nothing in this world is without charge.
For everything here is a price.

One of the things Frank had to leave behind was his violin.
An excellent instrument from Italian production of 19th Century.
It was given to him by his father Frantisek in times when money was not a problem for them.

Now there was somebody who could play his violin and maybe love it.
What a great coincidence in the last hours before our departure.

Frank put his violin in a plastic bag and on Sunday morning left with David for the tournament and to meet the stranger.

To his surprise the man was already there.
Frank opened the bag and put the violin in the hands of the man.
He took a look on the instrument, then picked out a sound and told Frank, "It is not exactly what I wanted, it is not very good instrument. Anyway, how much do you want for it?"

Frank smiled at him and answered, "If you would like this violin then take it. It is yours. I do not want any money."

The face of the man beamed with pleasure.
"Are you sure of it?" he asked Frank.
"Oh, yes, absolutely sure," answered Frank.
The stranger thanked, shook hands with Frank and disappeared.

Frank had the feeling that his violin was in good hands.
That would bring joy and pleasure to many people that would sing or dance or just listen to it's sound.

Vera Stanek

Because the stranger was a gypsy.
And gypsies know how to play a violin.

This weekend was really a bad one.
It was hot and the sand of the tennis court swirled in the air, and
that was the worst what could happen to David.
He had to scratch the match, again.

David stood outside the court and tried to pull himself together, to
catch his breath.

In this moment Frank took his hand and told to him, "David, if we
could go tomorrow through the border, we would not come back. I
promise to you, that in Switzerland are doctors that would help you.
But do not say one word, about knowing our plans, to your mother.
This is just between us, men.
Promise it to me!"

David promised and did not say one word to me.

The evening before our departure arrived.
We could not eat.
We could not sleep.
We were just a bundle of nerves.

We had an agreement with Eva.
She and Hans would be waiting on the shore of a border lake,
Bodensee, on Swiss side, at 1:00 p.m.
We had about 500 miles to drive.

By midnight we realized that it did not make sense to toss about
any longer.

We started our journey.
We put two suitcases with summer clothing in the trunk of our car,
David's tennis racket and utensils and three books.

For every person one book.
What to bring was the most difficult decision, because we had to leave another 300 books behind. How to find a most loved one among them?

I went, for the last time, throughout the apartment we built with so much love.

In every room another memory struck my head.

The picture we paid on for seven years and now I had to leave there.
The dark green brocade in the bedroom that was difficult to put on the wall.
David's glass cup he won in a tennis tournament not a long time ago.
The chest of drawers with the angel head, the nicest piece in our apartment.
Or...
It was hard.

But I said a *goodbye* to everything.
In silence.
So that nobody could hear it.

Then we closed the door.

We drove in the direction of the Czech-German border.
Nobody spoke.

Frank was behind the wheel of the car.
Having enough time, we drove slowly because we started two hours earlier before our planned itinerary.

We came to the border area at dawn.

Vera Stanek

The wired barriers that, together with watchtowers, marked the boundaries of the *nobody's land* were already visible in the first morning light.
The view was horrible.
My knees were shaking with fear, the memories came back.
I gritted my teeth, but it didn't help me.

To our misfortune the customs officers were changing their duty and so we were told to wait. So we waited.

For more than one hour we stood there together with another two cars.
I was sitting in the car with our papers on my lap.
I stopped thinking.
I just survived one minute after another.
Sometimes I shook, sometimes I put myself together.

The door of the customs house opened.
Few customs officers went out and slowly reached the waiting cars.

I breathed in very deeply.
It should help me to calm down; but it didn't.

The officer opened the door of our car and asked for our passports.
I put them in his hand.
He turned on his heel and disappeared in the customs house.
'If they want to stop us, then it happens now,' was my next thought.
I almost lost control, but I fought hard with myself to hold on.

Finally the door of our car opened, and the officer asked the common question,
"Do you have something special with you?"
"No, nothing. Would you like to take look to our trunk?" I answered.
"No, go!"

The gate on the Czech side of the border opened, especially for us.

It was August 1st, 1983 at 5:47 a.m.

Chapter 15

We cross the border to West Germany without any problems.
We are free!
But we could not believe it.

We drive through a small village and nearby woods on the right.
Suddenly Frank turns to the woodland way.
He stops the car.
We are still shaking.

We leave the car, sit down on edge of the woods and begin to cry.
We hug each other.
We managed it!
Finally.

The tears are for these sixteen lost years.
Years, when we were young and in the most productive phase of life.
When we thought we could change the world or at least leave our mark on it.
But we lost them locked in socialistic Czechoslovakia.

The tears are tears of happiness, too.
We waited for this moment sixteen long years.
Years, when despair changed with hope and belief that a day would come and we would be free.
Now the day is here.

Is it a miracle or not?

The tension slowly dropped out of us.
We were able to calm down and talk again.
But no longer about the past; it was behind us.

And not about the future; it was foggy and we could not see through it.

We were sure only about the present; we were here and would not go back.

The price for it was, for once, absolutely not important.
Now was necessary to restore the confidence in ourselves again.

We came back to absolute simple things like the feeling that we were hungry. Something to eat and drink was now the best way to recover our composure.
With every bite we gained strength and with it our optimism returned.

We continued our journey to Switzerland with a smile on our faces.
We looked forward, not back.

We met Eva and Hans on the border of Switzerland only 20 minutes later than we assumed to be there.

Together we drove through villages and fields that were as clean as someone vacuumed them just five minutes before. With every mile we came near to the mountains that showed up against the sky on the horizon.
It was so much of scenic beauty.
We did not know where to look first.

Finally we came to Ballwil, where the family of Hans and Eva lived. Hans was a teacher at a local elementary school and together with Eva occupied a house with a small garden.
There they prepared guest bedroom for us.

Not until we were there did we know, that we had arrived on a special day.
The National Day of Switzerland.

Fireworks and bonfires were lit on tops of mountains and their blaze illuminated the night sky.
It was a feast for the eye, an impressive spectacle, a fascinating experience.

We were absolutely excited, but terribly tired.
It was too much excitement in the past 24 hours.

The next day we confessed our intention to stay in Switzerland.
However nobody was happy.
Understandable.

To have for once a family to take care of was not a very pleasant though for anybody.

Of course we were disappointed, but to tell the truth what we were waiting for?
That everyone would be happy for us?
That all of them would hug us and offer a help?
No, that not.

But maybe we were waiting for an understanding at least from the members of Hans' family, for their belief in our ability to manage this change.
Unfortunately, it did not happen.
We were met with disagreement and doubts.

Despite his different opinion Hans went with us the next day to the immigration office in Lucerne.

An officer took us to his office for a talk.

We explained our intention to ask for asylum in Switzerland.
His first reaction quite surprised us.
He frankly wondered, how all three of us got the permission for an entry.

He told us, "It has been a mistake from our side. We do not give permission for a whole family to entry Switzerland. Then they could not ask about asylum. It has been a mistake from our side."

We answered simple, "They were two mistakes. One from you, the second one from the Czechs. They permitted this visit to all three of us, as well."

The officer tried to persuade us to change our mind.
He asked to take couple of hours before the last decision, to be sure, what we really wanted.

Finally we agreed to take another 48 hours.
We promised to think it over only to comply with his wishes.

We sat at Eva's home around the table and talked again.

There were five persons present; we three, Eva and Hans.
To the end we asked all to write their opinion on a piece of paper.
We asked for only a simple "Yes" or "No".
The result was quite clear.
Four times "Yes," one time "No."
Eva understood.
Hans not.

The decision was final.

The next day we went back to the immigration office.
We insisted on our decision to ask for asylum.

The officer began talking about the problems.

"First, there are now many thousands of requests for asylum. So it would take maybe a year or more until yours would come for decision."

"Second, the possibility to gain asylum is minimal. The Swiss government is on the way to a restriction of refugees."
"Third, the timing is wrong because the economy is on a standstill. You would have problems finding a job."

"Do you still want it ?", he asked.
"Yes, officer, we want it."

The visions were bad, but we were convinced that this was our last chance to be free. There did not exist words that could reverse our plans.
We believed in ourselves.
We were sure we would be successful.

It was maybe good that we were not clairvoyants.
So we could believe that we would be the exception. That we would be accepted from the Swiss authorities as real emigrants that came there not to be rich but to be free.

How naive we were!

Only we had a long way before us to understand it.

Priority number one was to find a job for Frank, but we did not know how to do it.

Until now the Party told us where to go to work.
Now we were alone in a free world and responsible for ourselves.
We knew, it was necessary to learn the freedom, and learn it quickly!

Frank looked for an employment agency and asked for a job.
Yes, they had a job.
He was told, if he wanted to work as a carpenter he could begin tomorrow.
Frank wanted it.

Vera Stanek

It was not easy.

The work was hard and sometimes it was difficult to endure it.
But the people were nice.
Mostly younger men from different parts of Switzerland tried to help
Frank. They put him on work where it was not necessary to carry
heavy beams or work more than five feet above the ground.

They did not laugh when he spoke German, either.
Since Frank's German was not perfect, but neither was theirs.
They themselves spoke different languages, and that is usual in
Switzerland.
Because Switzerland recognize four official languages. Moreover,
the spoken Swiss German is a dialect, spoken different in every
valley.

So Frank was happy at work, although it was hard to hold on.

One day he came home very tired from work and told me, "Vera, I
can not do it any more. It is so hard! I do not know if I can endure
the work!"
Tears welled up in my eyes when I begged him, "Frank, please, try
another day.
Maybe it would be better. Maybe tomorrow you get easier work.
Please!"

If you think I did not have a heart, then you are wrong.

But it was the first time that we had only money that Frank earned.
From Czechoslovakia we brought ten Deutche Mark and sixty
Swiss Francs.
That's together about fifty dollars.
Nothing more.

Frank's salary was not very high, and part of it he had to pay to the
agency for their arrangement of the job.

Besides, the fall was already on the way, winter was approaching, and we had only two suitcases of summer clothing!
We needed at least pants and jackets, only, where to find money for it?

We had only one possession yet, and that was our car, that brought us there.
The car we had to sell now.
It was the only way out from our misery.

Finally we were lucky to find an old-timer collector.
He needed only a few parts of it for a repair of another car, but he was willing to pay for it.
We got one thousand Swiss Franc, for us absolutely a fortune.

We were able to buy winter clothing in one of second-hand shops, and we were very happy we could afford it.

And I should be honest.
We were lucky to have such a son-in-law.
Despite his different point of view, he let us stay in his house and at beginning he fed us. Later we had given him some money at least for food.
Anyway what we could give him was not too much.

Moreover Hans lent us money to put David into a private school.
It was a special language school in Lucerne, and David visited it every day.

David came to Switzerland, knowing just two German words, "thank you," and "good morning."
So it was necessary to start immediately.
We assumed that an intensive course of the German language would be the best way to learn the essentials.
Later on we would decide what to do with him.

Everything at the right time.

The fall arrived and with it the fog.
You can not imagine what it could do to your soul, if you do not lived in it. There are days and weeks when you do not see the sky, not the sun.
Only the white fog.

You think, the world died out.

I was desperate.
Frank and David were busy, but I was at home alone, with the fog outside.

Perhaps you would ask me why I didn't work?
The answer was simple; I could not find a job.

I tried everything possible, but nobody wanted to give me a job.
Because in my person were merged the worst characteristics ever.
First and foremost, I was a woman.
Second, I was a foreign person.
Third, I was 45 years old and that meant in Switzerland, old.
And in addition, I had higher education than most men I met in interviews.
I was a lost cause.

They did not want to give me any simple job because of the university.
They did not want to give me an engineering job because a foreign university is not accepted as an education in Switzerland.
If you want to be accepted as engineer you have to have a Swiss university.
It was a vicious circle.

So I sat at home and slowly grew crazy.

I didn't have money for a drive by train to Lucerne, to walk at the very least through the streets and look into the shop-windows.
I didn't have money to go shopping or go to the movies.

And I could not go to the fields of village Ballwil as well, because the fog was everywhere, and I could get lost.

They were moments when I stopped believing in myself, when I was sure that I did not belong in this free world.
Then I cried my eyes out thinking that I was old and useless and that was the reason nobody wanted me.
After a while, I calmed down again, clenched my teeth and tried to cheer myself up, "Stop it! Chin up! It will be better. These days will go away and everything will be fine. You should just be brave and trust yourself!"

It was easier said than done.

However, I somehow found the mental balance, and in the end my eternal optimism prevailed.
I knew I had to do something, to put my brain into work again.
To be busy and to have no time to think about my hopeless situation.

I began to work on myself.

With an enthusiasm I began to study the German language from David's books.
I tried to read as many books as I only could, and of course I still tried to find a job; but all the reactions were negative.

I had to be patient, over and over again.

How I hated the word, patient!

Meanwhile other sorrows were in sight.
After three months of hard work David finished his language school, and Frank and I agreed to put him in junior high school.
Only it was not so easy as we thought.

The high school in Lucerne did not want him!
What?
Him too?
Oh, no!
The principal told us, that David didn't have the necessary Swiss education on the lower level and so they were not interested in him. Period.

We did not know what to do.
For a lack of opportunities in Lucerne we tried another high school in Hochdorf, a small city only two miles from Ballwil further away.

This time we were lucky.
The principal agreed to take David to the school. He told us, "Look. We put him in the class he belongs to because of his age. If he manage it, then it would be great. If he does not manage it, he can still repeat the class."
We liked the approach of the principal, and David was excited and happy.

On November 2nd he started to study in Hochdorf and this was decisive for the future of the entire family.
We stopped to look for Lucerne as a place we would like to live, and concentrated our efforts to find jobs in Hochdorf.

Almost at the same time Hans came home with the news.
The only company for farmer machinery in Ballwil was searching for a design engineer.

Frank went for an interview and got the job.

The heavy job of a carpenter was finished now and instead of carrying the beams it would only be necessary to hold the pencil.
He heaved a sigh of relief.
To his great surprise this was not easy, either.

Frank's hands, stiff from the hard work, shook when drawing the curves.
But with time they got used to this work.

Frank and David were happy because they worked, and I was happy because of them.
I persuaded myself that I had to wait for the opportunity.

Christmas was near and everything changed.

The fog disappeared as if you waved magic wand.
Trees and houses were decorated and in the evenings everything looked like in a fairy tale.
Small electrical bulbs were put on tree branches or twisted around the trunks, artificial icicles hung from the roofs of houses and sparkled into the night.

A magical world, we did not know before, opened before our eyes.
We were enchanted!

We forgot once again that we had nothing.
That David had to stay at home when I washed his only jeans and had to wait until they were dry.
That the room we shared, did not belong to us.
That we were the poor relatives, like many times in our life, again.

We had nothing and we had everything.
We had each other and we were free.

Our dream about the freedom was a reality.

I almost forgot to tell you about Eva.

She fulfilled her own dream by studying piano in music school in Lucerne.

"The nicest music school in the world," she proudly announced.
So we went to see, if she was right.
Yes, she was.

The music school in Lucerne is placed on a hill with an
overwhelming view of the surrounding peaks and the azure blue
water of a lake, with the city of Lucerne stretched as a coral bead
on the string around it.
It is breathtaking.

The school itself has classrooms in a small castle.
The rooms are decorated with antique furniture and wooden inlays
in different designs on the floors.
A gorgeous garden around the castle complete the entire
impression.
It is marvelous.

There Eva continued in her passion of playing the piano.

In the time around Christmas we made a decision.

It was time to move away from Eva and Hans and to *stand on our
own legs.*
We had chosen to move to Hochdorf.
It would be good for David, who would save traveling to and from
school by train from Ballwil. And it would be not problem for Frank
as well, since a ten minutes drive by train would not be lost time for
him.

Maybe, there was another reason, too.

We did not like to stay with Eva and Hans anymore.

Something was wrong with them and we thought it was our fault.
It seemed to us, that Eva and Hans stopped mutual communication
and we were convinced that our presence was the reason for their

unhappiness.
We had to leave.

In January 1984, we made the first step.

We rented a two-bedroom apartment, in an old house, in Hochdorf.
The apartment was not very big, but cheap and that was decisive.
We moved immediately.

It was not too much to move, because we had almost nothing.

Hans' parents loaned us a mattress with bed linens.
We put it on the floor and Frank and I slept on it for more than one year.
It was necessary to take it easy, because... the mattress and linens were short for our quite tall figures.
In winter our feet froze.

So we went to bed dressed up as if we were in the polar region, with thick socks on our feet and with our legs wrapped in a small blanket.
You know, the winters were cold in Switzerland and the heating was not adequate.

We bought the bed and desk for David, and that was all what we were able to afford to buy.
We didn't have money for more furniture.
We began from zero.

For once we found that there were zillions things we needed.

In a normal life you take for granted that if you are thirsty you take a glass to fill it with water. But we didn't have the glass.
We didn't have a plate to put our meal on or a knife to cut a bread or ...
The first three days we had eaten our meals by sitting on the floor,

because we did not have money for chairs.
We waited anxiously for Frank's pay-day to buy them.

Oh, you could not put yourselves in this situation.
You have to live in it to understand.

To understand how you would feel, to have on the last day of the
month only one dollar and fifty cents in your account.

Please, do not think I am complaining.
Not at all.
I just want to show you the feelings and the reality of this big
change.

It was not so bad.

In our living room we had an old sofa borrowed from Hans' aunt
and three small cabinets, donated to us by one of uncles of the
family
To decorate our walls, I put on a nail my small enamel locket, a gift
from Frank for my fortieth birthday, that I brought with me.
In a corner of the room stood a TV set.

How we were able to afford TV?

It is another story.

Soon after we moved to Hochdorf Frank complained about teeth
pain.
It was for us a tragedy. Just the imagination of a dentist's bill for the
treatment brought tears to our eyes.
But we could not do anything against it.
The pain was getting worse.

Frank finally went to a dentist.
Back home, he told me, "It would costs two thousand Franc to put

my teeth in good shape."
Tears began to well up in my eyes; two thousand Franc was
Frank's monthly salary from which we could not save one Franc.
It was really the minimum we had to have for the living of a family of
three adults.

It was necessary to take a loan.
But where?

We went to the bank.
No, they could not give us a loan, because we were not Swiss
citizens, and moreover we had only temporary permission to stay.
Sorry.

The same answer was repeated by our visit of a second bank,
then a third bank, until we understood that there would be probably
nobody who could help us.

We were desperate and full of sorrow.

By coincidence Frank found an advertisement of a small bank
outside of Lucerne that started its business and offered loans to
everybody.
We called them and asked for a loan, and we got it.
They agreed to give us a loan under conditions we had to accept.

We did not have another choice, there was nothing to do, only to
agree.

In the end we decided to take a higher loan.
Not only for two, but ten thousand Swiss Franc, since we needed
money for other things, in this time absolutely essential for us.

Firstly, of course, there were Frank's teeth.
Secondly, we were totally immobile without car. We had driven
sometimes to Lucerne by train, but it was not cheap and
uncomfortable yet. Not to mention buying furniture or going on a

Vera Stanek

trip; we had to have a car.
Thirdly, we had to improve our German language.
We needed to hear it and thought that a TV would be just fine.
The connection of spoken language and visual imagination was
exactly what we were looking for.

And we were right.
It turned out that these decisions were worth of the price.

We paid off the loan very precisely in monthly installments for a few
years, to tell the truth.

After we were debt free, the bank sent us every year a blank check
with an offer of any amount we would need, and this time with
excellent conditions.
We did not take another loan.
But it was good to know that if something happened there was help.
We appreciated it very much.

After we moved to Hochdorf, I set my heart on a search for a job.

To improve my chances I decided to go study, to have a Swiss
education with the certification.
I thought about it for some time, considered what would be the best
for me, and at the end I choose to study computer programming.

To talk about it was easier than to realize it.
The school was quite expensive, and I didn't have the money.

I knew I had to find any job to start.

I picked out one of the four local factories, the one with the
production of displays from plastic, and with "fortune favors the
bold" in mind I entered the building.
It was a good day, I chose, because the boss was present and
agreed to have a talk with me. I asked for any job and pointed out

274

two things, that I thought could be decisive.
My residence in Hochdorf.
My intention to go study.

The boss promised to think about it and give me a call.
In two days his secretary called with a message that on February
25th, 7:00 a.m., I could start working in production.
I was overwhelmed.
Finally!

I was so excited that I could not sleep.
I could not think about anything else, only about my new job.
I was not afraid of working; there did not exist a work I would refuse
or find too trivial.
I felt, I could move the mountains around me, or pour the water in
lakes from one to another by tablespoons...

The much longed-for day arrived.

I came to the factory without knowledge what was waiting for me.

There I discovered about twenty women, working on production of
plastic displays for pharmacy, cosmetics, tobacco, etc., to name
only a few.
There were five men among them, busy by operating the big
machines or by doing the most heavy work.

Like every new worker I was assigned to the packing team.

The work was quite simple
First it was necessary to put together cardboard boxes with
adhesive tape.
Then the finished displays were cleaned, wrapped in plastic bags,
slipped into the boxes and these were closed.
Afterwards were the boxes heaped on a transport pallet and
brought to storage.

That was all.

For me was everything new.
I did not work, until now, in a factory.
And I did not work with my hands, until then, too.

But I was eager to work. I was eager to learn.

There were no limits to my happiness that I could earn the much needed money.
My hourly wage, 5.75 Swiss Franc, opened up for me undreamed possibilities.
You know what it meant in one month?
One thousand Swiss Francs!

If I spent on my study only half of it, then there still remained the another half for all of us.Then we could buy maybe furniture or clothing... or go on a trip, because we would have money for gas.

Do you see how many new horizons opened for us with this job of mine?

So it was for me irrelevant that I was tired after nine hours of work every day, because I was happy to have a job.

After some weeks my supervisor had found that I could be of more worth at another workplace.
So I was transferred.

There were many different kinds of work to do.

Every display consisted of pieces of a plastic materials.
These were bent on long benches by the help of hot wire to a required form, then eventually glued together and finally decorated with gold strips or labels, etc... and packed.
The series were small, from one hundred to one thousand pieces.
It meant that there was still something new on our work tables.

I started to do this works with another group of women.
I glued and bent the pieces and to the surprise of the supervisor I
was soon good in every aspect of this work.
After two months there was another job, to make models for
production, offered to me, and with the new job, more money.

I agreed with the knowledge that I had to learn more.

For this work I needed to operate machines, like a table saw, drilling
machine, hand milling machine, etc. and work with wood.
But it was thrilling.

I remembered my father, his words about working with file, saw, and
other tools. In my mind I was about 40 years back in our basement,
watching his hands.

Now under my hands grew new beautiful displays, and I had the
feeling of satisfaction.
It was so good; I needed the feeling to be useful to the world.

You can take my word for it!

On every Saturday I went to school.

The classes took eight hours, with lessons in many different
subjects, from English to programming.
I had to study the prescribed texts at home almost every day, after I
cooked the dinner, sometimes late until night.
Having problems with the German language I had to memorize
some parts, but it helped me to improve my German.

There was no problems at all with the study.

I had only one problem to solve.

Vera Stanek

To explain to my colleagues that I could not go with them for a lunch for lack of money. I was ashamed to tell them the truth.
I could simply not spend 15 Swiss Francs for a lunch.
My budget was enough only for two bagels I bought behind the corner and ate on a bench in the park.
So I used excuses.

With the time going I was very good at them.
Sometimes I had to do something very important in the city.
Sometimes I was on a diet, sometimes...
I tried not to repeat it.

They were not suspicious.
How could they, when they did not know what it was not to have enough money for a lunch? So I could cheat on them without qualms.

Only one woman of our class recognized it.
She asked me for help in subjects like math and methodology, and I had not other choise than to invite her to our apartment.
There on Sundays afternoon I taught her.

Of course she had seen our poor furnished rooms, but she had let it go without notice. Just when she left I found some money on the table or under the only vase we had.

I did not ask her for the money, but when she paid me for my help I was not ashamed to take the money.
She was one of the few people that tried to help and I was thankful to her.
I bought a new skirt and blouse, for the first time new dresses, not from the second-hand shop, where we used to shop for clothing all year. I had the feeling that these two pieces were a status of going back to the normal human society.

After six months I finished successfully at school.
I became a "junior" programmer now.

The school promised in it's advertisement to find a job for
everybody who finish the study. So I used this offer and asked for a
job.
Only there were probably some exceptions.
Anyway, I was one of them.

I was told that I was too old to begin as a programmer, although
that I was the best of the class.
This job was just for young people and not for an old foreign lady.

So another dream melted away.

The hard work and money I put in my study were worthless.
I should reconcile with the reality, that there would be not better job
for me, without regard to the certificate with a Swiss stamp on it.

But I did not want to understand it.
I was still a stubborn person.

During the time of my study there were changes in our family, as
well.
The first was related to Frank.
The second to David.
The third to Eva.

One day I struggled with one display, a dispenser for many lipsticks,
that I just could not put together.
The task was quite simple.
If you took one lipstick through the opening in front of the display,
then another one should drop to the same position.
Only the lipsticks did not drop and remained jammed inside.

Once at home, I discussed the problem with Frank and after his
opinion the angle of the dropping was wrong.
While I was studying new texts for my school, Frank sat at the table

and calculated the angle by himself.

The next day I used his result and to my and my supervisor's surprise the problem was solved.
The lipsticks dropped!

Our sales man brought the dispenser to the customer who was absolutely overwhelmed; nobody, until then, was able to solve this demand.
He spent two hours taking lipsticks from the dispenser and putting them back and it still worked flawlessly.
Then the customer ordered five hundred pieces.

This story reached our big boss as well.

He came personally to my table and congratulated me on this good job.
I smiled, pleased with the praise and thanked him with words, "Thank you. But I could not take credit for this job. It was my husband who solved this problem, using his math knowledge."

The boss hesitated and then told me, "Ask your husband if he wants to work for me."

I came home that day very excited and in detail described to Frank what happened in the factory.
Yes, Frank wanted the change.

Frank got a job as a design engineer in the second factory our boss owned.

There Frank designed many different plastic products made by thermoforming, like packing blisters, trays, containers for gardening and so forth.
By using his knowledge, ideas and experience Frank invented new tools and machines that not just improved, but sped the whole process of production.

The boss made a good profit by giving the job to Frank.
And Frank was happy that he could use his brain again and prove his ability and skills for technical problems.

There were times when he was happier then ever, only...
Frank remained *just the Czech,* like other people in the company were *just the Italian,* or *just the French.*
There was not a person worthy of thoughts, if this person was not a Swiss.

But this we found out later.

David was successful at the school to a great delight of his teachers and us as well. He was happy and enjoyed the way of expressing fully and freely his own thoughts.
It was the first time in his life, when he could say what he really thought and it was very exciting for him.

After we moved to Hochdorf, we looked immediately for a doctor.

We wanted David to be healthy again, free of his problems connected to asthma.
We deeply believed that it would be possible.

The doctor made some tests, including a test of sensitivity to different materials, and the result was surprising.
David's asthma was in reality a strong allergy to grass and trees.

We asked the doctor about the healing process.
He told us, "Two third of patients with this problem could be treated and healed.

The rest not. You could only hope that David belongs to the first group."

The treatment began.

David came one time per two weeks, later less often, to the doctor's office for an injection, alternating *grass* and *trees.*
After three whole years he was given new tests and found fully recovered.
He really belonged to the first group, we believed he would.
Lucky David, lucky us.

Meanwhile, David joined tennis club in Hochdorf and began to play tennis again.
He was still very good; in his new club, the best .
Soon he started tennis classes for youngsters as a trainer and began to play at the club's championship.

When he brought the first place, a Champion of Canton Lucerne, to Hochdorf the celebrations were limitless.
He was written about in the local newspaper and from this moment he was in our village a very well known person.
And we together with him.

Because from this time we were *the parents of David.*
We were very proud of him.

And then there was Eva, with some changes in her life.

After two and half years of a life together, Eva left Hans.
So we were right, I am afraid so.
It was *something in the air* already in times we spent in their house.
In the course of time the problems accumulated, and Eva and Hans tried to find a way out from this situation.

They decided to live separated and see what would happen.

Eva moved to Lucerne to be near the music school into a small apartment with just one room and a small kitchen in the hallway.

By day she studied at music school and taught children to play piano.
Evenings she worked as a waitress in an Italian restaurant.
She needed money for her study and for living, because she did not want to take money from Hans.

She had to learn now what we knew already before.
That a life is an immense struggle.

Eva was intelligent and she had learned it very quickly.
The hope of her and Hans to be together again, was not fulfilled.
After another two years they finally divorced.

With her changed life she returned to her former passion to travel and see the world.
Only this time, especially to begin with, her purpose of travel had two parts: traveling and learning languages.
She spent some weeks in London to study English.
The following year some weeks in Paris to study French.

Later, she traveled for pleasure.
She visited many countries in Europe, she even went to South Africa.
Back home she brought many memories and great experiences.
But until this time she didn't find a country, where she wanted to live.
Not yet.

It was necessary to wait for some time.

Our life was changing all the time.

Shortly after Frank got the job, the big boss called me in for a talk.
He offered me another job; to change the workplace and work out offers for displays and production plans for both of his factories.
I agreed and was very happy.

Vera Stanek

I belonged now to another level of employees.

I did not work in production in noise and dust, but in an office by a nice table and a floor covered with carpet as the only woman among the men.
I was so proud on myself!
After all these disappointments I was finally on the way up!

I began my new job and as expected, I had to learn something new again.

Anyway it was not something brand new to me.
Now I was happy to have a good practice from my life as a professor when I had to learn, almost every year, something new.

To begin with I was happy to do another job because it was new and interesting.
Later I found that I was dissatisfied with the job, and what was more important for me, with the people around me even more.

I was used to working with women of different nationalities.
French, Italian, Turkey, Yugoslavia and I, Czech, together with Swiss women.
Who cared, that we sometimes did not understand each other.
We worked as a team by the sweat of our brow.
Our mother-language was not important; what was important was, that we all did a good job.
This was decisive.

But now I was among the men, Swiss men.
And they did not want to have a foreign woman in their center.
They let me feel it very soon.

My enthusiasm slowly disappeared.
I tried to fight against it but it was stronger then I was.
Only I could not allow myself the luxury of going away because we

needed the money and I needed the job.
We were waiting already three years for the decision of our asylum status.
But nothing was solved until now.
So I had to stay.

Not even a new supervisor I got improved my depressed mood.

His special working style brought me on the verge of insanity.
In the day he spent his working hours in production by talking with people and doing almost nothing. I was supposed to do his work together with mine.
In the moment I left for home he began to control my day's work.
Sometimes three hours, sometimes more.

He was good because he did overtime; I was not.
He was diligent because of it; I was not.

My reputation went down.

All of the co-workers just waited for the first mistake I would make.
In regard of this situation it would be almost a wonder if this would not happen.
But a wonder doesn't happen.
That I knew already.

The situation escalated.
I began to have difficulties holding food in my stomach before I went to work.
I was a bundle of nerves.
Only I wanted so much to survive!

Finally I made the mistake everybody was waiting for.
I do not complain .
I do not make excuses.
It was just my own fault.

Vera Stanek

One day I counted a size for an order of plastic foil and forgot to add an extra for holding the foil on the machine and it was wrong.
For once I saw only smiling faces around me and this made me suspicious.
I found my mistake.
I made correction.
I found the solution for it.
But it was too late.

The big boss called me in for a talk.
He told me, that I made mistake and that no one in the office wanted to work with me. So I had to leave.
But if I wanted, I could go back to my first work place, to the production, to my old job of making models.

I felt terrible.
I felt that I disappointed not just myself, but the whole family.
I was so ashamed!
I wished the ground would open and swallow me.
I wanted to go away.

Only I did not have a place to go to work.

I still had in my mind the desperate searching for a job and I heard the negative answers after an interview.
I remembered very well the vain waiting on a phone call that did not come.
No, I had no another choice.
I had to stay.

I took the offer and went back to work in the old factory.
The women took me back like a friend, as if I was not at all away.
It was a balm to my soul, and I felt a huge relief.

But I needed time to be the *old* one, I had to struggle with myself for many weeks.

My problem was in my mind.
I lost the faith in my ability and was sure that everybody knew about my incapability.

That it was a little different, I did not know then.

I did not know that in this company this was a typical case.
It depended often on a sleep of the big boss and a full moon.
Only in my case it was appropriate because I made a mistake and so I could blame only myself.

During the time I found that it was the best thing that happened to me.
In only three months I was happy again.

I knew for once, that it was very important for me to see the result of my work.
When I saw hundreds of displays on workplaces of our women then I knew that I contributed to this product by doing the sample of it so good that someone liked it and bought it.
I loved to do things for use.
A work that had sense.

I loved this world again and I stopped feeling sorry for myself.

I was the *old* one, again.

Meanwhile, Frank and I began to discover the beauty of Switzerland.

It was incredible, how much of magnificence could be concentrated in one place.

I was skeptical about pictures of Switzerland.
I had the feeling that it was a special effect of a skilled photographer.

Now I had to admit that I was wrong.
Because it was a reality, it was not a swindle!

When I came the first time near to these big peaks, I was overwhelmed.
What a majesty and eternity radiated from these giants!
I almost sank down on my knees.
I closed my eyes and only one thought crossed my mind; they would be there in their beauty when I would be dead.

Maybe another people, after some hundred or thousand years, would stand before them in admiration like me now.
I felt like an ant.
And it was good so.

It would be, maybe, not so bad if everyone feels sometimes like an ant.
Because then, I think, the world would be a better place to live.

Frank and I began to hike all the mountains near Lucerne.
Not too high because Frank does not like the heights, but regularly.

Every Sunday morning we left David with his homework or tennis and went hiking to a place we choose on the map.

Because we had no money for lifts, we hiked already from parking places up the hiking trails to about six up to seven thousand feet.
Mostly for five up to eight hours.
We had a backpack with bagels, a bottle of water, and one fruit bar for each of us. Every Sunday the same, because we had learned what we needed to have very soon.

One Sunday, at the beginning, we hiked one not very easy mountain, and we forgot to take water with us.
So we agreed to make an exception and buy a bottle of water at the top-mountain restaurant.

Yes, of course, they sold us a bottle of water, only this bottle was twelve times more expensive than in our grocery.
It was the most expensive bottle of water we ever bought.

We did not forget it.

Next to mountains we decided to see Switzerland as a complete picture.

We had visited the cities and villages around us and it was easy. By going three to four hours by car, we were already on the border of Switzerland.
So it was not a long way to drive.

The cities are not very big, but have mostly a historical downtown, some hundreds years old. Just to walking and looking around was an experience.

The villages are beautiful.
In some parts of the country the houses are built from wood, sometimes already black from intensive sunshine. But old or new, all the houses are in summer full of flowers; on window sills, on walls of houses, in gardens, all over.

And they are many lakes in Switzerland.
With the water deep blue or blue-green and mostly with mountains nearby.
Sometimes you could go around lakes on hiking trails.

We loved to hike around such lake in our hill country, only fifteen minutes far away from our village.

On hot summer days we drove there after the work and swam in it's cold and clean water.
In springtime or in fall we hiked around the lake. The trail was about 15 miles long, nice, with snow covered peaks of high mountains visible in the distance.

Vera Stanek

During the wintertime we walked at least part of the trail, just to
have a little exercise.

After these years, we knew almost every stone of this trail.

I would like to tell you one nice story.
It's from our trips around the Lucerne.

It was about one year after our arrival to Switzerland.
A nice summer day, not too hot, just great day for a trip.
This day all three of us went together to a tour around the
magnificent lake by Lucerne.

We drove around the lake and stopped in every village.
We walked through the village and spent some time on a shore
of the lake. We did not hurry this time, we just slowly roamed and
enjoyed the beautiful day.

We came to one of these small villages.

Frank with David walked before me and talked.
I stopped, sat down on a bench and looked on this deep blue water
of the lake and ducks that forced their way through the water. They
left an arrow of small waves with a white foam on the tops behind
them.

In this moment in one of houses behind me someone began to play
a piano.
The first tones of this composition came to my mind.
It was Beethoven's " For Elise."
An indescribable feeling came over me, the feeling of peace.
The feeling of a peace I was looking for, and found it there.
On the shore of this lake.
In this minute.
I was so touched!

I did not know what would happen to us.
I did not know the future.
But I knew that I would not forget this moment in my life.

The moment when I found the peace in my soul.

The winter brought another activities on the program.

The second winter we bought cross-country skis and clothing for all
of us in second-hand shop.
We were terribly excited.

Yes, we still admired the big mountains with down hills trails.
Only we didn't have the money for them.
Skiing is an expensive sport in Switzerland, like probably
everywhere else.

We had cross-country trails just 10 minutes by car from our
apartment.
It was more than a great coincidence!
If there was enough snow, we could go anytime we were in a mood
for skiing.

There were three loops, the longest about six miles, and the best.
A track in the snow led through forest and meadows with a view of
high mountains in far; it was wonderful.
Mostly on Sundays we were there, happy to be on skis again.
Just to feel them glide in the snow brought the feeling of happiness
to us.
We really enjoyed it.

For David only, we bought ski and clothing for down hill skiing.
He was the first one who got in touch with downhill trails on a
school trip.
He was good on skis and surprised all of his friends.

After three additional years we bought skis for Frank and me, too

We went skiing for a whole week to the Swiss Alps, to the French part of Switzerland.

There I discovered a hotel that I liked and booked a studio for us.
The picture of the hotel was very nice.
The studio was not expensive.
The trails nearby were promising.

When we came to the place we had found soon why it was so cheap.
However, it was too late.

The hotel looked very nice, indeed, but the studio was not nice at all.
When we opened the door we grew stiff.
The room was dirty, the pictures hung crooked, and the kitchen was covered with a layer of old fat. The carpet was full of stains and in the door was a hole, someone made probably with a ski boot.

What to do, was the question of the day.
Anyway it was Sunday, no one in sight to complain to, so we had to be flexible.

Nobody and nothing could spoil our first holidays in the Swiss Alps.
That we swore to ourselves.

Our first trip was to the grocery store that was miraculously open.
There we bought all necessary cleaning supplies.
After three hours of hard work the room looked like new. Only the floor remained stained and the door with the hole.
Everything else was *picco bello.*

But the stay was not under an influence of good stars.
The weather was terrible all week; fog, snow or rain.
After five days we packed our luggage and went home.

We comforted ourselves that next time would be better.
At another place, at another time and not in Switzerland.
We should listen to our fellow-workers when they told us that we
made a mistake going skiing in Switzerland.
They all drove to Austria to save money and have better skiing.

We promised ourselves to find soon, if they were right.

After four years in Switzerland we were finally invited to the
interview for our asylum status.

We were terribly excited.
The time of the decision was there; the uncertainty about our fate
would be solved in a few days.

We drove to Bern, to the main immigration office with a heavy heart
and extremely nervous.

What would we do, if the asylum would be not given to us?
Where would we go after four years spent there and another four
years older?
What other country would take us, if it would be necessary?

All the questions we asked ourselves many times, when we tossed
about all night, unable to sleep.
Now we were there.

We entered the entrance hall.

There were about a hundred people already, standing in groups or
alone.
People of different origins, mostly from Sri Lanka, Tamil nationality.
Because of a war there, they came to Switzerland and asked for an
asylum.

We got a serial number and joined them.
Again a number, what changed actually?

After some time our number was called.
A young man, in his late twenties, came and took us to one of the offices.
Three more people were already waiting. One lady about the same age as the man and a girl that wrote the minutes.
An older man was introduced to us as the translator.

We did not ask about the translator.
After four years in Switzerland we were fluent in the German language.
Maybe he was there to translate if we wanted to talk in a whisper, Czech, just among us.
But it was just a guess.

The interrogation began.
The first question for each of us to answer, "Why would you like to have an asylum there, why did you leave Czechoslovakia?"

I answered first.

I began with a quivering voice, my shaking hands held in my lap.
I told them that I am looking for a freedom a long 46 years.
First the war when Hitler...
The man interrupted me, "Go on, the war is not relevant to this case."
But it was.

Because I wanted to show him how much time I already spent under control of two different regimes and how eager I was to be free.
For the first time in my life to feel the freedom, to be a part of it.

So I talked about socialism.
How it was to educate children in saying not what they think.

About the falling morality and decline of society and the communist propaganda.
And about our attempt to escape 20 years before.

However, they did not understand.
They could not or, maybe, they did not want.

They were too young and inexperienced.
They worked according to the rules they obtained in a short training for qualification for this job.
Sometimes a light smile crossed their lips.
No, they did not laugh at my arguments, they just smiled.

Only in my mind I went back to the moment when someone else laughed to my answers.
When I felt the same helplessness and the same humiliation.

Later Frank spoke how we accommodated to the society in Switzerland with our good work.
Then David spoke about his school and friends.
But nothing of this had helped our case.

We could not answer the question if we were persecuted, with yes.
We could not answer the question if we were tortured, with yes.
And for sure we could not show scars of beating on our backs.

Or like one person told me, before we left, "Leave your hope behind. Because you could not come to the office carrying your own head under your arm."
She was right.

The commissioners came to conclusion that we were just economic refugees.
We wanted tear from the rich Swiss a *piece of a bread with a thick layer of butter* for ourselves and nothing more.
To want freedom was not the reason to get asylum.
Period.

Vera Stanek

Were we really so naive to think that wanting freedom is enough to get asylum?
Yes, we were naive.
Yes, we were stupid.

After four years in the country we believed, we showed them what we were and what we wanted.
Only it was not enough.

Fortunately, the Swiss officials were prepared on such cases, like us.
They were prepared already before we came.

We got an offer to get a mercy to stay in Switzerland.
It would be inhuman to send us back to socialist Czechoslovakia after four years of living in Switzerland.
We got a status of *homeless foreigners,* the last group of society, not enrolled in Switzerland. We should be thankful for it, anyway.

Without thinking too long about it, we took it.

We had no another choice.

We were too old now to go out and begin again.
We had built slowly our existence, nothing special in reality, but we were happy at work, and we had a place where we felt at home.
Moreover we loved the Swiss nature.
And we still believed that the people would take us among them, and that we would have friends to talk and laugh.

We believed that to be free and happy we had to pay a price.

So we paid it.

Chapter 16

To be free like a bird.

When you escape, you do not know how you will react to this change.
You do not know how it will affect your soul and your feelings.

Would you hold on and fight for a new beginning, or would you feel sorry for yourself and your decision to leave the country you were born in?

The problem is, you do not know it before.

Why?
Because everything is new and different!
You could not imagine this situation before it happens, you do not have the experience how to manage it, you do not know your reactions.

They were people, refugee, that after an escape were like newborns.
Full of energy, simply they were in their element.
And they were another people, refugee also, that cried and could not find the peace of mind they were waiting for. Because they could not stay without their old country, language, habits.

To escape is a leap in the dark.

We risked it.

We were positive, that it would be not easy.
That we would lose something and get something.
Like every coin has two faces, a life has them, too.

Vera Stanek

What we lost?

Our past.

We *closed the door* and left everything behind what was connected to us.

Behind remained our family photos; our wedding day, our brand new children, family trips in the snow...simply everything.
We could not look at our pictures and tell ourselves, "Do you remember this moment? How old we were? Do you remember how happy we were?"
We could not laugh about our appearances because of different hair-styles, clothing and grimaces on our faces.
The past was gone.

The former life remained only in our memory.
What was left were only the words.

Behind remained our cultural habits.
Our books, our records with music we liked, our pictures on the wall we loved.
Theaters, concert or exposition halls we visited and ...

Now everything was different.

We had no money to buy a book or record, because we had to eat.
We had no money to go to theater or concert, because we needed winter jackets.
We had to give up everything that made our life richer of cultural experiences, because we did not have the money for it.
We had to hold on at least for some years.

We had to remember what it means to be poor again and be happy to satisfy the basic needs of the family.
Anyway, we had enough practice.

Behind had remained our rank in society.
In the past we were, because of our education, in some circle
of people with similar interests in cultural habits. Now we were
nothing.
We belonged to the last group of the society, we were refugees.
We did not have ancestors living at least 500 years in Switzerland,
and we had problems speaking the dialect.

The result?

We didn't have friends; we were completely alone in the world.
There was no one person, that wanted to come to visit us, to have
a talk with us, to eat with us, to laugh...

We had just our family and that was all.

Behind remained our parents, with no hope of seeing us again.
They understood more or less why we escaped.

My mother did not speak to me for about half a year.
She did not want to hear that I, her pride, could leave the *wonderful*
life I once had.
My father understood why we escaped very well.
Frank's mother was not surprised.

It was the hardest part of our new life.
Because you could broke the ties to your past, but not to your
parents.

What else remained behind?

Socialism.
With it's inhuman face, gray days without future for us and David as
well.
We didn't feel sorry for the loss of it.
It was the main reason, why we were there.

Vera Stanek

What we got?

Freedom and a new life with other joys and sorrows.

We came to a different country with different people.
People with different habits, language, with a history we did not know.
We were aware, that to socialize with them would not be easy.
But we believed in people and hoped that with the time they would open their heart to us.

We were wrong.
We remained just another *foreigner* and nothing more.

Life was absolutely different, from food to our dreams.

For once we could buy everything we only dreamed of.
Like a whole bunch of bananas.
Pounds of oranges.
Strawberries in March.
And every amount of vegetables, not to mention the quality and diversity.

I could buy everything I wanted, if I have had money for it.

No, not everything, because I could not buy a friend.

At night I experienced *refugee dreams.*
It was new.
It came to me in first days of our escape and lasted a few years.

The dreams were in essence almost the same.
I was in our old country and tried with all my strength to go out.
Only it was not so easy because...

Airplanes did not exist, just so.

Trains were full of people, and I could not find a free place.
Cars were not available, and taxi drivers just did not stop on my
wild wave.
So I mostly walked with suitcases in both my hands, trying to
escape a person that every time pursued me.
I knew, I had to run, but I could not move my legs quicker. Because
my legs felt like a lead.The only chance I had was to sneak on all
fours for some miles, maybe, miles that did not end...

Until I suddenly awoke with a sweat on my forehead.

Then I opened my eyes wide.
I looked around to see the well-known contours of the furniture and
to convince myself that it was just a dream.
I lay in my bed, not sleeping, with a fear that my dream would come
back when I closed my eyes.
Because I was scared.

However we got a life we enjoyed.

We had jobs we liked, and that was a good reason to be happy.
We were surrounded by beautiful nature we admired and drew a
confidence and courage from it. That brought us the necessary
balance to our jobs.

We enjoyed the tidiness of Swiss cities and villages, the peace,
freedom...
We loved Switzerland.
Only we were not sure if somebody loved us.

Our life was full of contrasts between losses and gains

We had freedom.
But we didn't have friends.

We were in a country with wonderful nature around.

Vera Stanek

But we were just refugees.

We had jobs we liked and worked hard to gain respect.
But we remained *just Czechs.*

We were in reality happy.
But we were lonely.

We could go and see the world.
But we didn't have money for a trip.

What we had then?

A future.

Chapter 17

I am looking in the mirror.
Why?
Because I would like to see the "Cain mark" on my forehead.
It has to be there.
I am positive of it.

If it did not exist then the people would not change the smile in the moment I say the first word.
Because in this moment everybody hears it.
That I am not a Swiss.

I do not look different and my behavior is like I am one of them.
But I am not.

It is not just an imagination.
It is a reality.

My vision about the equal value of people with no regard on color of their skin or language or religion slowly vanish into thin air.

The world remain divided.
On rich and poor.
Black and white.
Communist and capitalist.
Moslems and Christians...
And Swiss and non-Swiss.

How long yet? I do not know .

Probably forever.

Our life stabilized at least in one way, we could stay in Switzerland. We didn't think what would happen later, we lived in the present.

"Take today how it comes and do not think about tomorrow," was now our philosophy of life.

With a passport in our hands we could finally travel outside the Switzerland.
We were eager to go and see Europe, because despite our ages, we did not known the West at all.

So we started immediately to make up for it.

Our first international visit took us to tiny principality of Liechtenstein, one of the smallest countries in the world, and a neighbor of Switzerland.

Why?
Because it was just two hours by car.

We were armed with camera to record this historical moment.
We had an exact imagination of the picture we would take; the nameplate of Liechtenstein and us.
Only the reality was different.
The nameplate of principality was in the middle of a bridge with no possibility to stop. So we gave up the idea and continued on our way.

After we spent a wonderful day there, it was for once not important if we had a historical picture or not.

The more one has, the more one wants; we were not an exception.

We wanted more trips, more to see, more experience, more memories.
We remained too long on only one place and were keen to travel.

There were only two small hitches we had to manage.

First, we had to have a visa to every country, because of our status, but the principality of Liechtenstein.
Although it was necessary to think in advance to get them, to compare it with hours of waiting in lines in Czechoslovakia, it was nothing.

Second, we had to choose places we could afford.

We worked out a special procedure where to go for holidays.
We covered the left side of a catalog with the description of the places and mostly with beautiful pictures and looked only on the right side for the prices.
When we found the cheapest one, that was our favorite.
It was for us more play than just selection.

Anyway we had fun and could be able to go for holidays two times per year.

Our first holidays abroad brought us to Italy.
On a small island near Naples, named Ischia, where we felt like we were in heaven.
The hotel was high on a slope in a garden full of bougainvillea, the sea was dark blue with white cliffs and small beaches, and the people were just great.
We had a splendid time.

We fulfilled our desire to go skiing in Austria.
For the first time we took Eva with us, and we all enjoyed the downhill slopes of the Alps.

We remained loyal to Austria.

There, we found the place that we were looking for all life long; a small village high in the mountains with many opportunities for skiing. For ten following years we spent one whole week vacation by skiing in these gorgeous mountains.

Vera Stanek

There we were very happy.

It was our love of a lifetime.

In the meantime were some changes in our family.

Eva graduated from the music school and decided to go to study
music history at the university in Zurich.
She began with big enthusiasm and soon she was number one, as
always.
Next to music classes she took English courses.
She studied Shakespeare's work, wrote poems and of course still
played piano.

However, this way of living did not last long.
After she came from her second visit to America she told us, "I
found a country where I would like to live."

She managed it in about one year.
She canceled her apartment and sold all her furniture and gave her
most important things like books and records to us.
Then she kissed us goodbye, and left.

Only this time we did not take it so hard.
Maybe because it was not the first time or maybe it was another
situation.
But we knew that we would stay in touch, without regard of the
amount of miles between us.

We all changed.

On this occasion Frank and I promised ourselves that we would let
our children go where they wanted.
No matter if they would stay in next town or on another continent.
Because we wanted them to be happy.

It was easier to say, than to do it, but we were sure that it was the right decision.

We were aware of the time, approaching step by step, when our children would open their wings and fly away to find their own world.
That we would remain alone.

Just Frank and I.

They were changes in David's life, also.
He went to study at senior high school in Lucerne the economy.
Despite the preference to the school, tennis remained his love and joy.
David found a new tennis club, new friends and a new team for playing in the national championship.
He was happy and socialized very easily.

Because of school and tennis he found many friends.

The young generation was different; more open and mostly with no prejudice.
At least among themselves.

We were very glad for David and were sure he deserved it.

Then events happened that deeply shook me.

My father died and I could not believe it.
In my imagination he was the person who would live forever.
However he was an ordinary man and, for once, he was not more.
His heart stopped working, without warning signs.
One minute he was there, the second he was dead.
It was the hardest moment I have had from the moment we escaped.

Vera Stanek

I could not go for the burial.

If I went back, I would be stopped on the border, and put into jail.
The usual practice of socialistic Czechoslovakia was precise; if you
escape you are sentenced in absence for some years in jail.
Period.

It was the first time when I hated both of the countries.
Czechoslovakia because of communism.
Switzerland because they refused to give my parents permission to
visit us when we asked about it two years earlier.

Why?
"They could ask for an asylum," was the answer.

What should we do?
We ourselves got a pardon to stay in Switzerland, with no rights
and an everlasting question, "How long will they let us stay here?"
We could only try to persuade them with a reference to the age of
our parents.
But in a vain.
They kept stubbornly to their official opinion.

Now my father was dead and I could not say goodbye to him.
It was the price for a freedom, too.
Too high a one, believe me.

That was not all of my sorrows.

After another nine months my mother died.
She did not want to stay in this world alone, she just did not want to
live.
The stroke helped her to not be alone, but to follow my father.

My parents went from this world.

Their ashes were spread together on a flower field, near a cemetery.
Where the wind brought them?
I do not know.
And never will.

Frank and I went on in our days full of work and weekends with hiking.

Some small changes reached us, too.

Frank got a special computer for drawing forms and to realize his ideas for improving old machines in production.
He was sent to computer classes and soon he was an expert in drawing.
Moreover, Frank understood exactly what he did, because he knew the laws of nature.
And that was almost an exception in the company he worked for.

But the time was still great for Frank.
He enjoyed his work and had a fun by doing it.

I got an offer, again.
To work in the preparation of production of our displays.
Up to now there was no documentation about individual orders.
When the customer, after some years, wanted the same product, then everything was done only according to an old sample, placed somewhere on a shelf.

In the same time was our company reorganized.
We got our own management and a new boss I liked because for his style of dealing fairly with people.
So I agreed.

I began to do drawings of all parts of a display, include all the necessary information of how to produce them.

It did not bother me, that I had only a desk and pen to do this job, because it was a technical job and I needed to use my brain to do it good.
My hands, used to work with saw, were slowly able use pen again.
And I found my work very interesting and satisfying.

These years were the most happiest years in Switzerland.

It was easy to recognize it.
When you go for holidays and you think, 'I would be happy to come back after three weeks,' then you know that you love your job.
I knew it at that time.

Later I got a computer, just small, simple one, for drawing my displays and was sent to computer classes.
It helped me to realize the imagination of our customers quite well and simultaneously I could improve myself.
Sometimes I drew displays in a perspective to show the customer how it would look in reality. I could use different variations, materials, shapes or sizes, yet before we started to do any samples.

I loved my work and was enormously happy.

But it was our nature that brought Frank and me the balance and peace to our souls and minds.

We continued in our *hunger* to see the world.

Every year during our holidays we visited another country or at least another place there.

So we went to Tunisia to come in touch with the *black continent.*
We were fascinated.

We strolled through narrow streets in the old city, Sousse, were bit by jelly-fish, and celebrated 200 years of the French Revolution, the remainder of former French influence in Tunisia.

As a highlight, I flew in a parachute sailing over sea.
From bird's-eye-view I have seen the magnificence of the city, no-ending azure waters of Mediterranean sea,and in far the yellow sand dunes of the Sahara Desert.
It was very impressive.

But David was eager to see the world also.

He successfully finished high school and went to work. After six months he put together enough money for his dream-trip.
David decided to see two continents and three big countries.

He started his trip in Australia, spending two months with our friends, and surviving an accident with, fortunately, no harm for him.
Then he flew to New York.
There he bought a car and drove to Montreal.
There he took a route from east to west, through all of Canada until Vancouver.

Crossing the border to the USA he continued on the West Coast.
He reached San Diego in Southern California, and going crosswise through the Southern States he achieved his last destination.
Eva's apartment in Florida.

His trip took him six months.
An experience of a lifetime.

He stayed in camps with many different people.
From forester to manager, from hippie to clerk.
He went alone, but he found many good people that let him not feel alone.

Moreover he learned that if he wanted to eat he had to buy or cook

the food by himself. Or do laundry with nobody there to do it for
him.
To be responsible to himself and to others as well.
It was a perfect education.

He changed, and it was good.
After months of thinking what to do with his life he decided to go
study at the university.

Independent of David we went to America, also, for our first visit of
the American continent ever.
We went to visit Eva in Florida

Totally excited we came to De Barry, near Orlando, to Eva's
apartment.
It was a great time of great experiences.

We swam in crystal clear water of a small river near the village.
We drove and sometimes we walked around.

As a culmination of our holidays we spent five days in Disney World
where Eva worked.
It was absolutely marvelous!

Surely, all the attractions were wonderful and we had fantastic time.
But we found that best of all were the people around us.

We stood one day in a line for an entry to Spaceship Earth.
Suddenly Frank squeezed my arm and told me, "Look at this line
and look at the people."
When I looked around I understood immediately what he meant.

There were two girls with fine, blond long hair, maybe Swedish
origin and next to them a Mexican family with many kids. Behind
them was an Afro-American man with a small and beautiful girl

sitting on his neck and a large, probably Chinese, family next to him.
All the people were American.

Maybe then we first time understood what America is.

And we promised ourselves to come again.

But there were other changes for us on the way.

After a "velvet revolution" in Prague the communist regime fell down.
Finally, after 41 years!
The people were terribly excited at the thought of changes to democracy and freedom.

We got many enthusiastic Christmas cards from a few friends still there.
We understood how happy they were, although we were less optimistic. It was the first moment, the rush of adrenaline.
No one knew, what the future would bring.
How Czechoslovakia would develop as a democracy.

The next year the Christmas cards were less enthusiastic.
The third year we got only normal Christmas wishes.
The life went on.

What was destroyed in 41 years could be not repaired in one or two years.
To have democracy and freedom means to change not just the economy or ownership, but especially people's mind.
However, this is a long process.

The people had to learn new moral values like responsibility, fairness or honesty.
And what was more important, to think on their own. Something that

Vera Stanek

the majority of them did not know before or had forgotten, already.
Besides, the bulk of the population did have not the experience with
democracy at all.

This new Czech event brought some changes in our lives.

About two years after the change we were asked by the Swiss
officials to give back our passports of mercy and to take the new
Czech ones.
With them we could stay in Switzerland like every foreign worker
with a permission to work.
We shouted with joy!

Not more the last place in society!
From now on at least one or two steps higher!
Thank you, Switzerland, many thanks.

Not that something changed in mutual relationship with the Swiss,
but we were happier than before.
Because the inner secret fear, what we would do, if ...disappeared.
We were more free, as well.

No, we did not think of going back to Czechoslovakia.

Why ?

In this seven years of our stay in Switzerland we changed.

We were positive that going back would bring only problems for us.
We would probably be foreigners there also.
In Switzerland we had our jobs, we knew the environment and the
people around.
Not to mention, that in this seven years we grew older and we did
not want another unsure change.
For us it was too late.

Other things had changed for us in connection with Czechoslovakia.

After some years of struggle Frank got part of his father's
ownership in his business back.
There were six heirs that fought among themselves for the best part
of it.
Finally they sold it and split the money.
Frank's legal portion was transferred to a Swiss bank and thanks to
the currency exchange it was not too much for Frank.
But it was enough to find our financial situation as great.

Moreover something nice happened to us.

One summer evening we got a call.

Our former neighbors and friends called from Prague. The message
was short.
"Our cousin is going to Switzerland for a visit. He will call you
because he is bringing you a gift. Please meet him."
OK. Why not?

In about a week we got the call and met the cousin.
He was in hurry so he put about three feet long cardboard roll in our
hand, then he said goodbye and was away.

Immediatelly after we came back to our apartment we carefully
opened it.
We were very curious what it would be.
It was something wrapped in a fine paper and in another protective
bubble cover. Gradually we unwrapped it, and...
Then we remained motionless, speechless and slowly began to cry.
Before us, on the floor, laid our picture.

Yes, it was the picture we loved so much, and with heavy heart had
to leave behind in Prague.

How it was possible that the neighbors sent it to us?

Vera Stanek

Before we escaped we gave them a key from our apartment and asked them to water our plants.
When we decided to stay in Switzerland we called them and said we were staying a little longer.
"How long?" they asked.
"A lifetime," was our answer.

Later we learned what followed.

Our neighbors *cleaned* our apartment of things that maybe some another people could use.
The words of this cleaning process were quite precise, "It remained not too much to the Bolshevik."
Period.

Now we had our picture back.
Somehow they knew what we liked most of all and they used the first opportunity to give it to us back. Later they sent us some of our former books, and by their visit to Switzerland they brought our photos to us
We were extremely delighted.
At last we were again people with a past, and that was good feeling, believe me.

We did not stay in touch with them over the years.
We changed and they changed too.
They were too busy for a friendship at a long distance.

But we would not forget them.
Every time I look on our picture I am so terribly thankful to them.

Thank you, friends for being there for us in bad times.

With our new Czech passports we went for second time to America.

This time to Texas, because Eva changed her job and state.

My imagination about Texas was quite simple; dust, sun and cacti.
What we found was different.
We landed in Austin, a city full of trees and lakes.

To see the country we rented a car and began our trips around
Austin.
We wanted to know how the people there live in all complexity.
We were eager to see it.
Why?

I would tell you the truth.
Our visit in Florida left us restless and left a big impact on our
thoughts.
We still had to think about the people in the line, because they were
exactly what we missed so much.
To have people around.
To have friends to talk with.
To enjoy life.
To share moments of happiness and sorrow.
To be not alone.

In our minds began to grow another dream.
To be there and be a part of this world.

Actually, it was just very harmless playing with the imaginations.
The vision was far away, since we had to work until retirement at
least eight years yet.
Moreover there was a problem; by working in Switzerland just ten
years, our pension would be very low and so we had to work to the
last moment, we only could.

Anyway we looked around Austin.

What we found were the eternal hills with junipers and oaks and the
blue waters of many lakes.
The nature was simply wonderful.
So different than in Switzerland, but so peaceful.

Vera Stanek

The people lived in wonderful houses, so unlike anything we knew.
In view of warm weather, they were built in another way and
therefore cheaper compared with Switzerland.
"It would be great to have one of them, just the smallest one would
be enough," we agreed.
It was so nice only to dream!

One day we came to a place named Lago Vista.

We saw a sign with an advertisement of a retirement community on
the lake.
'It would be probably marvelous,' we thought.
So I went to the first Real Estate agency we saw be the road and
with very bad English asked for a few maps and brochures.
Both were given to me by an older secretary.

Frank and I hit the road to look around.

We got lost, then we found the way again, but we were absolutely
excited.
We found it was the nicest place in the world that we ever saw.
The houses were spread out on the shore of the lake, some of them
hidden in big oaks. Narrow ways crisscrossed the small community
buried in hills; a heaven on the earth.

With a head full of dreams we left.

We visited other villages, saw many other places and swam in
different lakes.
Simply we enjoyed this visit very much.
Only this Lago Vista remained in our mind all the time.

We had just four days until our departure.
At the morning I asked Frank, "Please, let's come again to Lago
Vista.
I would like to see it a second time. Maybe we would be not so
excited as the first time."

So we returned to this place one more time.

We entered the Real Estate agency again to ask for information on prices of houses in this community.
This time another lady, the owner of this agency, greeted us with a smile.
At our request she answered, "You know what? I will show you some houses so you can get a picture about it."

We went with her for a drive through Lago Vista, and we liked it more than the first time.
We drove through ways with beautiful houses around, great yards full of lush green and we held our breath by views on lake and hills.

Deer walked peacefully through the roads and the air was full of the chirping of colorful birds.

"Where are we?" we asked ourselves, "Is it a paradise or are we already in heaven?"
No, it was not a heaven; it was Lago Vista.
A small village on the shore of a lake in Texas.

The Real Estate lady, named Ann, shoved us two houses on a golf course.
They were really nice.
Then she told us, "Come and look at a brand new one, not finished yet and really pretty one."

We came up to a big construction site with a white two story house and entered it. Inside were just construction beams, some isolation and general mess.
But there were already steps to the first floor.
We took them and came to the upper deck.

An unbelievable feeling came over me.
I stood there, looked around, and began to cry.
Before me lay part of the blue lake surrounded by a sea of green

hills that melted into blue far away.
It was this magnificent view that touched me so much.

Frank stood silently next to me.

After a while I took his hand and said, "Frank, please, let us buy this house. If we do not do it now, we would not do it later. Please..."
To tell the truth we did not need to discuss it for too long.
We decided to try to buy this house.

Do you think we were crazy?

There was only one question open.
We did not have enough money, this we knew for sure, and we did not know how much we could put together.
We needed some time to think it over.

So we asked Ann to give us one more day to think about it, and promised to come back the next day with a decision.

Terribly excited we went to Eva's apartment and with a pen and calculator in hand we counted all our money to find out, if we could afford to buy this house.
No, it was not possible.
We did not have enough money.

We talked with Eva about it and were absolutely disappointed with her reaction.

She was not happy for us and we did not know why.
We were so eager to boast about this big event, but she was very reserved and disapproving.
She made it clear to us that if we wanted to buy the house, we should buy it alone, because she did not want to be involved in it. Period.

At least in this moment Eva underestimated us.

There were times in our life when we were sure about a decision we made.
Like the decision to escape, to name only one example.
Now we were sure that to buy this house was the right thing for us.

Only the money was really a problem, and we did not know, what to do.

With a heavy heart we went to Ann's office the next day, after an almost sleepless night, and told her that we were sorry but we did not have enough money.
That we were really sorry!

Ann told us, "Stop worrying. I already thought about it and I think I can help you."
She called her friend Liz from the bank and these two ladies organized in one day everything what was necessary to buy this house.

We took a loan in America, because we decided to hold back information about this purchase in Switzerland.
Why?
We were almost sure what would happen.
Our boss would dismiss us the moment he knew that we bought a house in America.

In our last two days in Texas we came again to now our house, took some pictures and said goodbye.
To the two great ladies.
To our house.

Our first house in our life!

We did not know how we would manage to come here.
We did not know if we would have enough money to live here.
But we knew that our life changed.

We had a goal now, and we knew that we would do everything just possible to go for it.
We would work harder.
We would count every Swiss Frank before we would spend it to pay off the loan.
Moreover we would shut our mouths.
It would remain our secret.

After we returned to Switzerland some changes were awaiting us.

Our boss handed over the company to his two boys.
Both of them finished at the university in economics and public relations.
Now their father laid the company at their feet.
The changes were drastic.

First, the boys did not know what it means to work.
They did not spend one hour of working in production, they did not know how it feels to have a sweat on the forehead, and they did not know the company.
Second, because of their status as boys of very rich family they were often arrogant and not friendly to the people around them.

But right now they were in control over about two hundred people!

My immediate boss did not hold out long and after about a year he quit and went away.
The new boss, who fitted exactly the picture of our two big bosses, came soon.
It was hard.

For me began a special hard time again.
Because I was a woman, and did quite a professional job some Swiss men were not able to do.

Slowly but steadily the new boss put me on a second track.

"The company belongs to young and dynamic people," he told me many times.

What could I tell him? Nothing.

The only smart behavior was to shut my mouth and be inconspicuous.

Somehow I managed to stay, maybe because I knew my work and was still good.

Everything changed to the worse in only a short time.

Gradually people left our small company and those who stayed were people like me. Women who had almost no a choice to find another job.

I suffered, but this time I was not alone.

Frank suffered, too.

He had basically the same problem; he was older than me but at least he was a man, he was an expert in his job and worked for the sister company.

Not directly for mine.

But the changes were almost alike.

The immediate chiefs changed quickly because they did not understand the job.

Every newcomer was greeted as a savior with no regard to his knowledge for the branch.

It would be not a problem if the people had the will to learn.

But the word learn was not in their vocabulary.

Sometimes just to read an article was a problem for them.

So they began to show their ability by stupid decisions that cost the company lots of money.

This Frank could not allow; for him this company was his other *child*, that he knew almost to the last procedure, to the last tool.

He began to protest, loud and with arguments.

"The laws of nature could be not changed. Not by Swiss people,"
he told me.
He told the same to the people in his office with one exception.
He let the "Swiss people" away.

Only it was wrong.

He should work and not criticize.
Regardless of his clairvoyant ability to know already before, if a
decision was right or wrong.

Convinced about the correctness of his arguments, he forgot
something important; he was an old foreigner.

So what happened with him was the same as with me.

He was put on a second track and only because they needed him
they let him, at least at the beginning, work.
He had no more opportunity to say something.

Principally Frank was an introvert person; so he returned to his old
habits of talking not too much and put his ideas on the computer
screen.
But he suffered inside.

Our hiking changed, as well.

With our head full of sorrows we needed firstly to relax.
So it was almost a rule that we started our hiking by talking about
the problems and all the heaviness we had in our hearts. After
about one hour we began to perceive the nature with all the beauty.
When we arrived back, we were different people.

We were prepared for another week.
We were prepared for another fight.

But we promised ourselves to hold on.
We had the goal before us and with every week we were nearer to it.
It did not matter to us that it was in a far future.
It was a shining star on the dark sky of our lives these times.

After one year we paid off our loan.

We still knew how to save money.
Our house was now really ours and the tenants took the minimum care that was necessary.

Our life altered because of changes in Eva's life.

Finally she came with news that shook us by surprise; she was in love with her boss from Switzerland, Wolfgang.
We could not believe it, but it was true.

For once we understood her displeasure with our decision to buy our house.
She feared, probably, that we bought it because of her and if she would move in future to another place with Wolfgang, what would happen to us?
Only she did not know us very well.

We bought the house for us and our dream was to go there.
No matter if she would be there or not.

Wolfgang played a decisive role in our life.

He was a strong man who built his own orthopedic company and expanded his influence to the whole world.
He knew Eva from Switzerland.

It was he who asked Eva to go work for him to Texas, for the company he worked with, to take care of his interests there.

Now they were a couple.

They met on different places in the world by symposium, exposition or conference. Wolfgang was a rich man, and so Eva traveled in luxury, without sorrow about tomorrow.
Of course, it was very pleasant to stay in five stars hotels, eat excellent food just in the bests restaurants, and see the greatest places in the world.
But was she able to adapt to such life for long?
An entire life, maybe?

To know the answers on these questions, we had to wait.

From the moment we met Wolfgang, our life changed.

Wolfgang was a withdrawn man.
It was necessary to know him better to understand the core of his personality.
After we spent some time with him, we felt more relaxed in his company.
Anyway, it was a new experience for us.
We were not used to mingle among rich people.

Every year as a Christmas gift, we were invited on a trip with him and Eva.

So began our time of seeing places we could normally not afford.

We would always be thankful to Wolfgang for it.

The first time we met in Vienna.

There we felt immediately at home, because Vienna was basically the same as Prague, only much nicer and richer.
The houses were built in the same style as in Prague, but there every house showed up, that somebody cared.
The plaster did not fall on your head, nor did the dirty dust cover your face.
Vienna was, and is, a gem.

"The streets of Vienna are paved with culture. Streets of another cities with asphalt," I read in a travel guide.
And that was true.

The first time we strolled through the streets I remembered a small episode, I read not long time ago.
A stewardess on a plane told to passengers before landing in Vienna, "Ladies and gentleman we land in Vienna. Please fasten your seat belts and turn your watches two hundred years back."
I felt almost exactly the same.

I could imagine the people from more than hundred years ago walking solemnly in the same streets. Men with top hats and canes in hands, ladies in long dresses and with parasols getting onto carriages.
The time when music like operetta, a typical Austrian music comedy, and dance like waltz, ruled the city.
When people were dancing waltz in wonderful opera house or in the streets pubs and artist from whole Europe belonged to the life of empire.

Vienna is now another city.
Modern and vibrant with a lifestyle of this century.

But you could still feel the culture on every step.
Whether in museums, galleries, in opera house or restaurants.
It does not matter where you are.
Sit down on a bank in some park, close your eyes, and you could feel it.

Vera Stanek

They are some places in the world that did not change very much.
Vienna is, surely, one of them, believe me.

Then we went to Venice.

I was very exited because it was my dream from a long time.
To go and see the jewel of history, the most romantic city in the
world.
Now we were there.

We came, like everybody, by boat from the airport; already this was
exciting.
Not to mention the astonishment to arrive into the city with not one
car on the streets and with only boat traffic, transporting goods and
people in narrow canals.

Our accommodation was a palace some hundreds years old on the
shore of the Lagoon with a wonderful view of palaces, towers, and
domes of many churches.
We were overwhelmed.

Eager to see we dived to the narrow streets of the city.

And you know what?
I was disappointed, really disappointed.

I found, the city was neglected.
In some places were wonderful palaces collapsed almost in ruins.
The air in entire city smelled of stagnant water.
But what! Once we were there we had to look around.

We would let the city play on ours heartstrings and see.

This time we were right in giving the city a chance to let us see and
feel before we came to the final conclusion.

The second day the place did not disturb me so much; it was enough to see and with every minute I was more and more enchanted.
The atmosphere of this marvelous city was unique.

If just the stones, I walked on, could talk to me about the history.
About the people who strolled through its streets already some hundreds years before me.
Who they were and how did they live?
Did they love or hate?
"Please, talk to me," I begged them worthlessly.

I walked through the streets without perception of time.

I hear voices of the past, I saw people of long forgotten times.
A figure in a wide black coat with a mask on it's face, running on a small bridge and disappearing in one of the palaces nearby.
The door locked itself and only soft laughter echoed in the narrow alleyway.
Was it real or my imagination?
Do not ask me, I do not know.
Maybe it was just magic, but it does not matter.

And the third day?
I was in love with Venice.

Now I had just one desire that was to win a million dollars in a lottery and then I would immediately put my plan into effect.
Since I had already plan in my mind.

Frank and I would buy one of this palaces that was falling to pieces and we would completely rebuilt it.
We would proceed step by step.
The marble stairs at first, then walls, one stone after another, and finally we would furnish the rooms.
It would be our lifetime job, we would stop only if we die.

There was only one problem, the money.

We did not win the lottery and so it remained just a dream

We were charmed by this city and by its influence on our soul.

Until now I did not talk about the moon over San Mark's Basilica and that was one of the greatest experiences we ever had.

The last evening we had dinner in a extremely nice restaurant on the roof of our hotel. The night was warm and the full moon like a silver ball hung in the sky.
After we finished dinner, we came to our room.
Then I suggested to Frank, "It is too early to go sleep in such wonderful night! Come to the San Mark's Square one last time."
We changed into jeans and left the hotel.

In only five minutes we were there.

The place was teeming with people.
Two bands played popular music, painters exhibited their works on easels, people laughed and talked over glasses of wine.
The city was alive without regard to the end of tourist season.

It was probably the same a thousand years before and I hoped from my whole heart it would be the same thousand years after.

Frank and I had glass of wine and then we walked slowly among the people.
Until we stopped before the Basilica.

Some wooden beams laid on the street, prepared to be put together in a catwalk in a case of a flood, so people could walk on them through the Square.
We sat on them and were silent.
There were no words necessary.

The moon was directly over the dome which was now flooded in silver light, with some parts of decoration on the opposite side in a shade. It was like in a fairy tale, like in a movie with aspiration for an Oscar in photography.
But it was nothing from this, it was pure reality.
We were lucky to be there in the right moment.

That was all.

To go to Paris was a necessity.
You could be not in Europe and not see Paris.
It is quite simple.
So we went.

What to say about Paris in one word?
Paris has a charm and you could see and feel it on every step.

How the women swagger on the streets.
How the men talk in small streets pubs over glasses of wine.
How marvelous are the streets of Paris.

The influence of the former royal court on the culture and history of Europe left footprints on every corner of this city.

It is the Louvre with Mona Lisa of Leonardo da Vinci and others big artists.
It is the Museum D'Orsay, with impressionist paintings of Degas, Renoir or Manet and Lautrec and...
You know what?
I had tears in my eyes when I have seen all the paintings in reality, because I had loved them already for about 40 years.

Of course there is the Eiffel Tower with breathtaking view at this wonderful city.

Or the Gothic cathedral of Notre-Dame, not to forget the Avenue

Vera Stanek

Des Champs-Elysées and the bridges over Seine and...

What's my advice?
Go and see yourself.
You would love this city, like we did.

Next to the big cities we visited different places in Austria and Italy.

We went to the Austrian Salzburg with full four evenings of classical music.
We enjoyed operetta performance on the shore of a lake near Vienna.

And for the first time we came to South Tyrol, the most northern part of Italy.

A place where people speak two languages; German, because they once belonged to Austria and Italian where they belong now.
This means the best combination ever.
The people inherited the tidiness of Germans and the charm of Italians.

It is named the "Garden of Europe."

When we came to South Tyrol we were surprised to seeing no fields, only orchards with zillions of apple trees and nothing just apples.
When we looked nearer we saw that this was not all, that among the apples were vineyards, one of the best in Italy.

The wine was really excellent and we had the opportunity to enjoy it, to our great pleasure, many times.

We found friends there we liked very much, but life went on and we left.
Their life goes on today probably in the same way as then.

But our lives changed and an amount of miles between them and us grew.

However, I am sure, that if we would once come together, then a pitcher of wine would be put on the table, we would sit in the night and talk and talk and...

From the last pages you probably think that we were just on the trips.
But you would be wrong.

Frank and I worked on at our old places and with gritted teeth we tried to survive.
We had a dream.
We had a goal.
It was necessary to hold on.

Frank got deeper into himself and did what he was told to do, without enthusiasm and big involvement.
He protested rarely.
His strategy for surviving was passive resistance.

My situation worsened with every day.
Finally it escalated when my boss told me that he did not want me in a collective of young and dynamic people, that I was too old to bring something new.
It was devastating for me.

It did not help me that I was already the seventeenth person who was laid off because of the boss. Neither did it help me that our company shrunk to half, in people and in production also.
That the company I still loved so much struggled for surviving.

Now it was time for me to go.
But where? The jobs were not available for persons like me.
I was 56-years-old foreigner.

Desperately, I tried to find what to do.
Then a coincidence helped me.

I talked about my problems with a chief of a computer department,
who was responsible for computer systems in both companies.
During the last years I did some work for him about following
calculations regarding our company .
Now he told me, "Look, I could use you for a statistics of the
companies. But I need to talk to the boss first. Give me some time."

To my great surprise I got the job.

I was transferred into the central computer department where I was
responsible for all the calculations and all the monthly statistics of
both companies.
I could not say I loved it, but it was a work and I was paid for it.

The change of job brought a change to my person.

I had a small dark room just for me so I had nobody to talk with.
After I fulfilled my daily work, I went home.
I was not happy and not unhappy, it was a time of surviving.

Nothing else.

What lightened our spirits were the trips and our mountains.

There we found the relaxation and the strength to hold on another
week, month, year.

Meanwhile we reached our twelve years in Switzerland, a time that
was necessary to wait for a request for Swiss citizenship.
We agreed to ask for it.

David had received his Swiss citizenship some years before us.

The rules for him were different than for us.
Now was our turn.

We filled the petition and waited.

It was well known that we would have to wait another year and then we would be invited to an interview to a board of examiners in our village.
Only this time we were absolutely wrong.

We were invited to the interview in six weeks and in three months we had Swiss citizenship, including the passports.
Now we were equal to all the people around us.
On the paper, yes, in reality, nothing changed.

We began to think how we would organize our life in future.

Then something happened and everything was different.

One day Wolfgang called and asked if I could cook him his favorite food of pork roast, dumplings and cabbage.
I agreed and we made appointment for the evening of December 5th, 1995.

After a delicious dinner we were sitting and talking.

Suddenly Wolfgang turned to Frank and asked, "Frank when do you go for retirement?"
Frank answered, "Better not ask. I have to wait one and a half years yet."
Wolfgang smiled and announced, "Then it would be necessary to shorten it."
"Why?" asked Frank with surprise.
"Because I need you in Beijing, in China" answered Wolfgang,

Vera Stanek

"I am offering you a job as a general manager of my joint-venture company. For one year or maybe two. What do you say?"

Frank was speechless.

Then he looked at me and saw in my eyes the reaction; a mix of excitement with agreement, maybe a hope to be away from all the sorrows and problems.

Some second later he finally found his voice again, "Why not? When do you need me?"
"Starting in January 1997. You have some time to prepare yourself and Vera for this change" was Wolfgang's answer.

And that was it.
That was the big breakthrough.

That was the moment that changed our life and brought new future to us.

Immediately we began with preparations.

We bought some books about Beijing and China. We had to learn about this fascinating country with about a five thousand years old culture before we would come in contact with it.

There were many questions that went through our mind that we could not answer here and now.
How we would feel to be in communist country again?
How we would react on this situation?
What about our ability to be together with people of another race?
What about the culture, habits, etc.?

We did not know, how we would react, but we were eager to go.
Still, we had to wait another year.

What to do in the meantime?
First, we promised ourselves to be silent.
Not one word to our fellow-workers, not one word to anyone.
We knew exactly that an immediate lay-off would follow.

On this point we were as one.
When the time came we would go, alone; this was our imagination.

Among other things we agreed to go to Czechoslovakia.
We had Swiss passports now and we did not need to worry.
Frank had already been there many times to visit his mother and because of the heritage.
I was not there, until now, and I was really curious about myself.

How I would react to going back after twelve years of living in Switzerland?

We started our journey on Christmas Day.
Driving through West Germany we reached the Czech border in about six hours.
On the border my hands shook, I could not help myself.
It was still somewhere in my mind.
Nothing changed.

And in Prague ?

It was nice.
We visited the Prague Castle on a crispy winter day with lots of sunshine.
We stood by the low castle wall, looked on the red roofs of the old Prague houses and golden towers of churches and palaces.
The river Vltava, worked its way through many bridges.

I was happy to see it again.

There were no tears.
Only memories of a past life that was gone in exchange for a future.

Vera Stanek

Frank and I observed the windows of *our* old apartment.
We strolled through the small streets of the city, we listened to chamber music and we really enjoyed the time we spent there.

After four days we found that we wanted to go home.
Home? Yes, home.
Our home was a place where we worked and lived, and that was now in another country and another city.

We found that we changed.

We had problems talking to the few friends in Prague, we still had.
Although we spoke Czech, we spoke a different language.
It seemed to us, that we were for once people of two different worlds.
It was not easy for anybody.

We had our happiness and our sorrows, they had theirs.
Next to memories there was not too much to speak about, our lives developed in totally different ways.
So we left.

Now I have to tell you about David.

He had his own life now.
Maybe a different one than we though he would have, but so it is in life.

David decided to change his life radically.
After two years of a life that brought him no satisfaction nor the happiness he quit the university. He came to the point when he had to find himself and a life he would be happy with.

To make up his mind about the future David took a temporary job in an insurance agency and that was decisive for his future plans.

There he fell in love with a girl, Monica, and that was the start of his new life.

After a turmoil year when Monica finished high school, left a despotic father whom she lived with and moved in with David, they began to live for their dreams.
David changed jobs, and Monica went to university to study law.
They were happy together, and we were happy for them.

Soon we would be in China.
David in Switzerland.
Eva in America.
One family on three continents!

We all agreed on one simple wish now; to be once together on the same continent.
If this could once really happen it would be great, if not, then we would have to find a *Plan B.*
That was told many times in our family by similar occasion.
We would see.

The entire year of 1996, we spent in preparation for the big change.
To begin it was necessary to stay with our old habits.
Working, hiking, skiing.

We could not to show our excitement or change the lifestyle, it could be suspicious.
We had to stay in Switzerland almost an entire year yet; to be more precise nine months by our work and three months learning the know-how of Wolgang's company.
That was the agreement.

Until May everything was fine, but then the course of events accelerated.

In the middle of May one of the big bosses called me.

Due to worsening situations on the market, my position changed to a half-time job. He made it absolutely clear that he wanted my understanding and agreement, and of course no problems from my side.
He was wrong.

First, I had an appointment in the hospital for a surgery for my crooked toes, that gave me more and more problems, especially in walking and hiking.
After the surgery were two months of recovery necessary.
Second, I had two months of term of notice.
Third, I had some holidays to take, also.

When I counted everything together I was pleased with the result.
Yes, it would be all right if I quit immediately.

But it was not so easy.

We struggled for every week, later almost for every day. The big boss was furious; not because I was going away, but because I disobeyed.
He tried to threaten me by giving me an order to cancel the surgery with words, "You do not need surgery. Our insurance will not pay for it!"
I cried, I was upset, but I stuck by my decision even though I was a ball of nerves.

How many times in my life was I in a similar situation?
I did not known.
Only this time everything was different.
I was not in a desperate situation, I had the China adventures before my eyes.

But they paid back to me in a style that touched me on a tender spot.

Some days after I refused the offer, Frank was asked to come to

the office of his big boss. The discussion was short and ended with a dismissal, laid down on the table before him.
Reason? Officially, the bad economical situation and the necessity to cut jobs.
Unofficially, my behavior.

So we had it.

After 12 years of good work we were basically thrown out on the street.
Frank had just nine months before his retirement and that was a bit much.
The impact on him was not so strong as would be without the offer from Wolfgang, but it was really too hard.

Finally both of us managed it to the bitter end.

What was left?
Disappointment.
Tears in eyes.
Sore heart.

Our life did not stop, but continued at full speed.

In the following three months we had a lot to do.
We had no time to think about past.

Our stay in Switzerland was in the last stage, and our future began to take exact shape.
We decided to leave Switzerland forever.
After our stay in China we would try to go to our house, to Lago Vista, to America.

We were now much more confident that it would be possible, because meanwhile something important happened.
Eva became an American citizen!

Not only were we all very excited, but it opened a new way for us; to come as first grade family members, as parents.
Eva promised to help us and we knew that we would do everything that had to be done to come there.

That was in the future somewhere.
Now we were in a very busy present.

We had to learn, both of us, an absolutely new and different job in Wolfgang's company by changing workplaces almost every week.
We had to gain the know-how about replacement of artificial joints, knees and hips, including the production.

We had to cancel our apartment and find somebody who would like to take it over as soon as possible.
We had to dispose of all of our possession and this was the most difficult part.
They are no "garage sales" in Switzerland, because no one Swiss ever would buy worn out furniture. So we had to rely only on our foreign neighbors, but these people did have not money, at least not too much.

In the end we sold some things to Italian and Portuguese families. The rest we gave out to a few Croatian families. It was time of war in their country and they came to Switzerland to find a refuge.
They had no furniture or clothes, nothing.
So we helped them a little.

Our personal possessions, books, china, glass, we packed in 26 boxes.
On the top we added our skis, paintings and carpets.
All that remained in the storage in Switzerland, until the question of "when?" would be known.

Then everything took a quick course of events, like if you play a movie at an increasing speed.

We spent the last two weeks with David and Monica in their apartment, because our old apartment already went to the new tenants.
We celebrated our last Christmas with everything that was a family tradition, not knowing where we would be the next year
We had a farewell party the last evening before our departure with lots of food and wine.

We awoke to the last day, December 29th, 1996.

The day, when we said goodbye.
To David and Monica.

To Switzerland.

Chapter 18

Finally we land in Beijing.
It is 6:00 a.m.
The horizon changed the colors, the day is breaking .

Our plane stops on an airfield.
Few buses that would take us to the terminal arrived.
We leave the plane.

I do my first step outside and inhale.
Out of the blue it strikes me: the smell. The aroma of spices, frying
oils and exhaust gases that I would learn with the time, would be a
little different according to the particular countries in Asia.
But it would be there.
I could close my eyes, but I would still know where I was.
In Beijing or Bali or Thailand or...

Now we are here.
At another end of world.

Hello, Beijing, we are here!!

We drove through the streets and the light was getting stronger.
Some small parks among concrete houses were already alive with
people crowded to group and exercising.
But not really exercising!
These people were engaged in slow motion of shadow boxing,
taichi, in graceful and unusual movements, I have not seen before.

First impressions.
First excitements.

With a face pressed against the window of a car I was eager to see
as much as possible in these first minutes.

Vera Stanek

We drove through the streets of Beijing and it was a strange world that flew before my eyes.
People had different faces.
Streets had names I could not read.
Old houses had roofs I did not see until now.

Almost on every corner another surprise.
I was overwhelmed with new views, pictures and surroundings.

Finally we came to the hotel that would be our home for the entire stay in Beijing.
We would stay in its apartment tower, in a one bedroom apartment.
The idea of staying in a hotel was not bad.
There we could mingle among other foreigners and feel not so lost as if among only Chinese.
Surely an advantage because of our long stay.

Our new life began with many surprises from the very first day.

When I opened my eyes at the first morning after our arrival, I could not believe what I saw; it was snowing. The snow slowly fell to the ground and soon covered everything in a white blanket.
How was it possible when every guide about Beijing claimed that a snowfall was possible perhaps one time in ten years?
Were we so lucky to catch the right year?
One way or another, it was wonderful.

I was convinced it was because of us.
Beijing wanted to show us its beautiful face, not the normal gray day with layers of dust overall.

A little later I was positive that all the people of Beijing went outside to the streets and parks to enjoy this miracle. Naturally equipped with cameras, because every member of a family had to have a picture in the snow.
There was no exception.

A mother standing under a snow covered tree.
A father shoveling snow from the street.
And children....? Of course laying in the snow in the park and making *angels,* what else.

Everybody smiled, everybody was happy.

During short time there were working teams on the streets, armed with shovels, that began to clean the sidewalks and adjacent lanes from snow.
There were not snow plows or other mechanization in sight, but people in large numbers.
They gathered the snow and heaped it around the trees.

Because you have to know that the Chinese love trees.
Maybe they do not care about many things except the trees. All year long somebody looked after them so that at the right time they would bloom to beauty.
I did not imagine that Beijing was so full of a greenery!

I thought about other cities with green areas I knew from Europe.
And I remembered all the trees in Paris.
But to my greatest astonishment I had to confess to myself, that the trees in Beijing were more healthy than the trees in Paris.
On hot summer days they were the natural canopy above your head and you could stroll hours through the city and enjoy their shade.

But we came to Beijing to work.
It was necessary to organize our life after the company's schedule.
First to work and then to see.

Every morning our driver picked us from the hotel and in a drive of about 30 minutes he brought us to the company.
Only one time we needed about three hours, because we were

stopped in a jam.

No, not in traffic jam, but in a human jam!

We were stopped in one of the narrow streets of old Beijing in a crowd of people with bikes or handcars or... The people were crammed tightly together until any movement was possible. The situation was quite horrible and scary. There were only a few cars surrounded by hundreds of people, helpless waiting for a miracle. Finally the crowd began to move and after a while we were free to continue.

I could probably write a special chapter only about the traffic in Beijing.

Firstly, next to cars there are bicycles, the transportation vehicle for everything and everybody; from people to vegetables, from a load of chicken to a load of coal. There are eight millions bikes in Beijing compared to about twelve millions people.

Every person riding a bike goes the shortest way without regard to traffic in both directions. Bikers ride sometimes across the intersection of four lines highway, sometimes in the opposite direction as well. What's the matter? Cars have brakes or not?

But traffic accident happen not too often. The speed of all vehicles is not very high.

In view of this traffic situation, Frank did not try, not one time, to drive a car.

Our company was established only some months before we came to Beijing.

In the offices were employed about eighteen people.
Another thirty people worked in our production factory outside
Beijing.

Before we came there I did not know if I could also work at the
company.

At the first oportunity Frank asked the Chinese partners if it would
be possible for me to work there. He pointed out that I would work
for no pay, only as a hobby.
The Chinese answered simply, "We would be happy if your wife
would work. But in China everyone who works get money. So,
please, put her on your payroll!"

And so it happened, that I worked and had my own salary as well.

I had not an exact job description.

First I tried to organize the environment, our offices, our working
places and to bring a little hygiene to people there.
But it was not as simple as I imagined it would be, because the
whole company was a mess.

The people were sitting by tables, knocked together into the middle
of room, full of newspapers, ashtrays with stubs of cigarettes and
with dust overall.
It was really a sad view on an international company.
So I thought that it would be the right time to change it now.

One Friday Frank ordered a *cleaning afternoon.*
All employees were asked to help to promote the *look* of the
company.

To start with I asked the women to help me clean the windows.
I was surely not prepared for the answer I got.
They refused with words, "No one in Beijing clean the windows."
With surprise I asked confused, "Why?"

"Because outside is so dirty that in a short time the windows would be dirty again. It is a waste of time and work."
I was speechless.
I did not know how to behave, how to react, and what was appropriate to do.

Where were my dreams about improving the appearance of the company?
Do I have to abandon them?
No, and no again.

After two hours of hard work I cleaned all of them.
After three hours only two people worked, Frank and I.
Our employees chose to play computer games; it was for them more interesting than cleaning.

Frank and I had much to learn.
We were just greenhorns.
But it looked better in our company and it was the only joy we had.

For a future Frank and I chose to proceed in small steps rather than big ones. Sometimes we failed, sometimes we were successful.
But you could believe me that we did not give up.

Next to cleaning I worked with computer and was in charge of an organization of our replacement joints in the storage.
Then I was responsible for all purchases of joints from Switzerland, include all necessary paperwork.

In a spare time I wrote, in English, handbooks for Chinese hospitals about our joints and post-surgery exercises. I drove pictures of a tiny man gradually doing movements with knee or leg.
Why this? Because we found, that no one in China knew about it.
It was new to the doctors and to nurses also.
They all had to learn.

And I have to add that I had fun working, and it did not matter to me

that it was not easy.
I was happy to work in Beijing.

After a confusing first month I came up with a new idea.

I asked politely the General Manager, Frank, to allow me to work
just four days a week and my query was accepted.
I worked out a plan what I would like to do the fifth day.

Every Friday, on my day off, I discovered Beijing and not only this.
I began the day with swimming in the hotel pool, then I showered,
did my hair and nails and hit not the road, but streets of Beijing.
I walked for some hour and looked for interesting places where I
would take Frank on Sundays.

I discovered new parks, and found them great.
I peeped in concrete townhouses, and found them terrible.
I watched people, and found them fascinating, children or old ones,
it did not matter.

Then I went for lunch to MacDonald for Big Mac, my favorite meal.
Later I strolled through the Silk Street, looked for news in fashion,
but sometimes just to say "hello" to some of the sales persons.
After a short time I knew some of them quite well.

I loved these Fridays.
I loved Beijing.

And what about Frank?

Frank tried to put people together.
Until now they worked separately without the feeling of being part of
the team.
Soon Frank found, that a few of them had less interest in work than
it was appropriate for their position. So he fired them and found
new ones.
It turned out, that this decision was quite smart.

The people in the company began slowly work together.
In half a year there was a team of people that helped each other.
The company was on the way up.

But do not think it was easy work.
It was terribly hard work.
Because the mentality of Chinese is different from ours.

Moreover, some decisions Frank had to make were not in harmony
with views of his Swiss advisers. Their decisions were made from
five stars hotels, Frank's from everyday life.
So it came to a clash of views.

Already one month after our arrival to China we had the opportunity
to celebrate Chinese New Year, the "Year of the Ox."

Beijing was prepared to say *welcome* and celebrate.

All trees were full of small bulbs that sparkled in the night.
The houses were decorated with ornaments, on hotels and in the
streets were put many new neon lights. Big red inflatable balls with
colorful streamers were placed before shops.
Everything was shining.
It was just wonderful.

Frank and I agreed that we had to record this historical moment.

On New Year's Eve, armed with camera, two lens and a tripod,
immediately after the darkness, we left the hotel.
It was terribly cold, with the temperature less than twenty degree.
So we put on our warmest shoes, sweaters, jackets, not to mention
wool caps and gloves.
But nothing could stop us from our intention to make nice picture.
To see the spectacle.

We took the subway to the downtown and then we walked through the city.
It was marvelous.

We did not know which photo to take because everything was so wonderful.
We just shouted in excitement, " Look on this house! No, no, look on this! Please, took this picture, or maybe this one would be better!"
It was really something what touched our heart.
It was almost a dream.

However, with the time going it was getting bitter cold.
After about three hours, our camera stopped working; the battery refused to continue. Not until then we looked at our watches and found that it was later than we thought it would be.
In our excitement we forgot how quick the time passed.
We were not happy to go home, but the vision of hot tea and bed was not bad either.

This evening would stay in our memory forever, together with the beautiful photos we took.

From the begining of our stay in Beijing we decided that Saturdays and Sundays would be our days for discovering the city.

On Saturday morning we used to go shopping for food.
We walked to the department store to do our errands, and we came home by taxi with hands full of plastic bags.

For a reason I did not understand, the Chinese love plastic bags and they wrap especially food in many of them.
The already used bags are then visible on windy days. They are flying through the streets and wrapping around branches of trees.
It is not nice view.
Especially in winter, when the trees have no leaves and when only

the bags are their decoration.
It's too bad.

Saturday afternoon we mostly visited the parks in the city.

The parks were one of the biggest surprises we had in Beijing.
Because the parks were clean in comparison with the streets.

Sometimes, directly before an antrance to the park was a mess.
You had to wade through layers of plastic bags, papers, drinking
caps...
But when you walked into the park, then you were in another world.
Not even one paper or plastic bag on the ground, simply nothing.
It was something we did not understand.
So we took it as a nice surprise.

Moreover the parks were wonderful.

Waterfalls, stone bridges, flowers, trees...everything in an
unbelievable harmony. At every step you could find something that
brought peace and composure to your soul.

We loved to walk in the parks.
Sometimes in silence and lost in thought, sometimes in lively
conversation.

The parks were different not just in their architecture but also in
their mystery .

Sunday was our Big Discovery Day.

In the morning we decided if we go today north, south, east or west.
Because the streets of Beijing are arranged in these four cardinal
points. By the help of the map we chose our destination and then
we started.
Mostly by subway, at least part of the way, and then we walked.

We found, that if we would like to know Beijing better, we had to walk.
Because only then we could peep in the windows.
Watch the people on the streets.
See the real life.

Not the one a travel agency offers you when you are there for three days.
We had time enough, we were not in hurry.

Step by step we discovered Beijing.

We were overwhelmed with the intensity the city's appeal to us.
How amazing and totally different the city was; everything around us seemed to hit us with full strength.
There were not many people that had the opportunity to see what we have seen.

In these moments we were thankful to Wolfgang for giving us the chance to be there.
We believed that our work would show him how we appreciated it.

Our tours through Beijing brought us excitement in many ways.

We were warned to stay at home when the wind blew.
But we told ourselves, "We were here to see and not to sit at home," when one Sunday a sharp west wind blew through the city .
We did not care and fearlessly started our journey as always.
However, it was horrible.

The wind took in the air all the dirtiness from the streets.
Plastic bags flew around us, the grains of dust crashed in our faces, pieces of newspapers wrapped our legs.
Moreover the strong wind did not let us continue on our way.

After two hours we were back in the hotel and headed directly for

Vera Stanek

the mirror to see the damage. We looked on our picture and began
to laugh.
Compared to the white tiles in the bathroom, our faces and our
clothes were colored only in gray.
So we took a shower so long until we were sure that all the dust
was washed away, and I put all the clothes we had on immediately
into washer.

Our Sunday trips were for us a must.
An obsession with the city and a thirst for knowledge of Chinese
culture and habits.

On one crispy winter Sunday we took a trip along three lakes at
north-west of Beijing that were frozen, but very alive.
Children on small wooden sleds with iron blades on the base
romped around. They laughed and shouted with joy together with
their parents, looking after them.

Frank and I enjoyed watching them all.
The attempts of children at first steps of perfection, the proud looks
of parents wrapped in the coats and with collars turned up because
of cold.
It was an atmosphere of happiness and joy.

It was a normal Sunday in Beijing.

Anyway, the lakes were beautiful.
And Beihai Park, where our trip ended, was a pearl among parks.
We promised ourselves to come again in the springtime when
nature woke up from the winter sleep and when everything would
be in bloom.

We fulfilled our promise, we came again, but we were disappointed!

The lakes, beautiful in winter, were dirty now.
The surfaces were full of plastics bags and papers as elsewhere,

and above the water level stuck out many remains of household items.
On some places we discovered a few people with small fishing nets in hand. They skillfully picked algae and put them into prepared plasic bags.
We assumed they ate them in a dish or salad, but we could only guess.

It was the case, when we were happy, that nobody of the people offered us a piece.

Obviously we visited the Forbidden City.

We waited long for this tour, until we were sure, that the tourist season was over.
Because then it would be not necessary to box our way among zillion of tourists. Then we would have all the palaces only for us.
We were right.

On one wonderful Sunday in fall, when the sky was blue and without one cloud, we finally visited this famous place.

We admired marvelous structures of the palaces with all the creatures that decorate the amazing roofs. We found gorgeous secluded spots, peaceful, full of harmony and unbelievable beauty.
We were almost alone there.
Only a few visitors, Chinese, with us.

Of course, we visited the Summer Palace as well.

An immense park around a magnificent lake, with pavilions and Buddhist temples on the hills.
In former time it was an oasis of green and fresh air for emperor's court.
I am sure they loved it in the same way as we did.

Vera Stanek

In Beijing was so much to see and to do!

Slowly, step by step, we began to see the enormous diversity of Chinese culture.

On one side all the wonderful palaces and temples, parks and sculptures.
On the other side still the old residential places, the Hutongs.
An ancient Chinese houses in middle of the city, without running water and with one public toilet for an entire street.

There I met one day a girl, beautiful as a picture, painted by an artist.
She was perfectly dressed, with a make up on the face, and wonderfully styled hair.
I had to wonder how she could prepare herself in such way when she had only primitive conditions for it.
Anyway, it was her secret.

If I think about Chinese culture, I could not leave out the contrast that came to my mind already after short time I spent there.

People with a five thousand year old culture, with medicine famous in the whole world, with the only construction, Great Wall, seen from moon, and with history full of great emperors.

People with non cultural habits like spitting on the streets. They do it all; young and old, men and women, dressed in fashion clothes or in rags and tatters.
People with discipline.
People with love for freedom.

All this is China these days.

Our live in China worked very well, at least in the first nine months. The company held together and slowly began to go up.

Our young employees showed great progress.

These young Chinese people wanted to work, wanted to show that they have the necessary know-how. They were eager to learn.
We got instruction films and they learned how to do surgeries. How to use our special surgical instruments, used by replacement of hips and knees.
They practiced alone, on plastic bones, to know every detail that could be useful to the surgeon, his advisers and helpers they should be.

The difficult work from both sides brought results.

To put the company more together, Frank agreed with two days trip on one weekend in July.
He gave his approval to a proposal of going around Beijing and let our employees organize it all.

On one Saturday morning, we all, 28 people, gathered in front of the company's office building.
All present persons were counted and asked to get into cars of our company.
A minibus, Jeep and Audi.

Then we started our journey.

Our first stop was in a State Park.
The entry gate was decorated in the style typical for most of Chinese structures.
Through the gate we entered the park.
After a short walk we came to an enormous dragon, done from plastic as we learned later, that was fixed to small hill. Frank and I were pushed to the mouths of the dragon as the first ones.
By seeing our indecisive faces our employees burst out laughing.

What a surprise was waiting for us!
Through the door in the mouths of dragon we came to the first of elevators that brought us to the top of the hill.
We stepped outside and breathed out a cry of admiration.

Before us lay a green lake above small dam.

From the hilltop we climbed down to a small harbor and boarded a ship.
We cruised a passage with artificial pagodas high on the hills, artificial birds on the shore and high rocks on both sides of the lake.
It was magnificent.

On opposite side of the lake we disembarked the ship.
We rented canoes and paddled small river that flew into the lake.
We had a great fun!

During following lunch I carelessly asked the lady in charge of this trip, where we would go for a night. She answered, that after the lunch we would go and find a hotel.
'Oh, no,' I thought, 'they want to find now a place for 28 people!'

What was for me unimaginable, happened.

In the third hotel, we stopped by, were rooms available to all of us.
One of our employees came to us and explained, that they just booked a suite for us, allegedly the best they had in this hotel.
However I was upset and raised a protest.
"We do not go to any suite. We want to have the same room as all of you. Period."
After a few minutes of talking I won.

We were brought to a quite clean room, with TV, no air-conditioned and cold water in the bathroom.
We had what we wanted!

I clenched my teeth and went under the shower. The water ran, there was not a reason to worry, so I put shower gel on my body and...the water stopped running.

I screamed, complained to Frank who rushed up to my help, but in vain.

Desperately I tried to wipe off the shower gel away, at least from my face, but it was not so easy; to feel clean and fresh, I put on quite a thick layer.

Just before I went crazy a miracle happened.

The water ran again.

After I finished my shower, I felt clean and happy again.

Sometimes you need only simple things like running water to feel good.

At the evening we all had dinner together.

We were sitting by two round tables in a separate room.

Waiters brought big plates of different food and placed it on the table.

My table neighbor was Zhang Tao, one of the typical young people of China during these times. A young lady from Inner Mongolia, one of countries of China.

She came to Beijing three years ago and went to university and studied English. Then she was hired to our company as a reception lady.

When Frank came as a general manager to the company she asked for a job as product manager and got it.

She was smart and intelligent.

I loved her very much and I still love her.

After the waiters brought other plates of food she told me, "Do not eat it, it's a snake!"

I hesitated only moment and then I asked myself, "When would I have the opportunity to eat snake?" The answer was relatively simple, "Never."

So I took the first bite, then I took more.

If I would not know it, I would assume it was fat pork meat with vegetable.
It was not so bad.

But there were other things that were a shock to me.

Our drivers had on the table two glasses; one with red, the second with green liquid. They mixed drinks of this liquids for themselves.
That caught my attention.

Curiously I asked Tao, what does everything mean?
She tried to explain it to me in considerate words, but her answer was for my understanding just too much, although I spared no effort to deal with it.
The red liquid was the blood of the snake.
The green was its gall.
The two men drank it to improve their strength and potency.

Finally I came to only one possible conclusion.
Another country, other habits; only a little different from ours.

But the evening was a success.

Good food, karaoke and dancing to the popular Chinese songs.
Some of our people were absolutely excellent in dancing. They seemed to me as if they were born not to walk but dance.
Frank and I were absolutely enchanted and were among the last ones who left long after midnight.

The second day was planned a hiking trip to the mountains.

Frank and I were very eager to see the Chinese mountains.

It was a little different than we were used to in Switzerland.
I was almost positive, that all people of Beijing decided to go on this day for a hike. The paths were full of people; one line up, one line down.

After about three hours of fighting our way among the crowd we gave up and took off to another destination.

For us a big surprise and challenge.

We arrived on a farm with huge grassland around to ride horses to a great excitement of all our employees.

There were only two people that were not excited and that was Frank and I.

Finally, after a long hesitation, I sat on a live horse for the first time in my life.
But only under one condition that our driver would go next to the horse and would hold the reins.
I was afraid the horse could run away with me on its back and this I wanted to avoid at every price

It was quite cowardly, but I was really proud of myself!
Already the reality that I was on a horse's back was enough.

Only Frank refused the ride with simple words, "Over my dead body!"
He was the only person sitting on a bench and enjoying the attempts of our people trying to ride a horse.

What a smart man was my husband!

At the late afternoon we drove back to Beijing.
It was decided that before we would say goodbye, we would have dinner together.

Our employees had chosen a canteen of Patent bureau of China, where the kitchen personal cooked on Saturdays and Sundays for the public.
Of course it was necessary to know it.

We came into a big room with buffet tables around two long walls. The tables, with a burner in the middle, were arranged in neat rows. Until now nothing special.

But what struck me next was something I was not waiting for and that was the quality and quantity of food.
I had not seen, and probably would not see anymore, so much so excellent food all in one place!

There were crabs with red eyes, blue eyes, big and small in a row of containers.
Shrimps were there in tons, but mostly too normal to the people to pay attention to them. The fish were in different colors, some still alive, some already prepared for cooking.

Fine cut slices of lamb meat were red and fresh, in the amount to feed an army.
The chicken looked so great on the plates but nobody ate them; too common.
Legs of pork were marinated in big bowls without catching the attention of the eaters.

Vegetables and fruit were so fresh as it picked from the fields just ten minutes before.
All desserts, straight in rows and full of decoration, were colorful and made all mouths water.

Frank was helpless and did not know what to put on the plate.
He asked his table neighbor, a very pretty young lady, "What should I eat?"
She answered simply, "Follow me!"
Both disappeared.

After a while Frank appeared at his place.
His plate was full of crabs and shrimps that he cooked in a big pot of hot water.
He looked very pleased with his choice.

I decided to make the selection alone, although I did not know many sorts of the food either. So I looked at plates of our employees and then tried to find the same, only it was not easy. But in the course of time I managed it to my great satisfaction.

Opposite of me was sitting an engineer from our production factory. He fried something small on a pan. It smelled so good, that I could not resist and
asked him, "Please, tell me what is it? It smells so good!"
He began to laugh and told me, "Qua, qua. Take one!"

First I did not understand but after some seconds I had it; frog legs, what else.
With a little hesitation I took one piece and put it in my mouth.
It was good. So I took another piece and found it very delicious.
It was my first and last experience with frog legs.

This day, I tried the best delicacies that are probably on the worldwide market.
Food, that I would be not able to afford on another place in the world.
But I could, and all of us could, to afford in Beijing.

The two days were great.

We learned to know our employees better and I assumed, that it was good for both parties.

The summer was full of excitements.

One of them was even a historical event.
The day when Hong-Kong was handed over to homeland China.

Beijing was prepared for this celebration.

The streets were decorated with flowers in so many pots that everything looked as one sea of colors. The streets were clean, the shop windows sparkling...

It was absolutely beautiful.

On Tiananmen Square, the big watch that showed the time of hand over of Hong-Kong in days, minutes and seconds was surrounded by a big crowd of people, Frank and me include.

The watch showed the last eight hours and the picture of me on this place could document this moment.

We were invited to a big celebration party on the terrace of our hotel.

We all waited for a big fireworks from Tiananmen Square, but something got wrong.

Probably we were not on the right spot or it was only a little fireworks and we missed it.

But the party was nice.

In September we went for extraordinary holidays to Las Vegas.

There, on October 1st, David married Monica.

But this was not the only destination.

To enjoy little more of the America we spent the first part in Lago Vista.

We could not stay in our house, because we had tenants there, so we booked a room in a Lago Vista Resort.

We just wanted to feel the spirit of this place and be there.

This time we were not in hurry to go on trips.

We just traveled a little around, swam in *our* lake and enjoyed the place.

Simply we felt like in heaven.

With each day we loved Lago Vista more.

Every minute of our stay was unforgettable and we looked forward to spend the rest of our lives on this place.

We did not know when we would come, but we were sure it would not take long.

Two weeks in Lago Vista passed away so quickly like a dream.

Then we went to Las Vegas.

I was eager to see if what I heard about this city was true.
I was told, that no one could remain apathetic to Las Vegas; you either loved it or hated it. And I thought that it would be interesting to find out in which category I belonged.

We came to Las Vegas.
In a course of hours Frank and I felt in love with this exciting place.
There we met David and Monica, and Eva and Wolfgang.

The wedding was great.

The ceremony was in a small chapel, full of flowers, in a beautiful garden of the Hotel Flamingo.
David and Monica looked very happy, and the entire ceremony was very touching. Even Eva and I cried a little, but it belongs to weddings.

After we spent some time taking photos, we celebrated in an appropriate way for such occasion like the wedding cake, champagne, and excellent food.
The spirit was tremendous.

So we got a new member in our family.
Welcome Monica, we love you!

The next day we all took part in Wolfgang's wedding gift, a tour to Grand Canyon by helicopter. That brought a huge excitement to all of us.

The children had doubts about Frank and me. They were not sure if we, old people, could enjoy the flight.
What if we would be sick from some turbulences?
But finally they took the risk.

We started in the afternoon after a light thunderstorm.
The timing was perfect, the sky was magic.
The rest of dark clouds moved across the sky and through small gaps among them gleamed the sunbeams. Sometimes was sunlit just top of one rock or a small place on the bottom of the canyon.
It was gorgeous.

We landed on a plateau in Grand Canyon to have some snack and champagne.

But not all persons of our small group could enjoy it in full.
David was sick, Monica was white in a face, and Eva both of it.
Who then could enjoy it?
Frank, Wolfgang and I. While the children tried to pull themselves together, we enjoyed the rocks, canyon, nature and food.

The way back by helicopter was little more turbulent.
But our children survived it.
We landed back in Las Vegas in the approaching night when the lights blazed with colors and changed this city in a fairy tale kingdom.
What a marvelous view!

Among many of unforgettable impressions we could not miss the tension between Eva and Wolfgang.

We used some free time in our busy schedule and had a talk with Eva, only in a family circle. We sipped margaritas, nibbled on chips, and talked.
Yes, we were right.

Eva decided to break up her relationship to Wolfgang.
The attempt to live together failed for lack of things that could hold them together.
The result was a restriction in mutual communication about their problems and with it the ability to solve them.
Maybe, they both were too much of individualists and did not want to change their life up to now.

Four years of hope and struggle for a life together found the end.
Eva was sorry.
We were sorry also, for her.

The future would show us the consequences of Eva's decision, because we were still Wolfgang's employees.
Only we could not ask Eva to change her mind.
Eva was old enough to manage her life alone with all the responsibility for the decisions she made.
We could just stay near and keep ours finger crossed for her, nothing more.

We said goodbye to Las Vegas and flew back to Beijing.

In the time we were out of Beijing many things changed.

Our biggest competitor in orthopedic production and distribution left China.
It had big impact on the future of our company and on our future as well.

Our bosses in Switzerland used this opportunity to hire a Chinese general manager. To do it now was favorable, since many of experienced Chinese doctors were for once without jobs.
The hunting for Frank's successor began.

Frank hoped to be involved in this choice.
Maybe he could recommend some of doctors he already met, but

he was wrong.
The decision was made exclusively by the Swiss.

On next meeting of Board of Directors was made an
announcement.

Frank's job would be officially ending on December 31st, unofficially
on November 1st, when a new Chinese general manager would
take his job.
Because he is an experienced person he did not need Frank's help.

Our fate was completed.
We had to leave Beijing in a moment, when Frank succeeded to put
the people together, and when the company slowly began to rise.
After nine and a half months of struggle of surviving we had to
leave.

We considered it as unfair.
But we had to accept it.

To be honest, what we were waiting for?

The contract, Frank signed, was quite clear.
The first year the job of the general manager, the second year for
training of Chinese general manager.
Only Frank's help was now not required.
Maybe it was the reason with our unhappiness with this decision.

If there were another hidden motives, we better did not think about
them.

We did not ask ourselves how much of Frank's behavior, saying his
point of view that was not appreciated, made the difference .
We did not ask ourselves how much of Eva's behavior, breaking her
relationship with Wolfgang, affected the course of events.
It was better not to ask.

Leaving the company meant leaving our relationship with Wolfgang.

What would remain?
Many good memories together with gratefulness for all the trips, for giving us the opportunity to spend one unforgettable year in China.
A bit of disappointment that would, maybe, disappear with the time.
But maybe not.

Without regard of this, the life would go on.

All the work, all the love for people, all the evenings and nights when we tried to find solution for problems of the company, all this would be past.

There was not too much time left.

We had 14 working days to work in our company and two months to enjoy China.
Until now we were not one step from Beijing, since we didn't have the necessary free time.
So I came to conclusion, that a travel would be the best to do for our wounded soul.

However we had to hurry.

As a first destination I chose Tibet.
We had to go there and see the real mountains.
Because then, maybe, we would look on our sorrows with different eyes.
Maybe even, there would be no sorrows at all.

I found a Tibet travel agency near to our hotel, and it took me about two hours and I had everything prepared, although there were some restriction for a trip to Tibet.

First, you had to fly to city named Chengdu, where you should

acclimatize and especially, get the visa for Tibet.
Not until then you could take plane for Lhasa, the capitol of Tibet,
and the main tourist destination.

Before we started, we talked about our intention to go to Tibet with
our children.

Their reaction did not surprise us.
"You would like to go to Tibet in November? Are you crazy? It would
be cold!"
No, we were not crazy!
We were told that a November is very nice month in Lhasa.
Mostly sunshine and in the 50ties, sometimes the temperatures are
even higher.
We believed them, they were the experts.
They should know.

We started on November 4th, direction Chengdu.
The flight was pleasant and we looked forward to our adventurous
trip.

We were told, that someone would be waiting at the airport,
holding a poster with our names on it.
We came to the waiting area. There were lots of people with lots of
names on posters in the hands, but no one with our names.

After a while all the people were already gone, only Frank and I
stayed there alone, totally lost in a city with eight million people.
Our knowledge of Chinese language was limited to three words.
Thank you, please, and how are you.
Not too much.

We had not the smallest idea what to do.

We had in hand just a small English document with the name of
hotel, Tibet.

It was easy to remember, but how to tell it to the Chinese taxi-driver?

But then I remembered on this small episode that happened before, when we came to the waiting area.

A young man asked me, in English, if we are Mr. and Mrs. Smith and where we go. I answered him, that we are not the Smith's, but I mentioned hotel Tibet as our destination.
The man told me, that he works in the same hotel but for another travel agency.
Following the Chinese habit, he put his business card in my hand.

When we stood later alone on the airport, I remembered the card.
Now I took it out from my jacket.
It was the common Chinese card, one side in Chinese, the another in English.
And the name of the hotel was there black on white and in Chinese!
We were saved.

We came to the stand of taxi-drivers.
The third in the row finally agreed to bring us to our hotel.

That was one of the longest 45 minutes of my life.
We were in the power of Chinese taxi-driver without the possibility to say one word to him. And we did not know if he intended to bring us to the hotel.
I was very nervous during the entire drive and on a verge of panic.
But the story had a happy-ending.
We arrived in hotel Tibet and everything was just fine.

Immediately we looked for the office of our travel agency and in a twinkling of an eye we found it.

Slowly I opened the door; an unbelievable sight greeted my eyes.
There, laying on sofa, slept a man.
I did three more steps into the room and gave him a good shake.

The man sprang from the sofa and looked at me totally confused.
But now it was my turn. I asked, better say screamed to him in
English, "How could you sleep and not wait for us on the airport!"
His reaction quite surprised me although I would say he did the
best.
He escaped from the room.

Waiting what would happen next, I cooled down.

Another man came to the office. He apologized and tried to explain
us that our arrival would be in another two hours.
It was just too confusing for me.
But when we discussed the issue a little more we finally found, that
his time-table of flights from Beijing was two years old.
Only meanwhile the airlines changed the schedule.

To tell the truth, we did not want to rub it in.
We were happy to be there.

The hotel was nice and clean, the food was excellent, and we got
our visas.
What more did we want?

The next day we started for Lhasa.

We were welcomed with a few snow flakes.
Two people were waiting on us; our guide for next five days and a
driver with a Jeep. Because the rule for Tibet requires that every
person, or group of persons, have to have a guide and a driver.

We drove from the highest located airport in the world, more than
11,000 feet, to the city of Lhasa, a two hours ride.
We talked almost continuously with our guide, a young man with a
university degree in English.

Already the way to Lhasa was fascinating.

We drove at the foot of high mountains, along the river, surrounded by incredible bleak landscape around.
Then we came to Lhasa, to the hotel Tibet.
There were some surprises already waiting for us.

The hotel was in big renovation with just one wing left for quests.
On this day Frank and I were the only ones.

We came to our room, flooded with sunshine.
The view from the window to a beautiful garden and mountain ridges, with the tops covered with snow was wonderful.
Shortly I inspected our room.

I had the feeling, that probably somebody else already slept in our bed.
But the guide had already left for today so I had to manage it by myself. I did not hesitate long.
I simply turned the pillows with the other side up.

We had only a small radiator in our room; there was not other source of heating.
Besides, we were told, "We are sorry, but the warm water will be available after 9:00 p.m."
We had to take it how it was.

Before our guide left, he gave us advice.
"Because of the thin air you will probably have problems. Please, take my advice and go to your room and lay down. After two hours go out, but just for 20minutes. Repeat this for the rest of the first day. Tomorrow you will be fit to enjoy Lhasa."

We did not know, what to think about it.
But somehow we came to conclusion, that he probably knew what he was talking about. So we did what we were told to do.

When we came to our room after dinner, we found that we were

tired.
For once it did not matter, if somebody slept in our bed.
It did not matter that warm water would be late.
We quickly took a shower in cold water and fell in bed.
We slept like a log.

In the morning we woke about eight.
It was dark outside.

Frank felt good, but I felt bad.
I had the felling that my head was three times bigger and full bees,
humming without interruption "Bzzzzzz, bzzzzz..."
After the breakfast I felt a little better and hoped, that in a day or
two my problems would slip off.

Our guide came to pick us up.

Our magic tour to the Potala Palace, the Winter Palace of Dalai
Lama, began.
We slowly walked through the rooms in deep respect and tried
to remember the names of different Buddha. We admired gilded
carvings, paintings and all the magnificent statues.
We were overwhelmed.

The sacred places were terribly impressive and absolutely strange
to our understanding. Although we spared no effort to put together
all the information we got from our guide.

Later we visited the Summer Palace of Dalai Lama, placed in
beautiful garden.
And with it we completed the picture about the life of this
mysterious man.

To see the biggest monastery was a must.
Once there were eight thousand monks, now only eight hundred
monks.
But what struck us first were all the stray dogs in narrow streets.

Of course I asked our guide about the reason for this phenomenon and was really astonished by his answer.
"We, Tibetans, love dogs, the Chinese eat them. So we hide them here."

You have to know, that there are many Chinese in Lhasa now to a dissatisfaction of local population.

After the biggest, we visited the oldest monastery that is placed in the middle of the main square, surrounded by a Tibetan market with souvenirs.
There you could buy everything that represents Tibetan culture. The selection is huge; from gold and silver jewelry to facial masks and carved bowls.

It was a fascinating world that we did not understand in full.
But we enjoyed every minute of our stay in this amazing place.

My head problems stopped already the first day.
Frank and I were only terribly tired every evening and needed twelve hours sleep to be fresh for the next day again.
We were told, we should be very happy sleeping all night long, because some people could not sleep at all.

And there were not only the sleeping problems.

From the group of about 30 American, being in Lhasa in the same time as we were, two people died of a heard attack.

So take my advice.
If you would like to go to Tibet, go when you are young. The later on, the worse is the adjustment.

Our five days in Lhasa flew as quickly as the water in river.

In the very early morning, we said goodbye to Lhasa and in the complete darkness we drove to the airport. We had not a clue what

Vera Stanek

this early hour would bring us, but when we found it out, we were enchanted.

The sky was full of stars.
Millions and millions stars glimmered through thin air, one of the biggest spectacles that only nature could do.
I sat with my face turned to the side and my nose pressed against the window.
During two hours of our drive I did not speak and only muttered something like "ah, oh..." and that was all.
I was totally absorbed in thought about the infinity of the universe.

When we came to the airport, the dawn began.
The stars slowly lost the outlines, later the shine and before the plane started they totally disappeared.

But when I close my eyes I can see them.
They let their picture forever burned in my brain.

I thought this was the end of all highlights for today, but I was wrong.

Our plane started to a bright day with a blue sky and a sun above the giant mountains. We reached an altitude where just a sea of white fluffy clouds was laying under in valleys and above them loomed up sunlit mountains.
An unforgettable magic of nature, a great spectacle of lights and colors took place before our eyes.
And among them, the Mt. Qomolangma, the world's highest peak!

How lucky we were to see it.
How insignificant we felt.
How unimportant were our human problems.

Our souls were full of impressions.
We felt happy.

In a few days after our arrival to Beijing we started another trip.
Five days cruise on the Yangtze River with the following three days
stay in Shanghai. That was on our itinerary.

We came to the airport in Beijing and found it overcrowded.
"Of course, it has to happen exactly today when we are on the
way," I complained to Frank, "This is Murphy's law!"

The reason for this situation was a fog over Beijing that caused the
delay of all flights.

Resigned to our fate we found two places free, sat down and waited
for the departure. Only, there was a problem.
How would we find out when our plane departs?
They announced it in English, but ...
First, it was too noisy there, second, the pronunciation of English
was not very well.
What should we do?

A plan slowly emerged in our discussion on this topic and after a
while we found it brilliant.
Chinese flight tickets had different colors.
We assumed it was after the number of the flight.
So we selected a person with the ticket of the same color as we
had and when this person went to the gate, we just followed.
It worked very well.

We started our cruise in the city named Chongqing.

Due to the capricious nature there was not enough water in the
mighty Yangtze River and so our big ship could not come until
there.
We were put up in a hotel to sleep there overnight.

Morning we were told to embark a small river boat, and in about an
hour we would reach the ship, anchored down the river.
After three hours I asked the only person on the boat if Chinese

hours have another amount of minutes.
The man was not happy about this question, but he assured me,
that it would be soon. After four hours we finally arrived on the ship.

And it was better then we were waiting for.
We were only about fifty people on a ship for 500 people.
Pleasant surprise, indeed.

We sailed through three gorges, a unique work of nature, with
narrow canyons, mountains shrouded with clouds, submerged
rocks and waterfalls, which cascaded from the top of a high rock
cliff.

Every day we made one stop on some interesting place.

We walked through the cities with only skeletons of houses, with no
roofs at all.
Because everything that was useable was brought to higher places
where the water of the new dam lake would not reach.

What remained were thick white lines on walls.
They showed the people the future water level of the Three Gorges
Dam, the biggest project from the time of Great Wall.

It would bring electricity to huge parts of China and save lives of
many Chinese.
Because the dam would stop the notorious flooding of the
dangerous river.
Only, everything has it's price.

The terrace fields with the orange trees, built for centuries on the
banks of river, would disappear. The people built them mostly by
hands and with primitive tools long time ago.
Old houses or new ones would disappear, also.
Entire villages or cities would be flooded with water. The same
would happen to pagodas on the rocks that are not high enough to
be over waterline.

All the nature would vanish.
The gorgeous mountains that form the magic of three gorges would not be there or just their tops would rise from the lake.
Most of the beauty would pass from the sight.

But what is more important, the life of people would change.

All 1.5 million of people have to move!
To concrete houses in new cities that grow on tops of the mountains.

How do the people feel about this change?

The young people are mostly happy.
Their new flats would have running water and toilet, in the new cities would be enough opportunities to find a job.

The older people cry.
They refuse to move, they do not want to live in concrete apartment houses in anonymous life, they want to stay by their river.
The river that brought them for centuries livelihood, with its murmur they went to bed and awoke to a new day.
They sailed to nearby cities and they knew the neighbor.

Yes, they often had to escape when the river overflowed its banks and some of them died, but life went on.
It was the price for being close to the river and they knew it.

The future will show us the price paid for this enormous project.

The sailing through three gorges was captivating.
The peaked mountains raised directly from the water; the river was narrower, the water wild.
What a breathtaking scenery!

How expected, we passed by the construction site of the new dam.

Huge excavators and never ending rows of trucks dug and moved tons of earth.
The people were like ants among giants. They moved apparently with no destination from one side to the other side.
An impressive and fascinating picture.

We left the three gorges behind and continued on our voyage.

After four days we disembarked in Wuhan, another city with *just* eight million people. There Frank and I said goodbye to the mighty Yangze River.

We were happy we came on time.
In eleven years there would not be three gorges.
What a shame!

We took a plane to Shanghai, our destination for another four days. After our experience in Beijing we decided to walk through the city, although it took us about three hours to come to downtown.
But we gained knowledge about the city.

We peeped into the houses, walked through streets so alike Europe that it was remarkable. We entered many galleries and shops and visited the Yuyuan, a beautiful garden with a Zigzag bridge.
And we boarded a cruiseship to discover the harbor area with a power plant, shipyard, and iron and steel industry.
Everything was so giant and so amazing.

In four days in Shanghai we ran our feet off, but we were very satisfied with our trip.

We returned to Beijing and found that we had to slow down.
We had another plans to take care of and these were for us more important than another travel.

For example we did not know where to go.

We had our house in Texas but not the permission for residence.
In a family discussion we decided to use Eva as our sponsor to get green cards.
Only there was some time inevitable until the immigration office would handle the request, and during this period we could not enter America.

So there was one question actual.
Where to go in the meantime?

Eva began immediately to fill out the absolutely essential papers.
It was not easy because of our escape to Switzerland we missed some very important documents. Everything was more difficult then we imagined it would be.
And Eva worked very hard to have it all together.

Frank and I came to conclusion that we would stay in Asia and travel.

With this decision came the organization of our trips on the schedule.
We thought we would need three or four months until the immigration office would have our green cards ready.
In this time we did not know, how wrong we were!

I threw myself with a big enthusiasm into this work.
I found a travel agency, owned by Chinese woman from Hong-Kong and she was a jewel. In the next ten days she organized for us all the trips we intended to make, put together all the flight tickets, hotels, simply everything.

In the time that was left we still tried to see as much of China as possible.

Vera Stanek

Every Sunday our former driver and secretary took us on another trip around Beijing.

We visited a big and deep cave with lots of steps down; we were in a nice monastery on a windy and cold day, with fresh fallen snow on the walkways and frozen fountains.
And we went for the last time to the Great Wall.
Only this time we visited another part than the one, used by travel agencies.
Because there are many Great Walls around Beijing.
Some here, others there.

By a coincidence we choose a wonderful day in December.
A day, when everything was covered with sprinkling of snow, and with a sun high on the cloudless sky.
It was one of the days, I will not forget.

We walked slowly and admired the hills and mountains nearby.
But after a short time we found that something was wrong; there were almost no people. In two hours we met only three Chinese families with children.
That was all.
But mostly we walked alone.

I do not know, if it happened to anybody who visited China to be just one time in one place, alone.
But it happened to us.

You have to have just a lucky day, as we had.

Through the week Frank and I made the last arrangements.

We had two parties with our former employees.
One was organized by us, the second one by them.
There was lots of food, drinks and photos and from my side, tears.

I was so terribly unhappy to leave, but I could not do anything to change it.

Frank and I got many gifts.
It is a Chinese habit to say goodbye by giving a present to you.
We were overwhelmed by the flood of all the gifts; it was so nice.
In some ways you think, the people give you a gift because they like you.
Such thoughts are maybe wrong, but very human.
At least from our point of view.

Finally we had only a few days before we left Beijing.

Last was the visit to a Sichuan restaurant, we loved.
Last was the stroll through streets we walked many times so that we knew exactly where the potholes, wire strips that could strangle us, or just rugged pavement, were.

I had to confess myself that I did not understand so many things around me.
It did not matter if I tried, or not, this world held its secrets hidden behind closed doors.
It was as a puzzle I could not finish because I could not put the pieces in right place.
I did not have the ability to understand.
I was just an observer.

Anyway, it was a world that fascinated me.
I wanted to know more, I wanted to see more, I wanted to satisfy my curiosity.
However I had not more the time.
It was over.

Frank and I were forced to concentrate on our personal matters and to take care about all our belongings. Finally we decided to take on our trip just two suitcases, and the rest we sent to Switzerland to David.

These last days in Beijing were everything but pleasant.

Christmas holidays were sad.
We were alone, with children scattered around the world.
New Year Eve was not too much different; we fell asleep by the TV.
It was too much of excitement in those days.

On January 1st, 1998, we said goodbye.
To Beijing.
To China.

To the most exciting year of our life we would not forget.

But we promised ourselves.
We would come back.

To see the changes.
To smell the air.

To be there.

Chapter 19

We are on the way to our first destination, to Bangkok.
With Thai Airlines and the most beautiful stewardess I ever saw.
We are welcomed on the board with a bottle of champagne.
It seems to be a pleasant flight.

Because of the date, January 1st, the plane is almost empty.
Just about fifteen people on board.
Frank and I are in business class, some people in economy, and a group of ten men in first class.

The first class is divided from business class just by a curtain.
And the curtain is open, at least for now.
So I could peer in this space.
Inconspicuously, of course.

There is a table full of bottles of alcohol.
The group of men open some bottles of champagne and,
surprisingly, come to us with a glass in hand.
"Happy New Year" they wish us and smile.
"Happy New Year," we wish them, too.

How nice.
Not too many people wished us today a "Happy New Year."

After some time, the oldest man sat down in his seat.
The men immediately gather around him.
But what a strange picture I see!
Just two men sit on the seats next to him, the rest sit on the floor nearby.
The oldest man begins, in a low voice, talk to the group.

I do not understand one word, although I prick up my ears.
I am terribly curious.

Vera Stanek

The stewardess brings appetizers on a silver plate with an orchid.
I use this opportunity and ask her, "Who are these men?"
She smiles and add, "It is Mafia. But do not worry."

I am not worry.
I am just curious.

And it does not matter to me, if it is a Mafia or not.
They wished me a "Happy New Year."
And that was decisive.
At least for today.

We landed in Bangkok in the evening.
A wonderful tropical evening with the heat that went down to a pleasant warmth.
The streets were still wet after a short rain, the street lighting glimmered in small puddles of water.
The city had it's own smell.

In the morning we started our tour through Bangkok. As always, we walked.
In a city like Bangkok something unbelievable and normally this can't be done.
But not today and not in three another following days.
Why? Because it was a holiday.

The entire three days sidewalks were not crowded and the streets had almost no traffic at all. Because the people of Thailand were at home and relaxed.
"You are lucky," we were told at every step.
And we really were.

We visited monasteries with beautiful carved roofs and amazing architecture.
We spent one whole day in the Grand Palace and we could not believe how much wealth could be concetrated on one place.

Pure gold was on everything; from towers to monuments and sculptures.
We were breath taken by the view of all the diamonds and precious stones and a throne of mother-of-pearl.

We saw in Europe many palaces and castles, but nothing was like this. Perhaps the rulers in Europe were much poorer than in Asia. It seemed so.

Finally we succumbed to temptation and took a tuk-tuk for a ride.

What was a tuk-tuk?
A three wheeled vehicle with a bank in the back, a seat for the driver in front, and a canopy over head.
But what a drive it was!
Tuk-tuk jumped on uneven streets of Bangkok, the driver used the horn almost continuously, and we got Kleenex, to hide our faces from dirt.
It was an adventure!
We loved it.

The day, when Bangkok awoke to a normal working day, we left.
Our way to the airport was not easy and pleasant.
Traffic was slow and difficult, the air was full of exhaust gasses.
It was the exact picture of a travel guide's description.

Only we knew, that it could be different.
When you are lucky enough.
As we were.

Our second destination was Singapore.
A clean city and so different from the other we have seen.

I fell in love with Singapore on the way to the hotel already and soon I was absolutely enchanted.

Frank and I walked again, to discover and see.
We strolled through streets and watched the people; mostly young people in business dresses, eating lunch on banks by the river.

And we took the subway.
The subway with a special signs, like the notices: spitting on the floor - $100, eating in the train - $50....
I loved it.
I do not know if other people loved it. But the truth is that we did not see one piece of paper or one crumb of food on the floor.

If I were to be twenty again, I would go to Singapore.

First I would work in some of the restaurants as a waitress.
In the evenings I would go to school.
When I would finish school, I would stay there for some years, probably.
Because I felt that the city was alive.
It pulsated with people of different races, habits, food.
This mixture was colorful and it was very attractive.

The first evening, Frank and I went for dinner on the bank of the river.
There are crammed one restaurant next to another, all of them with an open place on the river bank, and with wonderful surroundings.

We were sitting by the river, that slowly flowed into the sea.
The food was excellent, the view as well.
When we lifted up our heads we could see thousands of lights of skyscrapers around, because we were sitting in downtown.

It was a magic of modern lifestyle that I found so charming.

We repeated our dinners at this place every day of our stay in Singapore.
And we loved it more and more.
We were not happy to leave, but our schedule was exact.

Next destination was Australia.

We went to Australia for a special reason; because of friends.

One of my best friends, Evina, left Czechoslovakia five years before
us.
Frank's co-worker and friend George, was there, as well.
Both of them were refugees as we were.

All the years we stayed in touch with them.
They visited us in Switzerland and our son David found in their
houses lodging during his trip around the world.
Now we were there to visit them.

We began with Evina in Melbourne.
She and her family took us to their house where we soon felt like
we were at home.
Evina's mother hid in her refrigerator Christmas cookies for us
which was so touching! Already the thought about somebody
thinking of us felt so good.

It was a marvelous week.

Evina took one week off, and we traveled around.
We enjoyed the big waves on the beach, took a ride through the
city and although not covered with snow, we visited a cross-country
skiing loop in the mountains nearby.

And what was my biggest impression of Australia?
The ferns that were about ten feet high.
I felt as I was in the time, when dinosaurs controlled this planet, but
I was thankful not to see them.

But most of the time we talked.
About our dreams, our problems and victories, or just about our
love to mountains or sea.

The week was too short.
Moreover, we did not know when we would see each other again.
But our plans were fixed.

We had to leave for Sydney.
To visit George and his wife.

We still had their last visit in mind, when we were sitting on the balcony of our apartment in Switzerland and talked and laughed through the night.
We looked forward to seeing them and to the opportunity, maybe, to spend similar time again.

But what we found was totally different.

George did come successfully through organ surgery. But something went wrong with him. We found another man than we knew before.
Bitter and unhappy with himself and the whole world.

It was the whole world's fault that he was an old and fat man, with just few friends among the Czech group in Sydney.
He had no friends among the Australian people although he spent 30 years of his life there, and he was an absolutely unhappy person, totally absorbed with the past.
What a poor man!

Very soon we found, that we are probably not so welcome as we thought we would be, but we did not want to make things even worse by going away.
So we limited the time spent together.

Frank and I took trips from our friends' suburban house to Sydney by train.
And this was excellent.

We visited the American Embassy and asked about the necessary

time to get a green card. We were told that it would take about two to three months.
Eva was almost ready to put our papers into the immigration office.
So we decided to stay in Asia.

We didn't have the wish to go back to Switzerland and wait there.
So we changed our plans.

We agreed to extend our stay in Asia by going to Thailand for not just a few days, but for some months, maybe.
Until we would get permission to come to USA.

From the decision to the action was a short way.

We went to the Thailand embassy and asked for visas for two months, because we estimated that two months would be enough to fill the gap we had in our plans.
We could not know then, that everything would be different.
In these days we were happy to stay in Asia, travel and nothing more.

After we organized all necessary stamps we began to enjoy Sydney.

We went for a cruise in Sydney harbor.
We were sitting in one of restaurants directly opposite the opera, having lunch and drinking a bottle of white wine and talking and watching the people, the opera house...
It was great.

We strolled through the tourist district and visited galleries.
And we bought a great painting, since we fell in love with the Aborigines culture and the great stories connected to every piece of art they did.
We were literally fascinated with it.
It was a very strong impression.
I still feel it in me, when I look on this painting.

With every day we enjoyed Sydney more and more.

Then came the last day.

The last time we tried to sit with our friends and talk, but I did not think about it as a nice time. The unbelievable bitterness of these people cast shadow on our last evening.
You could feel that both sides were happy about this ending.
We were sorry, indeed.

When we said goodbye at the airport I was sure, that we all knew, this was the last visit and the last time we would see each other.

We left for another place in Australia.
We went to Daydream Island, one of the islands in Barrier Reef.
Our friend Evina told us, "You have to go there. It is a dream."
And it was.

The whole island is very tiny; just 0.7 miles long and about 0.3 miles wide.
With one resort for about 500 people, three restaurants, some bars, pools and beautiful beaches.
That's all.

Due to school beginning there were just about 50 to 70 people.
The island belonged to us and this was wonderful.

The beaches were empty and no fighting for chairs was necessary.
Often we were there alone.
The first day we bought the necessary equipment for snorkeling and began to enjoy the snorkel paradise.

We lay on the water and watched the life under the water level.
It was absolutely amazing; lots of fish in all imaginable colors, some with black strips or fluorescent, a unique world we did not know of its existence at all.

Besides, there were corals.
Slowly moving in a harmony with a motion of water. Sometimes as a big branches of trees, sometimes as a fan, held by a gentle woman hand.
We were absolutely enchanted.

Our stay on Daydream Island was exactly this, what we were looking for.
A place, where we could relax.
We deserved it.

After ten days we left Daydream Island but it would stay in our memories.

We would still see the big moon raising from the sea and flooding the whole island in moonshine.
We would still see the slow motion of palms in a sea breeze and the underwater world with it's own life.

Magic place on planet Earth.

Our next destination was Bali.
To go there was my secret dream and big desire for a long time.
So I made a gift to myself for my 60th birthday which I was to celebrate two months later.

We landed on Bali shortly after midnight.
The night was warm and the smell of Bali was in the air.
Although different then in China, it was there.

In the morning we started our walk through the neighborhood.
The hotels and restaurants were built in a beautiful Balinese cultural style.
The gardens and pools with waterfall and flowers were extremely charming.
First impression - a paradise.

But then we started to have problems.

Our hotel was not directly on the beach.

A complimentary bus took hotel guests each morning to a small beach.
We used this offer and went also, but what we experienced was a bad dream.
Already before the bus stopped, some of the people sprang out to occupy the few chairs that were available. They began to push each other away; the fight for every chair was disgusting.
This was just too much for Frank.
He took me by my hand and said just one word, "Come."

We turned on our heels and left.
We walked on the beach back in direction to our hotel.
On the way we found a place under a big tree on a free beach and there we spent the rest of our holidays.

It was nice place with only one disadvantage; we became the point of interest of hundreds of Balinese sellers.
They tried to sell us everything, from a bottle of Coke to their own grandmother.
Sorry, just kidding, but it was not too much far away from the truth.

In the beginning we smiled and politely answered with "no, thank you" at all the offers.
With the time going we left off the "thank you." Because if you have to say it fifty-times in a day, then you are not very friendly anymore.
And there was another problem.
The people were friendly, they smiled but they were very persistent.
Some of them sat on my towel, touched my hands and tried to sell me their goods.

After a few days I was tired and I had enough of this trouble.

One evening after a hard day a man touched again my hand.

I could hold it not more and I exploded, "Do not touch me," I shouted. Desperate and with tears in my eyes I sprang, put all my belongings in a bag and ran away.
I needed time to relax and be friendly again.

For two following days we remained in our hotel garden by the pool.

I was quite surprised to find so many people there.

So I talked with one German couple on this topic, but their answer caught me off my balance. They explained to me, that they love Bali very much and this was their third visit already, but...
For two weeks they stayed only in the hotel by the pool.
They went outside just for dinner or on a trip, organized by hotel.
But nothing more.

I almost could not believe it.
But they both assured me, that they could not stand the beach sellers, so they solved this situation in their own way.
But what a way!
No, thanks, not for me.

Frank and I came to conclusion, that we probably did not understand the people, their culture and habits.
So we decided to come back to Bali, after we would go through our planned itinerary, since we were sure that it was worth the second attempt.

We found a small house on the beach for rent and we made reservations for one month, maybe more, depending on our next moves.
In view of this situation we did not go for trips now, because we would have enough time later.
We promised ourselves that we would find a place on Bali, that we would love.

The world was all right again.
However now we had to leave for Thailand.

In the last days on Bali we promised ourselves to be more understanding, more friendly, more... and looked forward to coming back.

Then we said "see you soon" to Bali and flew to Thailand.

We landed on Phuket, an island on Thailand's West shore.

We love islands.
Maybe it is because we spent almost our whole life in Czechoslovakia and in Switzerland, in countries without direct access to the sea.
So it was an excitement for us to be surrounded by water.

The hotel was great, but over budget, so we booked our stay there only for five days and in the meantime we would find something cheaper.
We hoped, this five days would be enough to find the hotel.
And it was.
We needed exactly three hours and not more.

What we found was exactly what we were looking for.
A small hotel, hidden in greenery on a gentle slope at one of the smallest beaches on the island.
Great!

Until our move there we enjoyed the luxury of the hotel we were in, the large and beautiful beach and were aware of all the differences to Bali.
The beach sellers there had another mentality that was a music to our souls.
They let us in a peace if we did not show an interest.
How refreshing it was.

2

The sea was smooth and deep.
Enough beach chairs for everybody.
The peace flooded our souls.
We were happy and contented.

After this wonderful five days we felt healed and looked forward to our new place.

But before we could enjoy the picturesque surroundings of the place we were put into a problem; in Indonesia, of which Bali is a part, broke out a riot.
The currency dropped down very quickly and the people went to the streets.
The tourist were welcome not with the flowers but with tomatoes and eggs.
We were confused.

After a discussion we decided not to go to Bali and stay in Thailand.

Anyway we had visa for two months and then we would see.

So we canceled the beach house on Bali and asked in our hotel, if we could stay for two months.

The owner, a Chinese family, was pleased and offered a change.

We could move, if we would like, into a bungalow behind the hotel, a private residence of the owner's children.
There were two big separated rooms with bath and shower and with a breathtaking view on the sea directly from the bed, because the main wall, turned to the sea, was of glass.

We did not hesitate long and moved immediately to one of these rooms, although there were seventy steps to get there.
Nothing could change our excitement about this place.

"At least we can do something for our health," we told ourselves.

Vera Stanek

We walked the steps up and down three to four times in a day.
But the place was worth it.

We were alone there, high on the slope and could enjoy the view on
the sea and a mini island at any time.
It was the nicest place we ever stayed in.

With two months of holiday in sight it was not bad situation at all.

In the first weeks we were just lazy.
We went to the beach every day and swam in the sea, ate fresh
pineapples put on ice for coolness, and got the best out of life.
Evenings we sat in one of many restaurants directly on the beach
and admired the nights with a sky full of stars.

The happiness we found on this place acted on our soul as a balm.

Later we took the plans of our house to the beach and *furnished* it,
on the paper only, after all the experiences we had by furnishing the
flats we had lived in until now.
Frank, very skillful in drawings, put on the paper the ideas we
agreed on. Sometimes there were fights about every corner for
many days, but we did not stop before both of us were happy with
the solution.
After about one month we were through.

We knew, that it would take some time until we would have our
house in such shape, as we would like.
But hey, we were retired now, we had enough time to spare.
For our house.
For ourselves.

In the meantime Eva sent our request for a green card to the
officials.
Now we could only wait on a call from one of our children with,
"Pack your suitcases and come."

Eva tried to call the immigration office to ask how long it would take, but mostly without success.
She could only talk to an answering machine, never to a person.
Finally she reached, at least, the right message with quite devastating news for us.
The waiting period was extended to 270 days.

We were exhausted.
For once we were with our back to the wall.
We did not know what to do, where to go.
How to react on this terrible news that changed all of our plans.

We had now about one third of the time behind us and planned to stay in Thailand for two months, total. But what would we do then?

First it was necessary to calm down.
Then use the brain again and think about plan B.
So we did.

We made up our mind to stay in Thailand.
As a next step it was necessary to extend our visas. We visited the police station nearby and asked what to do. They were exact, "Bring two photos, filled out questionnaire and 500 Bath (local currency) per person. We will extend your stay for one month more."
But one month was for us too short time.

"If you would like to stay longer, there is only one way how to do it," told the official and described us how to do it.

Anyway, after three months it would be necessary to leave Thailand.
The practice was strange, but official; we had to drive to the border of Malaysia, go through the border, and immediately back.
They would then give us visas for another two months.

We had no another choice.

Vera Stanek

We took the extended visas for one month, and at this very moment
we did not care what would happen in more than one month.
It was necessary to take everything slowly.
Step by step.

Now we had the next attraction, the Thai New Year, in sight.
We had no clue, how overwhelming the celebration would be.

The New Year is celebrated with a sprinkler of cold water.
Barrels with water, cooled with bags of ice, are placed on streets,
and when you pass by, a big pot of this water is splashed on your
face.
Occasionally, your face is painted with a yellow color.
It should bring you a lucky year.

Sometimes you get a real shower from a passing truck where a
group of people use buckets for sprinkling.
It is a big fun.

Frank and I were warned already before, so we spent the day by
the hotel pool.
To see everything a little nearer, we courageously went for lunch
outside the hotel.

We came to the restaurant already soaked through, but on this day
everything was allowed. After lunch our faces were painted, and
totally splashed with water we returned to the hotel back.
We changed clothes, and hoped the year would be good to us.

About this time I read in local newspapers about a painting course,
organized by one of the best hotels nearby.
Spontaneously, I decided to take part on this course.
I thought, that it would be a nice change.

The last time I painted was 45 years ago, in the school, where I
enjoyed the classes.

Actually I did not think about painting at all, but now I had time and I had the opportunity. Why not use it?

One of French painters, with his own painting school in Bretagne, came every year to this hotel, and there he spent 14 days teaching painting.
Everyone could take part on his lessons.
It was not too expensive.

I enrolled and was pleased with the atmosphere and the group around me.
We were only eight women between 25 and 60 years old.
Not one man among us; probably the men were not so brave, or they did not want to make a fool of themselves.

The week was full of excitement.
We painted some objects of every day life, a portrait, my first in the life, some collages, etc.
You can believe me, that we all had great fun.

I still have all the paintings hidden on the bottom of our closet.
Someday I will paint again.
Only I need to have time to spare.

I enjoyed this lessons so much that I immediately took part in another course.

I enrolled in cooking classes at one of the best restaurants on the island.
Because I loved Thai food, so I wanted to learn the secrets of its cooking.

Our class was full with 15 people, men and women, who were eager to learn.

In the restaurant, under the eyes of a chief cook, we got the basic know-how.

Vera Stanek

Just the spices and vegetables, most of them I saw for the first time in my life, not to mention all the fish that came directly from the sea on the table.
But we took it seriously.
What we cooked, we ate then.
At the end we got an apron with the name of the hotel and a diploma.

It was great for me, because I lost my fear of cooking exotic food.
You could ask Frank, if you do not believe me.

I became a very good cook of Thai food.

However, now it was necessary to make the trip to Malaysia.
We were short of time, already.

We were told that taking a bus would be the best way to go there.
Although the drive would take about five hours we agreed to use this way, too.

It was a *ride of death.*
I had many times in my life terrible fear, but this was something special.
During the whole way I had in my mind only one thought and it was death.
Even though I longed to live, go to Texas and enjoy the life.
I did not want to die on Thailand's roads.

"The driver is a criminal," Frank told me, and I agreed without hesitation.

I knew that I am in another country with another driving habits.
But I could not understand what I experienced.
Why the driver lighted a cigarette at a gas station?
Why was it necessary to pass another car over double lines on the way up the hill?

Why the driver passed most of stop signs...?

To the culmination of everything we were the only non-Thai passengers.
We were absolutely helpless.

The ride seemed to us as an eternity.
Finally we arrived at a city on the border, and all the passengers had left.
On the bus remained only two persons, Frank and I.
It was the situation we feared most, but there was no way out.

Silently we continued on the way to the border.
I could almost not breath from fear; only gloomy thoughts went through my head.
However nothing happened.

Before the drive we agreed to pay extra money for the drive to the border.
Now we were remembered by the driver.
He told us, that he would cut open our throats if we did not pay him.
To underline this situation his hand showed exactly what he meant.

But do you know what happened in this moment?

I could not explain it, but I stopped shaking.
I did not cry or feel dizzy, nothing of this sort. I was only aware of the fact, that we didn't have a weapon to defend ourselves and that we had to resign to our fate.
I sat with a stone face and waited for what would happen.
And to my greatest surprise, nothing happened.

We made a stop on the border and Frank and I went to Thai customs where we filled out all the necessary papers.
Then we went through the border, walking, and after about 10 minutes we came to the Malaysia side.
The lady on the customs looked at our passports and then she

asked, "Do you go there - or there?" and pointed with her hand at direction of Thailand or Malaysia.
"There," we answered and pointed with hands to Thailand.

That was it, that was the entire procedure.

We got the right stamp and could stay another two or three months in Thailand.
Wonderful!

Our *friendly* driver took us back to the border city, this time without threats and intimidation. When we paid him off, he even recommended a hotel to us.
There we stayed through the night.

The drive back was not too much different.
When we at the end reached our beach hotel alive and healthy, we could almost not believe it. It was an experience that we would not like to repeat.
I could swear to it.

Free from sorrows about our stay in Thailand we began to enjoy our extended vacation again, although there were many changes in sight.

Most of the tourists left, and only a few of the intrepid travelers came for a holiday.

You could see people you were not used to seeing before.
A young beautiful girl and an old white-haired man, locked in each other's arm.
A handsome young man with diamond ring on his finger, holding hans with an old man, ugly as a sin.
People with tattoos on their whole body and pierced nipples.

It was different.

And the sea was different, too.
Big waves knocked against the shore and brought all the mess from the sea to the coast. Everything from empty bottles, bulbs, trunks... to the TV screen.
Sometimes it was awful.

To save our good spirit we decided to discover the island, Phuket.

To be mobile, we chose a scooter as our transport vehicle.
We thought it would be nice to see if we could manage it.
And without doubt, it was an adventure.

One day in the morning Frank left the hotel to rent the scooter.
I was really surprised that Frank went to handle it alone.
But he had a reason for this behavior.

Frank had not driven a scooter for about 50 years. In addition he was not used to driving on the left side of the road as the regulation was in Thailand.
So he wanted to make a small tour alone.

Frank drove to the top of a small hill near the hotel and everything was just fine.
When he later drove down the hill he was surprised when all of a sudden a small truck came directly at him. The driver of the truck pressed the horn and waved.
Frank was confused, but only shortly.
Of course, he drove on the wrong side of the road; his habits predominated the regulation.
Thanks heaven, it was just for a short time

We started our journey.
We came to the places on another side of the island, saw villages with people working in the fields, and fishermen on small shaky boats putting their nets into the sea.
We saw the life of Thai people in reality.
It was amazing.

Not just hotels, beaches and restaurants nearby.
But something totally different.

Later we went on many such trips and got used to going on the left
side of road.
Everywhere we came we met the smiling faces of Thai people.
The symbol of their lifestyle and hospitality.

Slowly came the rainy season.

According to the local people, it was not so bad this year.
For us it was bad, because we were not used to it.

With the rain strange creatures rose from the ground, like five
inches long caterpillars, black and poisonous.
And as a peak of the surprises, new snakes.
Honestly, I hate snakes and I fear them.
Our hotel owner told us, "Take care in this time. If you see a green
snake, do not worry. But if the snake is black, be very careful. It
could be cobra."

'Oh, no!' I cried in my soul, 'No snake, please...'
But there was nothing to do.

I began to look on my every step.
In the evening we took a flash lamp with us and lighted our every
step behind the hotel. Altogether I had enough of all the creatures,
our home pet, a lizard, included.
On some nights the lizard crept from his hideout.
It crawled through our tile floor, made a noise, and I hated it.
I just woke up, and could not sleep.
Moreover I imagined the lizard crawling in my bed... and I could not
close my eyes in fear of this terrible moment.

I have to admit, that I really do not like lizards.
I do not like caterpillars.

I do not like snakes.

I just grew up in a country where they did not exist, and I am happy for it.
I apologize, but this is the truth.

So we decided to say goodbye to Thailand.
To this beautiful country with smiling people and bad drivers.
To the country with a wonderful sea and poisonous snakes.
To the country we learned to love.

We spent four marvelous months there.
There we enjoyed in full the sea, the food, the people.
There we were very happy.

But it was necessary to leave to the only place available to us, Switzerland.
Our permission for America was still not ready, so we needed a place to stay.
And in Switzerland David and Monica were waiting.

Maybe it would be not so bad an idea to come back.
We would see.

We came back to Switzerland in the last days of June.

Soon we found that *something in the air* would not let us breathe freely.
In only one month we were the *old* people again, unhappy and dissatisfied.
If it was the clear and fresh air, or the people on the streets, or the language, or what, we did not know.

We tried to find pleasure by walking through the streets of Lucerne.
We tried to hike again in the mountains we once loved so much or

swam in the beautiful lakes.
But nothing would help us.
We found that we had to go out as soon as possible.

To our surprise it was Wolfgang, who helped us to get out.

He stayed in touch with David and Monica the whole time and during his visit in their home he offered us a stay in his friend's apartment, high in the mountains.
The apartment was in a small village in Austria just a few miles from Italy and Switzerland.
We agreed without hesitation.

Some days later we left Switzerland

After a five hours drive, we came to the village Nauders at the altitude of four thousand feet.

It was the first week of August when we arrived, the peak of a summer season.
The days were warm, the sun was high on the sky, and the mountains were majestic.

Slowly we began with our everyday routine; breakfast and go.
Every day we chose a route after our mood.
We did not have to hurry, we had enough time to discover the mountains all around us.
It was the first time in our life, that we could enjoy the mountains in full.
With unlimited hiking every day, in a quantity we could endure and enjoy.

Anyway we prepared ourselves for a long stay.

We hoped to spend all our time there until the much longed-for call from our children would arrive.

But before the call came, we tried to work out our fitness.

You can believe me, that it was the time, when we were in the best shape of our lives. It was very easy to understood, why.

The routes, we took every day, required a lot of effort.

We hiked to the altitude of six to seven thousand feet, five till seven hours every day. With two bottles of water in the backpack and cheese, rolls, and some fruit.
Sometimes a piece of chocolate as a special bonus for strength hiking.
On the hiking trails at lower altitude we picked some wild berries, like raspberries and later blackberries.
In the evening I cooked dinner.

It was a marvelous time.
Without worries, snakes... in a nature, that changed directly before our eyes.
An experience we did not have until now.

In the summer time the meadows were green, full of wild flowers.
The forests were the natural canopy above our head.
That brought us the welcomed shade at least on parts of the hiking trails.
At higher level were the slopes covered with only sparse vegetation, sometimes with rocks, but it was not wild and bleak nature.
It was exactly what we liked.

In the fall the meadows were mowed and the hay was brought to the barns.
The forests changed colors from green to yellow.
The peaks of mountains got the first snow that shimmered in the beams of sun and changed the whole spirit.
The high rocks we watched from a far were no longer sharp and terrifying, but they looked under the white cover more peacefully

and friendly.

One day we came to the place we knew very well, since we were there already many times.
The trees in the forest changed colors.
We climbed a steep way in the middle of yellow and red leaves, later we came into the orange needles of larches.
We felt as if the world stopped moving and we were in a fairy tale.

We left the forest,
Our way continued to a meadow with a few larches.
The ground was already covered in a thin layer of snow.
Then I halted my pace, raised the head and almost stopped breathing.
The sky became dark with clouds and against them glittered orange larches on white snow.
What a combination of colors!

I could not turn my head away from this spectacle.

I knew that a photo would be great.
I knew that a painting would be great, as well.
But nothing could bring the atmosphere in which we were surrounded.

Because there are moments in the life when you perceive with all your senses.
And that was this moment.
When I close my eyes today and think about this moment I still see it.
The magic combination of colors, that only nature could give.

At this time we were almost the only tourists in the village, the hiking season was over.

We didn't have much clothing, because we did not know, that our journey would be prolonged through so many different weather

zones.
So we used the well known system of layers of T-shirts and sweaters, and without interruption we continued on our hikes

On days with blue sky and sunshine we still hiked to the high altitude.

We found a small log cabin with a table and benches outside and this became our favorite place.
We reached this place mostly around lunch.
First we cleared the snow from the benches, then we sat down and slowly ate our rolls. We almost did not talk.

We just watched the magnificent scenery.
The wonderful white peaks around us, the bare trunks of trees with icy layers from the side where the winds blew, and only two pair of footsteps, that headed to this place.
This of Frank and mine.
Nothing more.
No one human being in sight.

We felt as the only people in the world.
This was not overdone.
Because to all the beauty we were alone, terribly alone.

Yes, we were happy to be there.
We loved all the nature around us.
But little by little we began to lose our happiness.

The waiting for the permission to immigrate to USA was endless.
It was eight months already, an entire 240 days, and nothing.
There were moments I could almost not bear it.

I had enough of sleeping in hotels or someone else's apartments.
I wanted my own bed, I wanted to stretch my own bed linen over my body.
I had enough of doing nothing.

I wanted to furnish our house, work in the garden, or write this book, an idea I held in my head a long time already.

And I had enough to be alone.
I wanted to have friends, cook for them, entertain them and be with them.
I wanted to be in America.

When I saw an airplane high in the sky, I envied the people on the plane so deeply, that I could almost not breath.
I had such imaginations, that the people on the plane were on their way home.
In my vision they had a place where they belonged, where they could open a book they liked, put a disc in the CD player or talk to friends.
To do everything that I could not to do.

Our books were in storage in Switzerland, our CD's, also.
And how many friends we actually had?
Only a few.

Two friends in Czechoslovakia, maybe.
Our friend Evina and her family in Australia.
No friends in Switzerland.
I was in touch with some of our employees in China, but were they friends?
Then there was Ann in Lago Vista, our future friend, maybe.
What was left?

Our children.

The winter was approaching, our stay in the mountains became uncomfortable.

We were not prepared for cold and snow, we did not have the

winter tires on our car. Every day could be the day when our small village would be cut off from the outside world.
It was necessary to leave now.

We packed our few things and returned to Switzerland, to Monica and David.

It was already November .
We were sure, that the call that we waited for would come every day.
But days passed by and the call did not come.

Monica was in the middle of studying for the last exam to be a lawyer.
After a few days we found out that we were a disturbing element, although we tried hard not to be.
Our presence in their two bedroom apartment was not convenient.

We decided to go for some last trips.

We began with Prague and spent an entire week there.
We assumed it was our last visit; we did not know if we would come again.

We had enough time to stroll for the last time through the places we loved, places of our former life and of our youth.
It was really nice.

Prague welcomed us with snow and frost, but we were prepared and had enough of warm clothes.
We walked to the Prague Castle.
We listened to a Mozart quartet in the beautiful renovated hall.
We went to the opera at the National Theater.
And we made some special shopping in Old Town.

It was nice to shop in Prague.

There were many things available everybody likes; glass, pottery, rose china...

Frank and I decided for pottery, wall decorations and wine goblets.

One day we came to a small store on the bank of river Vltava to look for goblets.
A lady in her sixties, a salesclerk, offered help. We began to talk.
After a while she looked at us and asked, "You speak Czech, but you do not live there. Am I right?"
With a smile we agreed.
Then we asked her, "How did you find it out?"
She said simply, "Because you look happy."
It was really a surprise.

Probably we were different although we did not think about it, but it was just so.
We confirmed it again by meeting with our friends.

The time changed us all, of course.
But the experience from our last visit was the same; there was nothing to talk about apart from the past. The depths were deeper now.
We belonged to two different worlds.

Anyway, it was good to talk to them.

We left and our hearts were not heavy, because we were not sorry to leave.
The past was closed.

There was just the present.
And the future.

Before we could organize the next trip, the call arrived.
Eva had the authorization already on the table, and she sent a fax

immediately to us. The time, necessary for this approval, lasted at the date exactly 270 days!
Our green card was confirmed.
It seemed as nothing could change the decision.

I was overwhelmed and cried with happiness.
Finally it was there.

Of course we were eager to go immediately, but it was not so simple as we thought it would be.
It was necessary to wait until the American Embassy in Switzerland officially sent us the permission, and it could take one or two weeks.

To wait was in this moment no problem at all.
We were so happy, that nothing could change it.

What to do in the meantime?
Go for the last trip in Europe, to a small island in Mediterranean Sea, Cyprus.
Why Cyprus?
Do you really not know it ?
The goddess Aphrodite was born there, and we had to see her birthplace.

We flew from Switzerland in a snow storm.
But Cyprus welcomed us with pleasant spring weather with the temperature in high sixties.

We were not exactly prepared for this weather, in December. So we left our shorts and T-shirts at home.
So our first concern was to look around and buy them.
But the shop in our nice beach hotel was prepared for such guests and in a couple of minutes we bought everything that we needed.
We were rescued.

Immediately we started to enjoy the island.

We took long walks on the beach or relaxed in beach chairs and read.
We simply found pleasure in being by the sea again.
And meanwhile we discovered the island.

Our vacation's package included a car-rental.
Althout that Cyprus is a *left ride* nation, it was not a problem for us.
We had enough experience from driving left in Thailand.

We hit the road.
But the problem in Cyprus was not the left side of driving, but the circles.
We did have not problems to drive on the left side of straight roads, but a circle was something special.
Moreover the authorities of Cyprus loved the circles very much.

At the beginning we needed more than one attempt to find the proper lane.
But with the time, Frank was better and better.
For sure he was not worse than many of the locals.
We enjoyed our trips very much.

First we decided to drive to the mountains. But we drove into such thick fog that it was not possible to continue, and we had to turn and go back.
Anyway it was interesting to see rural countryside, the villages and the lifestyle of its people.

Then we stopped at Aphrodite's birthplace.
Exactly on this place, how was the saying, she emerged from the foam of waves and rose from the sea.
Secretly I took one small dark red stone with white fibbers and put it in my bag with a thought, that maybe Aphrodite stepped on this stone long time ago.
Who knows.

I still have this stone in the bathroom.

When I brush my teeth everyday, I look directly on it.
And then I remember Aphrodite.

We drove through many interesting places and visited many
archeological excavations.

I had a special feeling.
If you dig a hole in Cyprus, then you find a treasure; wonderful
mosaics, pillars, amphitheaters or even a head of the Zeus, mostly
some thousands years old.
It was the culture of Greeks that left traces all around.
And not only the Greeks.

I tried to remember the long forgotten pieces of history, but there
was not too much left.

So I promised myself to change it.
Sometime in the future when I would have more time to spare, I
would read about this fabulous place, and I would remember this
unforgettable trip.

The days we spent on Cyprus reached the end.

We gained a small view into an old culture and history,
Into skills and know-how of people that lived there a long time ago.
It was good to be there.
It was good to see it.

We returned to Switzerland.

The necessary papers for our immigration were there, waiting for
our arrival.

Frank immediately called the American Embassy.
He talked to the person responsible for the whole procedure.
"When you would like to go?" asked the official.

"As soon as possible," answered Frank without hesitation.

The two men talked for some time and then agreed on the following arrangement. The American Embassy needed 14 days to fill out all the papers, but Christmas holidays delayed the process.
It was necessary to set up our appointment for the new year.
For January 4th, 1999.

However it was December 17th, 1998, already.

Our last Christmas Day in Europe was in sight.

Eva flew from Austin and spent some days with us.
It was nice to be surrounded by a family again and to have the opportunity to be with our children.

On January 4th we left Lucerne for the American Embassy in Berne.
We came back at the evening with all the stamps and papers in our hand.
Our immigration was a reality.

From this moment we began to live in an accelerated speed.
In five days we organized everything.

A travel agency found the first possible flight to Austin via Houston for January 10th, 1999.
Afterwards we called some moving companies until we found the right one. They were able to bring all our possessions from the storage in Switzerland to Austin.

Meanwhile we went for the last walk in Lucerne.
We slowly walked on a shore of the lake.
The last time we enjoyed the view on all the mountains around.
Lots of them we knew well, because we hiked in them many times.

It seemed to be similar to our departure to China.
But it was different.

Two years ago we were in a rush to go to a special country.
To go for work and for adventure at the same time.
Now, we were going to the country of our dreams.
Not for a visit.
Not for staying one or two years.
But forever.

And that was the divergence of these two moments.

We had a last dinner with David and Monica.
We thanked them for being there for us, for all their effort to make
our stay in Switzerland as comfortable as possible.
We were aware, that it was not easy.

On January 10th, we left Switzerland forever.

We kissed David and Monica.
We said bye-bye to Europe.

We said goodbye to the life we had until now.

We closed the doors behind us and did not look back.

We just followed our dream.

Chapter 20

We are landing in Houston, the first place on the American continent.

We move with difficulty around the main stream of travelers. Since today we are not ordinary visitors, since today, only a little later, we will be residents.

My hands shake, my voice, as well.
I am terribly excited.
Frank, too.

By the help of a customs officer, a lady, we have all our immigration papers ready in relatively short time.

The very important moment for us is here.
The lady takes our passports, opens them, and then she takes a stamp.
With a smile she asks me, "Should I?"
"Yes, please" I answer and tears stream down my face.

We are there.

We are residents of United States of America.

It was wonderful summer night.

The heat of the day slowly ceased and a lovely cool breeze made the night warm and enjoyable.
The hillsides were flooded with the moonlight, the lake shimmered as a silver plate. Million of stars shining in the endless firmament put all the scenery together in a magnificent spectacle.

Despite the late hour, Frank and I decided to go swimming.

Vera Stanek

Not exactly swimming; just to let the nicely warm water embrace our bodies.

We lay on the water's surface, our hands extended to our sides.
We looked at the stars and we did not speak.
It was not necessary.

I tried to find all of the constellations of the stars I once learned at school.
Some of them I still recognized, like the Big and Little Dippers, Orion...
And I felt sorry I was probably not attentive enough to know them all.

After a while I stopped thinking about the stars and closed my eyes.
I let my body float on the water and my mind wander into the space.
I lost the concept of time.

A touch of Frank's hand brought me back to a reality.
A thought flashed by in my mind.
I squeezed his hand, then broke the silence and very slowly in a low voice, not to disturb the magic of the night, I asked, "Please, tell me, Frank, is it a dream or not?"

"No, it is not a dream, Vera, it is real," I heard the answer.
He said it so silently, that I almost did not hear it.

An infinite peace and composure overtook me.

Through my mind went my entire life.
The war.
Communism.
Switzerland.
China.
Trip through the world.

Everything was past that would be, I was positive of it, remembered.

But our life there, this is the presence.
This is our future.

We do not need to escape anymore.

Because after all the struggles we found the place, where we belong.
The place we love with all of our senses and hearts.
The place where we are at home.

Our dreams brought us there.

Here we stay.

Forever.

It was July 5th, 1999.

Printed in the United States
30528LVS00002B/1-33

9 781414 029894